C000060477

FOR THE SAKE
OF WALES

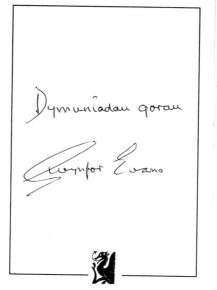

Dymuniadau gorau

Gwynfor Evans

FOR THE SAKE OF WALES

the memoirs of

GWYNFOR EVANS

translated from the Welsh by

MEIC STEPHENS

Welsh academic press

Published in Wales by Welsh Academic Press.

Welsh Academic Press is an imprint of
Cyhoeddwyr Annibynnol Cymreig Cyf.

First Impression – 1996

ISBN 186057 0062

© Gwynfor Evans 1996

The right of Gwynfor Evans to be identified as author
of this work has been asserted in accordance with the
Copyright Design and Patents Act of 1988.

English language translation © Meic Stephens 1996

Original Welsh language edition, edited by Manon
Rhys, published 1982 by Gwasg Gwynedd.

All rights reserved. No part of this publication may be
reproduced, stored in a retrieval system, or transmitted,
in any form or by any means without the prior
permission of Welsh Academic Press.

British Library Cataloguing-in-Publication Data.
A catalogue record for this book is available from
the British Library.

Typeset by WestKey Ltd, Falmouth, Cornwall.
Printed and bound in Wales by WBC Book
Manufacturers, Penybont ar Ogwr.

Jacket designed by daDa, Bethesda.
Printed by Design 2 Print, Llandudno.

Contents

i Alcwyn fy mrawd

Foreword

Since you have opened this book, and started reading my Foreword, it's safe to assume that, as a reader, you enjoy autobiographies. You are in good company. For the autobiography is a very popular literary form. The interest of autobiographies for the general reader probably starts with a curiosity about other people's lives. For writers, however, especially of political memoirs, the motives may be somewhat more sinister. Politicians who write their memoirs are usually guilty of trying to control the writing of history. They want to get their version of events in first, before future historians set to work. This is why, generally, I am very suspicious of political autobiography, regarding it as a form of literature which is mainly fictional and nearer the novel than a work of criticism or history.

However, I have read Gwynfor Evans's book twice — once in the original, discursive and very readable form so expertly edited by Manon Rhys, and then in this English version made by Meic Stephens, which so well matches the conversational style of the Welsh. Now a book which is more of a conversation than a series of essays is arguably less easy to translate than a collection of speeches, let's say. Meic Stephens has succeeded not only in conveying the conversational warmth of the original but in coming uncannily close to the author's own way of speaking. In this book it is as if you are engaged in a face-to-face conversation with Gwynfor Evans. Given his importance as a major figure of twentieth-century Wales, this quality alone makes the book worth reading.

But the real reason why I wasn't able to put it down, in either Welsh or English, is that this is not a conventional, boring political memoir in which the author sets about cataloguing events in an interminable tale of self-justification and self-agrandisement. It is only those who are unsure of their place in history, or of their own salvation, in this world or the next, who feel compelled to write in that way. This book has far more of the flavour of self-deprecation and self-effacement than the ego-centredness which seems to be the cardinal sin of nearly all politicians. But as Gwynfor's touching description of the stomach-pains he felt at meetings of Carmarthenshire County Council, and later in the House of Commons, makes clear, he was never the conventional politician. He was, however, and still is, always a brilliant propagan-dist, the courteous but determined communicator of a message, whether in his own popular versions of Welsh history, in his numerous Plaid Cymru policy pamphlets, or in the thousands of speeches he has delivered to audiences throughout Wales and far beyond its borders. It is a simple, direct message about the value of community, and it is at the heart of this book.

Such a message has to arise, as it did for Raymond Williams in his theoretical and literary works, from a warm personal experience of an upholding and uplifting community life. It is a sense of community, in which family, extended family, and networks of friends are the sustain-ing force. Some commentators have remarked upon Gwynfor Evans's personal shyness, though I must say I have never encountered it. What has always inspired him, and enabled him to write this book, is his love of people. On every page there are references to two or three individu-als, nearly always of a complimentary nature. I counted more than six hundred names, including a far too generous reference to the author of this Foreword, before I gave up counting.

It is not political ideas, or religious conviction, or moral authority, or personal integrity (though all these are virtues in the person of Gwynfor Evans) which shine most clearly through the pages of this book. It is, rather, a love of people everywhere, expressed in an open and positive caring for the national community of Wales and its constituent parts.

Patriotism and Nationalism have become dirty words in some quarters. It is because these words, and the theory and practice which surround them, have been hi-jacked by those who seek to hold on to, or take hold of, state power. But listening to Gwynfor Evans describe his love of people, places, landscape, and history, particularly in his references to Meirionnydd, almost persuades me that it might be possible to rescue these words from those who misuse them.

This book confirms that it was the distinctive leadership of Gwynfor Evans which ensured that Welsh Nationalism, as embodied in Plaid Cymru, became a progressive and non-violent force in the political life of Wales and Europe during the second part of our century. This is what makes it essential reading for Nationalists and non-Nationalists alike.

Diolch eto, Gwynfor!

Dafydd Elis Thomas

Translator's Note

This book was first published in Welsh by Gwasg Gwynedd in 1982. Its original title was *Bywyd Cymro* ('A Welshman's Life') and it appeared as the fourth volume in the popular series *Cyfres y Cewri* ('The Giants' Series'), which consists of autobiographical accounts of the lives of some of the most distinguished Welshmen of our time. The text was compiled by Manon Rhys who transcribed and edited it from tapes recorded by Gwynfor Evans earlier in the year of its publication.

No account or study of Gwynfor Evans's life and work has been available in English up to now. The enthusiastic reception given to *Bywyd Cymro* prompted Ashley Drake of the Welsh Academic Press to commission me to translate it into English for an even wider audience, so that more readers might have some idea of Gwynfor Evans's enormous contribution to the national life of Wales. This task of making an English version of his memoirs I carried out during the summer and early autumn of 1995.

I am glad to put on record that from first to last I had the advantage of advice and practical assistance from the author, to whom I am indebted for many valuable suggestions and for his warm approval of the final text. A few references to matters which might have been unintelligible to readers with no knowledge of things Welsh have, with the author's permission, been deleted or enlarged upon. I also enlisted the help of my friend Sam Adams, who cast an expert eye over the English idiom, making sure that it did not too often reflect its origins in another language. The author has taken this opportunity of correcting a number of small errors in the Welsh text and making some emendations, both additions and deletions, so that this English version may now be regarded as a new, revised, definitive edition of his book. For any infelicities that may remain I alone should be held responsible.

At the same time, although some fourteen years have passed since its first publication, the author took the view that no attempt should be made to bring his book up to date. The reader of *For the Sake of Wales* is therefore asked to bear in mind that many of the people mentioned here are no longer in the land of the living and that, with the passing of those years, the fortunes of Plaid Cymru, the condition of Wales, and the state of the world have all changed, not always for the worse. Nevertheless, the book stands as a major statement about the life and times of a great Welshman and the plight of his small country.

Like all Welsh patriots, I have always held Gwynfor Evans in the highest regard. I shall never forget the pleasure of carrying him on my shoulder the morning after his historic victory in the Carmarthen by-election of July 1966. Thirty years later, the rendering of his book into English has only increased my admiration for him. I think my feelings on completing this work can best be expressed in the words of Manon Rhys in her preface to *Bywyd Cymro*, which might be translated as follows: 'For the first time we are given here a glimpse behind the public persona of Gwynfor Evans and the privilege of sharing his most personal experiences and feelings. This is the story of one of the great souls of twentieth-century Wales. I shall always cherish the experience of working with him in the preparation of this book: for a little while I have been able to share in his joy and his sadness, his fears and his great hopes for Wales and the world.'

Meic Stephens,
Whitchurch, Cardiff,
Owain Glyndwr's Day, 1995

Chapter 1

Barry Town

From my home in Somerset Road overlooking the Barry docks we
could see the hills of Somerset, from the Quantocks to Exmoor, on
the other side of Severn. But whenever the melancholy foghorn of
the lonely lightship Breaksea sounded, the Land of Summer, and the
docks sometimes, would be lost from view. Then we would hear the
shunting of coal-trucks, and the sound of coal being tipped into the
hold of a ship, coming up muffled out of the darkness beneath us.

The docks had been opened exactly twenty years before I was
born in September 1912. The area had a cosmopolitan character,
and the rest of the town had a very mixed population, too. Out of a
population of some thirty thousand the Welsh were in a minority
among the large number of immigrants from Cornwall and Somerset
and the counties of Gloucester and Hereford. Several of my friends'
families had come from beyond the Severn estuary, and some from
the four corners of the earth. Our two next-door neighbours were
ships' captains, Welsh-speakers both of them, one from
Pembrokeshire and the other from Cardiganshire, but they were
both childless, unfortunately. Since they spent a good deal of their
time at sea, we didn't see very much of them. Across the way lived
two Englishmen, ships' engineers, and they too were often away
from home for longish stretches. I was very friendly with the son of
one of them, Duncan Milliken, and also with his neighbour, James
Cadogan, who later became Treasurer of County Durham. My best
friend in the Elementary School was Vivian Trigg, whose father, a
carpenter in the docks, came from Cornwall. The parents of Alan
Michel, my closest friend in the County School, were from the isle
of Guernsey, where Owain Lawgoch made a name for himself
fighting for the French against the English. Alan's father was a
coal-trimmer in the docks. The families of other friends had escaped
from the poverty of more romantic places like Italy or one of the
Arab countries. The Kalamatousis, Kastavounis, Veliadis,

Angelinakis and Germanacos boys were all Greeks, and every one a sailor's son. Chris Germanacos was at College in Aberystwyth with me. He was a splendid runner and in later years became Director of Education on the island of Cyprus.

The town could be a very rough place at times. I remember no policeman would venture on his own of a Friday or Saturday night past the large pubs of Holton Road and down Thompson Street, or anywhere near the docks. There were always fights – they were known as 'affrays' – among the seamen, often Arabs, and knives would flash and there would be stabbings. My father used to tell a story about the burliest man in the district, Inspector Evans, who was a member of our chapel. One Friday evening he was standing outside the Victoria Hotel, a pub known as the Vic, when he saw three or four police-officers trying unsuccessfully to overpower an obstreperous drunk. 'Leave him to me,' said the Inspector, and he wrapped his mighty arms around the man in a bear-hug, squeezing the wind out of him. One of the best things that could happen on our Sunday School trips was when Inspector Evans took one end of the rope in a tug-o'-war and all the children under eleven years of age strained at the other.

Only a very small minority of Barry's townsfolk were able to speak Welsh. There was a sort of colony of Welsh-speakers, mainly from Dyfed, though many had come from the industrial valleys, and some from Gwynedd and Powys. The local people thought 'the Welsh' lived up in the Valleys of Glamorgan and in West and North Wales. From a historical point of view this belief of theirs was not entirely without foundation, because after the Normans had conquered and taken possession of the Vale of Glamorgan, and built their castles there – the conqueror Fitzhamon landed at Porth Ceri on the outskirts of Barry – the 'Welshry' was to be found in the hills on the far side of the Garth mountain. For three centuries, according to Griffith John Williams, the main language of the Vale was French. But, strangely enough, the Welsh language flowed back to repossess the whole area and turn the Norman families into Welsh people. It continued to be the language of a good part of the Vale of Glamorgan until the early part of the present century. The memory of country-poets such as Dewi Esyllt of Dinas Powys and Ioan Trithyd of Llantrithyd survived into my own time. The largest village in the district before the building of the docks had been Cadoxton. It had been so thoroughly Welsh-speaking in the 1870s that immigrants from England and Scotland had found it necessary to learn the language.

In summer the people of the Valleys used to flock to the two beautiful bays at Barry, crowding along Holton Road, the town's shopping-centre.

> 'Mae ynys yn y Barri,
> Ac awel ym Mhorthcawl,
> A siwrnai yn y siarri
> I rai a fedd yr hawl;
> Paham y treuli ddyddiau ir
> A nosau haf yn Ynyshir?'

('There's an island in Barry, and a breeze in Porthcawl, and a trip in a charabanc for those who can pay the fare; why then spend the fresh days and summer evenings in Ynyshir?')

Those are the words of Robert Williams Parry, who was, like Gwenallt Jones, a teacher in the County School. Barry people used to make fun of the noisy ruffians – the 'Shwnies', as they were called – whom they thought 'uncivilized' Welsh folk come down to interrupt the respectability of our town.

The parents of my uncle, Dudley Howe, had come from the other side of Cowbridge in the Vale of Glamorgan. Their Welsh was rich and melodious, but as was the custom of the time, they didn't see fit to pass it on to their children, any more than did the parents of Geoffrey Howe, the Tory from Aberafan. They established an 'English Cause' at Bethel in Cadoxton, a chapel that has been closed these many years.

The eight hundred or so Welsh-speakers in Barry belonged to six Welsh chapels in the town. Four of them had very small congregations; the one Dr Glyn Ashton attended had hardly more than twenty members. The largest was Tabernacl, our chapel, which had about three hundred members in the 'twenties. My grandfather was its first minister and he managed to increase its membership to five hundred, as he did in his other two chapels in Llanelli and Melin Cryddan, Neath, where he had been their first minister. Melin Cryddan was turned into an English chapel sixty years ago. My grandfather died in his early sixties in 1916, after a long illness. In his time as minister you had to be in the evening service a quarter of an hour before it was due to start if you wanted a seat, although as I remember it in the early 'twenties the chapel was no more than half-full most of the time. By the end of the 'thirties it was only a quarter full. It had taken fifteen years for the congregation to be dispersed. By that time four of Barry's Welsh chapels had closed. Today only two remain, with a membership of about two hundred and fifty between them.

The Welsh language disappeared more quickly in Barry than it did among the Welsh of America! When I was a child in Tabernacl most of the children of the first generation, who were then in middle age, could understand Welsh but were unable to speak it. One of them taught me at the Sunday School, where the smallest children went, and another in the young people's class, where we had keen discussions about the football-games of the previous day. The language was English and, anyway, there would have been little point in talking to us in Welsh. There wasn't a single boy, and only one girl in my generation, who could understand and speak the language. The preacher used to deliver the children's address in English, so that we could understand at least something during the service. The Welsh sermon and the long prayers gave us an opportunity for playing games like Noughts and Crosses and Hang the Butcher. One of our favourite games consisted in each one of us opening the hymn-book, *Y Caniedydd*, ten times in succession, and seeing who could hit upon the largest number of hymns by Williams Pantycelyn, who was well-represented in its pages. Indeed, only a few families brought up their children to speak the language. I can think of about ten whose children were born between 1905 and 1920, and they were mostly families with only one child; there was none among them with more than two children. Despite the efforts of the local branch of the Honourable Society of Cymmrodorion, the Welsh language was fast dying in a town with a population of about forty thousand by this time.

Typical of the downright Englishness of the place was the Phillips family – the father a dairyman who hailed, like his vivacious wife, from Carmarthenshire. They both spoke Welsh fluently but their English was quite poor. It was the father, John Phillips, who carved Tabernacl's very beautiful oak pulpit – a masterpiece of craftsmanship. Both he and Mrs Phillips were extremely anxious, like everyone else in those days, for their children 'to get on in the world', and since Welsh in their view was a hindrance, they spoke not one word of it at home. Ivor, the youngest son, became a town councillor for a while. It was with him I composed and performed, in English of course, the operetta for the special meeting of the chapel's Cultural Society that welcomed the girls from the Training College. They jumped at a chance like this because it was only for this Society and the Cymmrodorion that their Principal, Ellen Evans, would allow them out on evenings when they should have been studying. The second Phillips boy became a Secondary School teacher but the oldest son kept a small shop in the back-streets of Barry that sold milk and sweets. Their subsequent careers hardly justified their being deprived of Welsh.

Then there was Griff Griffiths, one of the town's most colourful characters. Griff and his elder brother had walked all the way to Barry from Caernarfon in their early 'teens to look for work. From what Griff said, his brother had sixpence in his pocket when they arrived and he had nothing. He found work cleaning engines on the railway and in due course married a lovely woman from Breconshire who spoke a delightfully pure form of Welsh. They opened a chipshop in Hannah Street on the poorest eastern side of town, while Griff continued to clean engines during the day. He had a bass voice as deep as the sea, which we heard twice on Sundays from the front row of Tabernacl's gallery. For years he used to rush home from work to sing, twice nightly, in the Theatre Royal, changing each time into his evening-dress and then back into his overalls. He eventually gave up the chipshop and the engines to open a bakery, and then a bread-shop, and soon added two cafes to the businesses he owned. After a while he built the district's largest restaurant – the Merrie Friars on Barry Island, a short step from the resort's promenade. This astute businessman was a born Nationalist, who never refused me when I asked him to help Plaid Cymru. Whenever I went to ask him for a contribution, this hulk of a man would fumble in his waistcoat pocket and say in his nasal voice, 'I'll see if I' got a blinkid quid.' It was quite natural for him to address me in English. It was my language, and English was the language of his home, too, where he reared two sons who had distinguished careers in London, both becoming Fellows of the Royal Society of Surgeons. Neither of them had a word of Welsh and in this respect they were typical of the children of the town's Welsh-speakers. One who insisted on speaking Welsh on every possible occasion was Arthen Evans, the hard-working secretary of *Undeb y Cymdeithasau Cymraeg* ('The Union of Welsh Societies'), who lived near us in Somerset Road until I was twelve. I am ashamed to say that whenever I saw Arthen coming I would make off in another direction, though it wasn't so much him I was trying to dodge as his language.

It was more difficult for our home to be Welsh-speaking than it was for most. My father and mother were shopkeepers and when I was a child their working-hours were terribly long. They wouldn't shut their shops till nine o'clock on Saturday night, eight o'clock on a Friday, and six on all other nights. It proved difficult to find anyone to look after the house who was Welsh-speaking. For years the work was done by a young woman from Barrow-in-Furness, and for that reason the language of our home was English.

Chapter 2

My Family

I have been fortunate all my life in having about me relatives and friends whom I have admired and loved. My mother, Catherine Mary, was a very special person of whom I shall say, as T. Gwynn Jones said of Emrys ap Iwan's mother, that everyone was fond of her, that she was always ready to help other people, and that she was of gentle disposition. She was born and brought up at the New Inn, a public-house in Cydweli which for many years afterwards was a shoe-shop. It was there, by the way, that the popular broadcaster Hywel Gwynfryn's father was born. The pub was owned by William Richard, my mother's father. Like his father before him, he served as Warden of the large church at Cydweli. His father, too, was called William, and his trade was that of shoemaker. This William, my great-grandfather, was married in 1811, an important year in the history of Methodism, to Elizabeth Gower. My grandmother, Sage Protheroe, was the daughter of John Protheroe, a blacksmith, and Lettice Treharne of Y Trallwng, a farm at Llangyndeyrn. So I belong in one way or another to the families of Gower, Treharne, Protheroe, and Richard.

As a young girl my mother went to live with her aunt Sage in Llanelli. This aunt, whom we called Auntie Ben, had been a member of Caradog's Choir in Aberdare. She was the wife of Ben Jones, editor and proprietor of *The Llanelly Mercury*; that is to say, he was the general editor. The editor of the four Welsh pages was Myfyr Hefin, the brother of Ben Bowen, the poet who 'talked too much about Wales and eternity' – I have restricted myself to Wales! The only one of my mother's close relatives whom I ever met was her father's brother, a dignified man with a limp; his leg had been lost in an accident on the railway-line. He had been a stationmaster at Ayr in Scotland and later at Cardiff General Station. I never heard a word of Welsh fall from his lips. At the age of fourteen my mother went to work in a shop. After marrying, she kept her own china shop until well into her sixties. During her 'teens she went, like so many girls from Wales in those days, to work in one of the large London department stores, at a wage of five shillings a week, living over the premises. In the company of friends from Cardiganshire, she attended the Calvinistic Methodist chapel on Clapham Common, going to the Sunday School as well as to the services. One of the young teachers used to ride to Sunday School on a bike: his name was David Hughes Parry, and he was later to play a prominent part in the life of Wales. My mother was a zealous chapel-member all her life, regularly attending the week-day meetings – the Prayer Meeting, the Cultural Society, and choir-practice – as well as Sunday services, despite the long hours she had to work in the department store. She came to Barry to work in D.L. Evans's clothes-shop, which happened to be close by my father's business in Holton Road, and where again she lived above the shop. So often did she have rabbit for dinner there that she could never face it after marrying!

My father was the eldest son of an Independent minister in Llanelli. He wasn't born in Llanelli but at Cae Siencyn, a farmhouse at Llangadog which had walls three feet thick, his mother's home. It was her father, Daniel James, and her brother Walter, who were farming there at the time. The Jameses were known as 'the great vein', and they worked several farms in that part of the Tywi Valley, such as Llwyn Siac and Ystrad Walter between Llangadog and Cil-y-cwm on either side of Llandovery town. By today the tribe has died out as if they had never been. In his book on the history of Methodism in Carmarthenshire, James Morris names Cae Siencyn as one of four houses visited by Howell Harris, one of the great leaders of the Methodist Revival in Wales, who often came to Llangadog, no doubt because his father's home was there. Other frequent visitors were William Williams, the hymn-writer known as Pantycelyn, whose descendants still live in the neighbourhood, and Daniel Rowland, another of the great Methodist leaders. Some believe, says James Morris, that it was at Cae Siencyn the first Methodist meeting was held, and in discussing the Calvinistic Methodist cause in the district of Llandovery in the last century, he writes of my great-grandfather: 'Daniel James of Cae Siencyn was a very good man, of gentle character, and highly respected in the district. He was the brother of the late John James. They were and still are a robust family and one prominent in the cause of religion.' Daniel James's wife, that's to say my great-grandmother on this side, was Elizabeth Davies of Penybont, the next farm to Wernellyn, where I was later to live for some years. The Davieses were a leading Methodist family and among the very first Dissenters in the eighteenth century. During their time one of the Circulating Schools run by Griffith Jones was held at Penybont, in 1753-54 and again in 1758-59, as well as an evening class. It is recorded that thirty-two pupils attended the day-school and thirteen in the evening.

My father was brought up in Llanelli and became one of the first boys to attend the new Secondary School. At the age of fourteen he was apprenticed to an ironmonger. When the family moved to Barry, in his eighteenth year, he found a place with an ironmonger there by the name of Hooper. By the age of twenty-one, with capital of four hundred pounds which he received as a loan from his Uncle Walter James, he had opened his own shop in Holton Road, and went on to build up a large business there which grew even bigger with the help of my brother Alcwyn in the next generation. He achieved all this without sacrificing his life to his work. It could not have been said of him, 'born a man, died an ironmonger'. He was involved in all kinds of movements and philanthropic causes, such as the Seamen's Mission. He was for many years Secretary of the town's Chamber of Commerce, and he also served on the Council. In discussing the granting of borough status to the town in 1939, *The Barry Centenary Book*, edited by Donald Moore, has this to say about my father and uncle: 'It was agreed that the Borough's first Mayor and Deputy Mayor would be Dudley Howe and Dan Evans, the two champion boosters of the 1930s, the two men who had dominated the efforts of the Council and the Chamber of Commerce to shrug off recession and to develop confidence . . . Inevitable attention focussed on Councillors Dudley Howe and Dan Evans who had seemed to run Barry for as long as most people could remember. A cartoon in March 1944 depicted 'Dudley and Dan', and in so doing confirmed their symbolic status as the twin representatives of the old order, of what was now seen as the Establishment in Barry.' My father never had anything to do with party politics, but both he and my mother were great admirers of Lloyd George, whose picture hung in our home. This was the cause of the only quarrel I remember between my father and his Socialist brother, Idris, who was a minister in London. It was some time in the mid-'twenties. Idris had dared to make a disparaging remark about Lloyd George. My father could stand it no longer. 'There's the door,' he said. 'Get out and never come back!' The picture came down surreptitiously towards the end of the 'thirties.

My father had a beautiful baritone voice. He used to sing in light opera and was in great demand for concerts in town and throughout the Vale. One year, while performing *Don Quixote*, he fell awkwardly from his horse, and for a whole week he lay in bed during the day and sang in the Theatre Royal at night. He turned down an invitation from the Carla Rosa Opera Company to join it as a professional singer. Many of the ballads he used to sing still reverberate in my head. I often hum to myself the exciting duets he used to sing with Maggie Thomas, the splendid soprano from the Rhondda, and with T.R. Williams, the sweet tenor from Bala (our nickname for him was Baldy Williams – he was a teacher at Gladstone Road), or with Griff Griffiths, the deep bass voice from Caernarfon. Of all the singers I ever heard, my father was the one who gave me most pleasure, though I heard many of the best in the great concerts he arranged at the Theatre Royal. I remember hearing Mostyn Thomas there, his chest like a huge barrel, singing a whole verse in a single breath.

My father had a small orchestra in chapel before it acquired the magnificent pipe-organ for which he had raised the money. I inherited the gold watch that was presented to him by the chapel in gratitude. As there was no electricity in those days to work the organ's big bellows, it fell to lads and young men and one or two well-built, middle-aged men to turn the wheel in a small room under the chapel. We lads of sixteen or seventeen jumped at this chance of missing most of the service. Two of us would turn the wheel together, and when we gave up (a dozen bars of a hymn were enough for us), two others would leap to take our place. But it proved too much for us lads when the organ was officially 'opened' by the immortal Caradog Roberts. Four of the chapel's strongest men were called for that night. I shall always remember the perspiration on the faces of John Davies and Willy Lloyd as they furiously turned the wheel while Caradog Roberts played 'Y Storm'. My father used to play the harmonium sometimes, before the days of the pipe-organ, or else he played the fiddle in the orchestra, and after the advent of the organ he played it himself on some occasions. I was allowed to do the same from time to time, but it was my brother Alcwyn who was the better organist, and he still has that job. My father led the singing for half a century and was head deacon for most of that time. But his most magnificent achievement was the mixed choir of a hundred voices or so which performed every one of the great oratorios at least once, as well as several other classical or light pieces. Once they performed 'Blodwen', the work by Joseph Parry whose picture hung in our hall. Morgan John Lloyd, who lived in Barry, made fun of this extravaganza. Despite having no voice to speak of, I sang in this choir for many years, first as an alto and then bass, in a vain attempt to compete with Griff Griffiths! I had great admiration for my father's talent, especially since his musical education had been confined to the piano lessons he had received before his apprenticeship in

Llanelli. Whenever the tenors or altos or some other voices were unsure of the notes, he would lead them with perfect authority.

I confess that at sixteen years of age I had another reason, apart from my admiration for its leader, for being such a diligent bass in the choir. When Glenys walked in with her two older sisters, wearing a soft round black hat with a wide brim, a school-hat, my heart missed more than a beat or two. Glenys was a good-looking, vivacious girl, with a good figure, big blue eyes, red cheeks, wavy black hair and perfect teeth that were often to be seen, for she smiled like an angel. I courted her for three years. Whenever she felt relaxed in my company, and in happy mood, she would say, 'Oh, Gwyn, you're choc-o-late!'

My parents' hero, and the most important influence on their lives, had been my grandfather, Ben Evans, the minister of Tabernacl. They both worshipped his memory. I can hardly recall him, for he died young, when I was three. But I heard a lot about him from my parents, and from his sister, Auntie Jane, who was a martyr to rheumatism and lived with us, bed-ridden, for the last eight years of her life. After I went up into the sixth form, I made her bedroom into a 'Welsh room'. Auntie Jane was a gentle woman who had been employed in the service of the Dillwyn family of Penllergaer as a seamstress. She displayed her independent spirit by going to New York when she was eighteen in about 1870. I held her hand as she lay dying.

Ben Evans hailed from Felindre, near Pontarddulais, and was the son of a weaver who had gone there in the middle of the last century from Alltwalis, a district near Pencader renowned for its weavers. Of the weaver's four sons, three entered the ministry. The fourth was for many years a professional soldier in India. At the age of nine, Ben went to help his father's brother, who was known as Ifans y Gors, on his farm at Salem, near Llandeilo. This farmer was minister of the Salem Chapel that gave its name to the village, and also of Carmel at Llansadwrn, and on top of all this he was the neighbourhood vet. I once heard about his being called out in the middle of a sermon to see to a sick cow. Ben was a farmservant with this man when he began preaching, and when later he decided to go in for the ministry he received some of his education at the school which in due course became the one run by Watcyn Wyn, who removed it from Bacwai in Llangadog to Ammanford. (Bacwai now has a more dignified name – it's called Heol Gwallter, after my Uncle Walter who used to live there.) This was as much formal education as my grandfather had before going to the Memorial College in Brecon. During the first years of his ministry he was confined to his bed for twelve months, and used to say that the year had been more valuable to him than any college because it gave him a chance to read avidly. Despite his lack of formal education, he was for many years Chairman of Barry's progressive Education Committee. He was also an unusually powerful preacher. When I began visiting other parts of Wales, some twenty-five years after his death, people would come up to me at the close of meetings, mainly in the South but also twice in the North, to talk about the sermons he had given, quoting the text and sometimes even the sermons' heads. No doubt this says as much about the listener as the preacher. His great gift was inherited by Idris, my father's brother, who after studying at the Universities of Wales and Cambridge spent the rest of his life in London.

During the Revival in the early years of this century many turned to Jesus Christ at my grandfather's meetings in the docks. One of these was John Jones of Coigne Terrace, a saintly man. His handsome features used to shine when he stood among the deacons, facing the congregation and singing the hymns. At his side stood David Rees, who was a labourer in the docks, and he too had been converted by my grandfather's preaching. David Rees was one of the purest men I have ever known. When singing, he would be lost in the hymn, waving the hymn-book from side to side with the beat. Almost all the deacons in my grandfather's time were dock-workers. The academics and other posh people used to go to Ebeneser, where D.H. Williams, Chairman of the Central Welsh Board, was minister. But a good number of the workers in my grandfather's chapel were coal-trimmers who worked in the dust of the ships' holds. I used to see them coming home sometimes blacker than colliers. In fact, the chapel was popularly known as 'the Trimmers' Chapel'. To some extent, I have to admit, this was a result of propaganda by the chief trimmer, a Welsh-speaker and a good Independent. His surname was Lewis, but he was known to Welsh-speakers as Bola Mawr ('Big Belly') and his son as Bola Bach ('Little Belly').

Another great character was James Evans, the weaver, Ben's father; he too led the singing and was head deacon in the Independent chapel at Felindre in Pontarddulais, which is still a Welsh-speaking village situated in the natural bowl of the mountain between Tawe and Dulais. Whenever Tom Jones, a Barry grocer, who came from Felindre, wanted to pull me down a peg or two, he would say there was nobody in our family to compare in ability with James Evans. He hailed from Alltwalis, but his father, also a weaver, came from Llanfihangel-ar-arth, where my daughter Meinir now lives. I obtain my knowledge about our ancestors, by the way, from my son Guto Prys: he is the authority on our family-tree. With the help of the lineage drawn up by Gweirydd ap Rhys, my wife Rhiannon's great-grandfather, who yet again was a weaver, Guto has traced her ancestry back to Rhodri Mawr and Cunedda! As is now evident, my own roots are more humble! James Evans was an important man in Felindre. When I went there many years ago with Dr J. Gwyn Griffiths, the editor of *Y Ddraig Goch* at the time, for a Plaid Cymru meeting, it was held in Nebo Chapel. That is where all the village's meetings, of whatsoever kind, were held. It has continued to be a Meeting House and has not declined into a Temple. After the meeting was over, two or three of the older people said they could remember the funeral of James Evans. It seems that the oratory at the graveside was so terribly long-winded that lanterns had to be sent for. There was one occasion when I had to write about James, on behalf of my Aunt Jane, to Raratonga in the Pacific Islands. A letter from a missionary living on that island had appeared in *The Missionary Chronicle*. He had bought a second-hand book while on a long vacation in Wales – Fox's *Book of Martyrs* – in a shop similar to Ralph's in Swansea, I suppose. Inside the cover was the name James Evans, weaver. The letter asked whether anyone could tell him anything about the weaver who had owned such a book. So I wrote to Raratonga with details about my great-grandfather.

Sometimes, again on my Aunt Jane's behalf, I would have to write to New Zealand, to the widow of William, another of James's sons, who was a minister in Wellington. His wife had been the first woman in the Commonwealth to obtain a degree. This fact is recorded on a tablet in the University of Wellington, with the words 'To honour Mrs W.A. Evans, a former student of this college and the first woman to graduate within the British Empire. Bachelor of Arts, the University of New Zealand. A.D. 1877.'

I have in my possession an elegy by someone calling himself Habacuc which won a prize in the Eisteddfod at Pontarddulais. I am sorry to say that it doesn't compare with the work of the great Gruffudd ab yr Ynad Coch, though it sometimes ascends in the genius of its doggerel to the heights of the Cockle Poet, our equivalent of William McGonagall. But not often. It opens effectively enough:

> *'Tra'r haul ar orsedd ei ogoniant dillyn*
> *Y bore Sadwrn olaf yn y flwyddyn (1893),*
> *Yn ardal hyfryd y Felindre enwog*
> *Yr hon sydd mewn prydferthwch yn odidog . . . '*

('While the sun on the throne of its lovely magnificence on the last Saturday of the year 1893 in the fair district of famous Felindre which is splendid in its beauty . . . .')

Habacuc brings his long poem to a close with these impressive lines:

'James Evans, Ha! yng ngwlad yr aur delynau
Mae heddiw'n tiwnio tannau'r nefol odlau.'

('James Evans, ha! in the land of the golden harps he is today tuning the heavenly rhymes.')

It was thus my great-grandfather won a place for himself in the literary history of Wales!

Chapter 3

Childhood

The Great War was in mid-course when at the age of four I went to primary school. Although I fell in love immediately with Mary Rowlands, the seven years I spent at Gladstone Road School were on the whole unhappy ones. I remember seeing long columns of soldiers marching to the band's defiant sound down the slope a hundred yards from the school, from the Buttrills camp, to board a ship that was to take them to France. The two things that made a deep impression on me were the goat at the head of the band and the tears of some of the soldiers. One of the things that have remained on my conscience ever since that tender-hearted time was my threatening to shoot a boy who was even smaller than me, with a pistol that was only a piece of wood, and making him give me a lump of his horse-chocolate – horribly bitter stuff that resembled chocolate only in its colour. Very few children could afford to buy it in those days and I wasn't one of them. I was given a halfpenny a week as pocket-money until I went to the school for older children, when it was increased to a penny. The whole penny usually went on sweets, either all at once or else a halfpenny at a time. Whenever I spent the whole penny it was on caramel chocolates, which were my favourites because they lasted longer. I was in my seventh heaven when the penny went up to fourpence on my admission to the County School.

I was a sickly child who caught diptheria very badly on two occasions, the first time when I was four and the second at the age of eight. Of the first illness what I recall most clearly were the huge, beautiful warships in a book the like of which I had never seen before. Of the second, I remember my Uncle Dudley coming into my room one Sunday morning between visits from the doctor who had stuck a pin into my back, and the word 'crisis' reaching my ears as I lay in bed. None of this had any effect on my spirits. I went on making armies with the pennies and halfpennies I was given, with the heads fighting against the tails. I was sadder one evening to see, for the very first time, my father weeping, and from the conversation he was having with my mother at the bedroom door I caught the word 'deflation', which has remained in my ears ever since. I came to understand later that the value of the shop's stock was falling at an alarming rate. The physical weakness which had overwhelmed me meant that I had no reserves of courage. Vivian Trigg, my friend, who was much bigger and heavier than I was, insisted on fighting me on the way home from school, and he would floor me easily. Whenever my sister Ceridwen was a witness to this terrifying scene, she would run home screaming that I was being murdered.

My feeble constitution and small stature continued to trouble me until I reached the fifth form of the County School. As I stood no higher than my friend Vivian's shoulder when I was in the fourth form, I was at a serious disadvantage in trying to win the affections of black-eyed Lillian, one of twins, with whom I fell hopelessly in love when I first saw her in a flame-red dress at some party or other. The other twin was Vivian's sweetheart. Sometimes I was ashamed of my physical weakness, as for example in the Chemistry class. The teacher, a keen Liberal from Llanybydder, had won a prize for hurdling in the Olympic Games – it was this prowess rather than any knowledge of Chemistry that had got him the job. This chap couldn't stand me any more than my Uncle Idris before me. Whenever there was a noise in the classroom, while he was writing his interminable equations on the blackboard, he would shout without turning his head, 'Evans, get out!'. It was he who looked after the school's athletics and one day when I was in the fifth form he asked for volunteers to go down to Gladstone Road School to fetch poles for the games. My hand shot up, of course. 'Evans,' he said, 'you are too weak to carry a matchstick.' Sometimes my feebleness seemed to be getting the better of me, and many a time I was sure I was going to die. The trials of adolescence, no doubt.

The mention of Chemistry lessons brings to mind the Welsh classes at the elementary school. The same teacher taught us in all subjects from the first year to the last. It was the Welsh lesson that gave him the best chance for taking it easy, not that he made much effort in any of the other lessons; it would have been difficult to find anyone quite so lacking in inspiration. But in the Welsh lesson he excelled himself. His arrival was a signal for Ron Dawe to be sent to his family's small shop on the corner of Regent Street to fetch two things – a bar of chocolate and a copy of *The Racing Times*. The teacher would spend the Welsh lesson scoffing the chocolate behind this important paper, while mechanically asking

the class, 'What is horse?' '*Ceffyl*', chanted the class of fifty.
'Again.' '*Ceffyl*.' 'Again.' '*Ceffyl*.' We would learn about four
words in a lesson.

I have sweet memories of holidays at Llangadog during that
dismal period. I was a taken to be a bit of a lad among the country
people because I came from a town. Little did they think of
Llangadog as a town, although years before, the old village doctor
had written the cautionary lines,

> *'Ni ddylai'r un bachgen sy'n byw yn y wlad*
> *Fynd lawr i Langadog heb siarad â'i dad.'*

('No boy who lives in the country should go down to Llangadog
without telling his father.')

Indeed, over the mountain in Brynaman, Llangadog was known
as Tre-wanc, on account of its great number of public houses. Of
course, it couldn't be compared with the enormous town of Barry,
the glorious size of which was somehow reflected in me. Even my
inability to speak Welsh was respected because I came from such a
big place. Old Evans, the caretaker of the YMCA hall, explained to
my friends that, if I had so wished, I could have put them all in the
shade by speaking a more grammatically correct Welsh than the
impoverished form of the language that they habitually spoke. I used
to stay with Walter James, the auctioneer, my grandmother's
brother, about whom I shall speak later.

My Uncle Dan, or Danny as he was known, Walter's son, lived
with his parents in those days. It would have been better if he'd
continued to do so, poor fellow. Danny took great delight in dogs
and horses – any kind of dog, all kinds of horses. For most of his life
he was a judge of corgis at Cruft's. It was his friend, Griff Griffiths
of Bryngwyn, who looked after his sheep-dogs. He used to exercise
them by taking them to sheep-dog trials up and down the country.
He was a keen devotee of these events. We used to set off on our
bikes, with the dogs running behind us, their pink tongues slavering.
I remember in particular a trip over the Black Mountain to Abercrâf
at the top end of the Swansea Valley, when I was nine and Griff a
mature old man of twenty-nine. I was often in Abercrâf thereafter,
well into my thirties and forties myself by then and speaking at
street-corners, and on a few occasions listening to opera in Madam
Patti's beautiful little theatre at Craig-y-nos.

Bryngwyn, Griff's home, is one of the smallholdings built for
ex-soldiers on Sir Mervyn Peel's estate, Dan-yr-Allt. One evening he
showed me and Uncle Danny James the chief wonder of the new

house, namely the bath, a luxury that had been confined up to then
to the Dan-yr-Allt mansion. It was obvious that Uncle Danny had
seen such wonders before. But we had been taken there that evening
because there was more than a bath to be seen. The bath was half-full
of salmon – a catch taken from the river Tywi by Griff and Danny
in the small hours of the previous night. That was the moment it
dawned on me that Meg and Fan and the other dogs had more
important work than rounding up sheep and winning at trials, and
after that Griff and Danny were even greater heroes in my eyes. Some
time later, Danny was appointed to the magistrates' bench at quite
a heavy cost to himself, it must be said, as he was to confess to me.
I heard that he was a most meticulous magistrate who was especially
lenient to poachers!

Sometimes I would round up ponies with Jeff Lewis from the Post
Office, who would ride them skilfully at races. On other occasions I
went by bicycle in the company of Boysy Lewis, who later studied at
Jesus College, Oxford, to distant places like Llyn-y-Fan, where
Cadair Arthur ('Arthur's Chair') is said to guard the great depths of
the smaller of the two lakes. Sometimes a gang of us would go for a
picnic in the cart belonging to The Welcome, the home of my best
friend in the village, Arthur Rees. Arthur later went to Cambridge
and became a brilliant forward in the Welsh rugby team under the
name of A.W. Rees. It was with him and Alfie Light and others that
I would bathe naked in the river Brân, running around the field
afterwards in order to dry off; only the village snob wore swimming-
trunks. We did this in full view of people crossing the Brân bridge,
and unfortunately, on one occasion we were spotted by Arthur's
older sister, who was going to be a doctor, and the shock was almost
too much for her. When we went to Arthur's home later on, she gave
us a sharp telling-off that I remember to this day. However, I never
regretted it, I'm sorry to say. I liked to feel the wind and the sun's
warmth on my body. Years later, after selling tomatoes at
Llanwrtyd, I would sometimes go through Abergwesyn to Cwm
Irfon, before cars could go that way or any bridge was built over the
river, and wander the mountain-top with nothing on, or lie in the
river with my body streaming with water from the Irfon falls. Willie
Davies sat in the next desk to me when we were ten years old. He
used to love to hear about my holiday exploits. He had never had a
holiday, and when I talked about my nude bathing in the river, he
would listen with his eyes like saucers. More than once he would beg
me, 'Tell me about it again, Gwyn'. Poor Willie died young, without
ever experiencing such freedom and joy.

The Frondeg family at Bacwai, that is Uncle Walter and Aunty

Mary and their son Danny and daughter Blodwen, were exceedingly kind to me. English was the language of their home for the most part – Uncle Walter was an auctioneer and head deacon at Gosen, the Calvinistic Methodist chapel where he was a bit of a tyrant. He would interrupt a sermon mercilessly if the content was unacceptable to him. '*Ych a fi*, let's have a bit of the Gospel now', he would exclaim whenever some preacher, poor chap, tried to convey the social gospel. He owned a shiny yellow Renault, the 1912 model, which had a bonnet like a sea-wave, with room for one person to sit in front at the driver's side – usually Uncle Walter himself – and barely room for another two in the dicky-seat at the rear. The back-seat was a narrow plank set across two iron bars, and it was there I sat. Auntie Mary and Aunty Blodwen used to fear for their lives in the yellow Renault if Uncle Walter was at the wheel – he was such a reckless driver. He would often go over twenty miles an hour! It must be remembered that in those days the surface of the roads was made up of loose stones, and that there was no such thing as tarmac. Once, the car skidded and when someone happened to come by, they found Uncle Walter lying unconscious in a ditch, the vehicle itself a yard or two away. But the steering-wheel was still in his hands! The reason for this was his great weight. For most of his life he weighed more than twenty-one stone. He might well have said with Keats, 'I cannot see what flowers are at my feet'. Getting his boots on in the morning was an awful ceremony that called for all the combined skills of the maid Miriam and Aunty Mary, a little woman about a quarter the size of her husband. With many an 'Ugh' and exclamation from Uncle Walter, they managed with all their strength to pull the huge boots on to the feet that were stretched out on a low stool. Then they would ritually tie his shoe-laces, while the giant's eyes gazed thoughtfully at the ceiling. Uncle Walter enjoyed rude health despite his weight. He was over eighty before he was troubled by any serious illness. The doctor told him then that he would have to lose weight. He came to Barry to convalesce, to his daughter Blodwen's house, she having become by then Uncle Dudley's second wife. We went for a stroll together down to Barry Island, where Walter decided to see how many stones he had lost by dieting. He stood on the scales, put a penny in, and the hand shot wildly around the dial and, with a loud click, banged against the twenty-stone mark. 'Damn it,' said Uncle Walter, 'no more of that diet for me,' and he went on enjoying his food to the end of his days. Yet his last years were sad enough. During the Great Depression the butchers who bought stock in his marts and sales went bankrupt one by one, until Walter found himself thousands of pounds in debt. His son Danny, who followed his father in the business, spent most of his life, and all honour to him for this, struggling to pay off the debts, which he eventually managed to do.

Chapter 4

School and Student Days

Although going up to the County School was like entering another world, I wasn't much happier there until I reached the fifth form, when my increasing strength and physical stature brought a new confidence that secured for me a place in the school's hockey and cricket teams. The Barry County School was renowned for its success at games. The headmaster placed great emphasis on them. One of the boys in the same fifth form as me was Ron Boone who for many years played rugby for Wales as a winger. He was a very talented lad. He could entertain the Debates Society on his own for hours on end. He had also been the principal soloist of the famous Romilly School Choir that toured Europe and America. The choir's leader was W.M. Williams, the father of Grace Williams, the composer, who lived a hundred yeards from us in Old Village Road, where six thatched cottages were all that was left of the old village of Barry. Another form-member was Gus Risman, a true friend, who in a few years was to become captain of the English rugby team in the Northern League. Our prowess at cricket can be accurately measured because there was at that time a competition between the secondary schools of Wales, although it was restricted in fact to schools in eastern Glamorgan and Gwent. The Schofield Shield was awarded to the winning team. For five years in succession, including the three that I was a member of the team, we won the Shield. Some of the boys played for Glamorgan, including Gus Risman, Ron Boone, and Alec McKay, my predecessor as captain, who later became Cardiff's Director of Education. I also played for two years in the Welsh boys' team against a team of professional players at Cardiff Arms Park. A great deal of our time went on these games, and we continued practising in the nets even when the examinations were being held. I went on playing cricket and hockey for the University College of Wales at Aberystwyth for two years and later for St. John's College, Oxford. We also had a lot of fun in the chapel's cricket team on the bumpy field at the Buttrills. The state of the pitch was mainly responsible for my greatest feat, which was to take ten wickets without a run against the Royal Engineers. They nevertheless scored twenty extras! I'm not much of a batsman; it's my brother Alcwyn who has the eye for that.

The headmaster's enthusiasm wasn't wholly given over to games. Edgar Jones was an extraordinary man; Geraint Vaughan Jones, the scholar and novelist, is a nephew of his, by the way. Every Friday morning, after the school's religious service, all the boys, some five hundred of us, had a concert lasting three-quarters of an hour. We sang from *The National Song Book* the songs of the four nations in the countries of Britain. We listened to the greatest European music and to the headmaster himself reading extracts from the finest English literature. Imagine five hundred boys sitting for an hour or so in two large classrooms with a partition pulled back, for that was how the hall was arranged. About a hundred sat on chairs, with more than a hundred perched on their laps, and the rest sitting on the floor or the window-sills. In the sixth form the headmaster gave us talks about archaeology. Other teachers spoke about philosophy and art and various other subjects. Edgar Jones made sure that there was an eisteddfod in the school on St. David's Day. Glyn Ashton used to win all the Welsh prizes and it wasn't until he had left that I had any chance at all. But in my last year I won a prize for an English lyric, pushing Hrothgar Habbakkuk into second place. I don't remember what the subject was, but I do know that I wrote about a pretty blonde from Aberdare who was a student at Barry College, which was next door to the school. My poem was heavily influenced by Wordsworth's 'Lucy': 'And there I left her singing still'. This little success made up for my shame in the elementary school when the teacher had written, 'No signs of a Wordsworth' in the margin of some uninspired verses of mine.

The staff at the County School were of exceptional quality. Most fortunate for me was the arrival of Mr Gwynallt Evans, straight from University, as a teacher of Welsh; I was his only pupil in the sixth form. The pleasure I derived from his tutorials has remained with me to this day. Under his instruction I warmed to the *Mabinogion*, to Ellis Wynne and Williams Parry and Kate Roberts and many another writer. As he was so young he mixed easily with us, even playing in the school hockey-team. Our History teacher was none less than David Williams, the father of the present generation of Welsh historians, a gentle, kind man who carried his learning lightly. Under his influence my best friend, Alan Michel, won a Meyricke Scholarship to Jesus College, Oxford. After a while as a don at Wadham College, Alan entered the diplomatic service.

The two years I spent in the sixth form were of great importance to me. That was the time when I first became aware of the wonder of Wales and the curse of war and the importance of international life. I was an internationalist before ever I became a Nationalist. I was encouraged to sit the examination for one of four scholarships that the League of Nations Union gave to enable pupils to study its affairs in Geneva. One of the boys in the same form as me who won a scholarship was Glyn Daniel, who in due course was to have his own Chair of Archaeology at Cambridge. We went to Geneva – which was better-known to us as the home of the League of Nations than as the city of Calvin – in the care of Gwilym Davies, the author of *Urdd Gobaith Cymru*'s Peace Message; he spent most of the year there as the League of Nations Union's Welsh representative. The other two who came with us were Gwilym O. Williams, later to become Archbishop of Wales, and Ellis Williams, who was until recently headmaster of the Grammar School at Abergele.

Prior to this trip, a walking tour of the Pyrénées in the company of Alan Michel had awakened in me an interest in the life of other countries. I was sixteen when we sailed from Barry in a small merchant ship to spend six weeks walking through northern Spain and south-western France, mainly in the Basque Country, where most men, as far as I could make out, did little else than wander the countryside on their bikes, wearing a beret and carrying an umbrella on their backs. They seemed to spend the rest of their time playing pelota! We slept in a small tent until the last week of the trip, when it was wrecked by a terrifying storm. We went into the nearest hamlet soaked to our skins to seek shelter and dry off our clothes and packs. The place consisted of a small cluster of houses, nothing more. We spotted a light in a shabby-looking café, a wooden building. The family were up and trying to catch the water that was pouring through the holes in their roof. They were kind enough to give us shelter, but there was no fire to dry our clothes. When it grew light we had to run for miles in order to dry off. We were now in some distress, with little money and nowhere to shelter. We reached Bayonne and began looking for a boat that would take us home. We were given to understand that there would be no boat for a week, but mercifully, the keeper of the Seamen's Mission took pity on us and for a whole week we slept on a billiards table in the club of the movement for which my father had done so much. We came back through the worst storm I have ever seen at sea, and then, after four days, to my great joy, the Mumbles lighthouse came into view.

I can see now that my seventeenth year was something of a turning-point in my life. In addition to the teachers' lessons and what the headmaster did for us, my fellow-pupils played their part. I enjoyed long conversations with Alan Michel and the company of Glyn Daniel, among others. Glyn's parents were Welsh-speaking and his father was headmaster of Llantwit Major Elementary School, yet they passed on nothing of the language to their son, unfortunately. It was Glyn who introduced me to *The New Statesman*, which I was to buy and read avidly, much to the disgust of Saunders Lewis, up to the late 'sixties. My class included some exceptionally gifted lads in whom the Old Barrians still rejoice. I have mentioned a number of them already. Three were given knighthoods – Brian Hopkin, who was to become one of the top men in the Treasury, Arthur Davies who was head of the World Meteorogical Service, with its headquarters in Geneva; Hrothgar Habbakkuk, for twenty years Principal of Jesus College and in due course Vice-Chancellor of Oxford University; and Elfyn Richards, who designed some of Britain's finest aeroplanes and became Principal of Loughborough University. Someone else who influenced me was the poet J.M. Edwards who lived in the town; he was always ready to help me with the finer points of Welsh grammar.

I had made good use of the town's library while still a pupil at the elementary school. By the age of twelve I had read almost all G.A. Henty's historical novels, dozens of them, and over the next year or two I devoured the detective-novels of Edgar Wallace, as well as Zane Grey's books which I borrowed for twopence from Dod Adams, the tobacconist, and read when my parents thought I was working hard at my homework. But at the age of sixteen I began borrowing books on political, historical, and social subjects. It was a book by Leyton Richards that made a pacifist of me. I still remember his descriptions of war. Soon, on the recommendation of David Williams, I had read R.H. Tawney's *Religion and the Rise of Capitalism* and his *Equality*. At College the work of G.D.H. Cole, whose thinking was so similar to that of D.J. Davies, was also to have an influence on me.

At the age of seventeen I was gripped more and more by my reading of Welsh: the language of W.J. Gruffydd and Kate Roberts, Williams Parry and Parry-Williams, and many another writer, gave me more of a thrill than any I had found in my reading of English literature. It's more than likely that I experienced something akin to a conversion in this year. Wales came alive for me. I awoke to the fact that we have songs and hymns that are splendid in both their music and their poetry. I found it exciting to sing them at the piano in a loud voice, even if no one else did. If only I could have sung as well as my father! Whenever my spirits were low I would cheer myself up by singing, no,

shouting at the top of my voice, I'm afraid, the words of the tune
'*Moab*' or '*Hermon*':

> '*Ar lan Iorddonen ddofn*
> *Rwy'n oedi'n nychlyd . . .*'

('On the banks of the deep Jordan I linger languishing . . . .').

The mournful sound of '*Tynged Morfa Rhuddlan*' always had the
same effect on me:

> '*Ciliai'r haul draw dros ael bryniau hael Arfon*'.

('The sun withdraws beyond the noble mountains of Arfon').

When I was in happier mood I took even greater pleasure in the
rumbustious sound of '*Llais hyfryd Rhad Ras sy'n gweiddi
"Dihangfa!"* ', or in the quiet beauty of '*Bugeilio'r Gwenith Gwyn*' –
'Watching the White Wheat'. In time my appreciation of the
splendours of Welsh hymns and hymn-tunes grew more profound
and perhaps my taste became rather more sophisticated, too. But
they have never ceased to excite me.

The enchanting loveliness I saw everywhere in my wandering
through Wales made a deep impression on my mind and feelings, and
to this day the beauty of its landscape can make me catch my breath
and bring me to tears. It has always vexed me that the English see so
much more of this beauty than the Welsh do. When I was young, it
was they, not our own people, who walked the hills and slept in the
Youth Hostels. Despite all this, it was some while before I became
aware of Welsh Nationalism, or even realized that I belonged to a
nation that had a claim on my allegiance. But I had begun to turn in
that direction. The moment at which something like a conversion
seemed to take place was a debate, in English of course, that I had
arranged just after my sixteenth birthday for the chapel's Cultural
Society. The topic I chose was 'that Tabernacl must be turned into an
English chapel'. I spoke earnestly in favour of this motion, giving the
reasons that were so popular at the time: that religion is more important than language, that Welsh was dying anyway, and so on. One of
those who spoke strongly against me that evening, and who advised
me to buy a Welsh dictionary and grammar and to learn the language,
was John Davies, the chapel's Secretary. He was one of the finest men
on earth, a man whom I learned to admire greatly and respect as one
who was foremost among the saints. He hailed from Cardiganshire
and had come to Barry to work in the docks, like many another Cardi.
At the time he drove a goods train. He was a big man, physically strong
with bandy legs and the face of an angel. He was also a sincere

Welshman who later became a Nationalist. I glow as I think of him now.

Just after my eighteenth birthday I went to study Law at the University College of Wales, Aberystwyth. The line from Carmarthen through Tregaron is long closed, but in those days it went via Cynwil Elfed, through a small valley that was 'narrower than a cockerel's strut', namely the leafy Cwm Gwili, and it never failed to excite me. Aberystwyth was a small college of some six hundred students at that time. Nine out of ten undergraduates were Welsh, with a sprinkling from England, India and Africa. I expect the sophisticated student of today would consider us rather immature. The first-year students, or freshers, were initiated into College life in weird ceremonies that were to be abandoned soon after the war. As part of these rituals we would all have to take off our trousers and wear pyjamas. Then we would walk along the prom and down the High Street with the older students prodding us from behind and pretending to whip us with bamboo canes and the branches of a banana-tree. On our return to College the trousers were hurled from the balcony to the floor of the Quad and we each had to search the pile for the right pair. I heard that it was my friend J.R. Jones, that fine philosopher, who had led the pyjama-procession along the prom the previous year, holding a chamber-pot in front of him in which to collect money, like an acolyte, his face as straight as a saint's.

The social life of the College was a full and hectic one. The Debates Society on Friday evenings and the Students' Christian Movement on Sundays would fill the Examinations Hall of the Old College; the buildings up on Penglais had not then been built. Even the International Relations Club, of which I was Secretary and later Chairman, could fill the Hall at times. The Welsh soirées organized by the Celtic Society, to which the poet Gwenallt Jones made such a great contribution, and at which Amy Parry-Williams was the star, were always full to overflowing. The beautiful Amy was serenaded in a song written by Gwenallt that was sung in one of these musicals to the tune 'The Rose of Tralee':

> *'Roedd hi'n brydferth a thlws fel rhosynnau Mehefin*
> *Ond nid ei phrydferthwch a aeth â'm bryd i;*
> *O na, ond y gwir yn ei llygaid yn gwawrio*
> *A wnaeth i mi garu perl Coleg y Lli.'*

('She was lovely and fair as the roses of June but it was not her beauty alone that won me; oh no, 'twas the truth in her eyes ever dawning that made me love the pearl of the College by the Sea.')

I could follow the Welsh of these occasions without much difficulty, however degrading it was to have to ask my friends to turn to
English in conversation with me. Apart from in the Welsh Department where T.H. Parry-Williams was Professor, the only Welsh to
be heard in lectures was at those given by T. Gwynn Jones, who held
a personal Chair. I used to go to listen to the great poet sometimes.
Of course, not a word of Welsh was used in the administration of the
College, nor was there any awareness that part of its responsibility
was to provide leaders in the life of Wales. As far as I could make
out, the Principal, who knew no Welsh, wasn't aware of Wales at all:
Stuart Jones was a Classics scholar and not at all close to his students.
Only once did I dine with him, and that was when R.T. Evans, the
M.P. for Carmarthenshire, came to speak to the International Relations Club. The talk over dinner that evening wasn't about international affairs. Instead, the Principal took up most of the hour trying
to persuade R.T. Evans to invest money in the Dolau Cothi gold-
mines which were in his constituency. The old Roman works had
been reopened under the supervision of the Principal's son, Commander Stuart Jones, the author of *The Last Invasion of Britain*; he
was the fourth person at table. After the gold-mine failed, the
Commander sometimes used to call at the greenhouses in Llangadog,
selling paint.

The Principal showed his political colours clearly on one occasion
when he chaired a talk by Gareth Jones, the brilliant son of my old
headmaster, Edgar Jones. In the summer vacation of that year
Gareth had described for me what he'd seen during his journey
through the Soviet Union the previous spring on behalf of *The
Manchester Guardian*. This was in 1933 when Stalin was starving
millions of small farmers and others to death as a consequence of his
collectivization of the farms. On coming out of a railway-station in
the Ukraine, Gareth had seen corpses lying at the side of the road
and hungry people, who had been in academic posts, had crowded
around him begging for a crust of bread. After his articles appeared
in the press he wasn't allowed to go back to the Soviet Union. I
invited him to address the International Club about what he'd seen
on his trip and the Principal had agreed to take the chair. Although
the speaker drew on his personal experience of Stalin's tyranny,
Stuart Jones had the effrontery to say at the end of the lecture that
he didn't believe him. As far as he was concerned, nothing so heinous
could happen in the Soviet Union. Two years later Gareth was killed,
by persons unknown, bandits probably, while travelling in China.

It must be remembered that this was a time of terrible economic
depression when hundreds of thousands of Welsh people were

languishing in poverty and on the dole. It seemed as if Capitalism was about to disintegrate. Many a generous-hearted young man turned to Communism and some, such as Burgess, Maclean, Kim Philby, and Anthony Blunt, members of a circle with which Goronwy Rees – who later became Principal at Aberystwyth – was connected, were spies for the Soviet Union. I felt no attraction to their Marxist-Leninist creed, and deplored the oppression of the Communist regime that some of my friends were wont to defend. But I joined the influential Left Book Club and read the red-jacketed Gollancz books with zest. If Keir Hardie could be called a Socialist, I was a kind of Socialist before ever I became a Nationalist. By the way, I met Hrothgar Habbakkuk at a meeting of the Left Book Club in Barry. A book that confirmed my attitude towards the totalitarianism of the Soviet Union, which was generally accepted by the British public during the war, was Arthur Koestler's *Darkness at Noon*; it made an indelible impression on me. Yet, although the tyranny of the left is as odious to me as that of the right, I respect the Marxist-Leninists of Wales for the reason that they seek a society which is not corrupted by market forces. Another book that left its mark on me, on account of its author's personality as much as its content, was *The Making of a State* by Thomas Masaryk, the Czech Nationalist statesman who had clear vision and was indefatigable in trying to realize it. There was, too, a similarity between the policies of Plaid Cymru and the Guild Socialism that was preached by G.D.H. Cole. I read his work early on and at Oxford I attended some of his lectures. The lecture theatre wasn't large enough to hold the crowd who came to hear his first lecture. Cole asked us to be patient: there would be plenty of room, he said, in the second lecture. It was true, for about a dozen turned up and only five for the third lecture. I don't know how many were at the fourth – I wasn't.

There was a vigorous group of pacifists at Aberystwyth. This was the time of the famous motion before the Oxford University Debates Union – 'that this House will not fight for King and Country'. We sold literature, held meetings and organized some very effective anti-war exhibitions in the Town Hall. But the strongest group in College was probably the Students' Christian Society. Two of the prominent Englishmen invited to address it were William Temple, who later became Archbishop of York, and Canon Charles E. Raven. The S.C.M. held a large British conference every four years. It happened to fall during my time at Aberystwyth and I was one of those who attended it in Edinburgh. The conference was held in the great Usher Hall with its banner bearing four words of Latin above the stage: '*Ut omnes unum sint*'. Our leader was Dr Gwenan Jones, of blessed memory, a fine example of Penllyn's culture and one of the greatest of all Welsh women; she was of very strong mind and convictions, a pacifist and Nationalist. She edited the magazine *Yr Efrydydd* for many years. After leaving College I kept in close touch with her through *Urdd y Deyrnas* and also came into contact with her in the ranks of Plaid Cymru. It was she who stood for the Party in the University constituency during the General Election of 1945. Throughout the war and for years thereafter she worked to remarkable effect with the Committee for the Defence of Welsh Culture and *Undeb Cymru Fydd*. Her booklet, *Cymru a'i Chymdogion*, was one of the publications which prepared the way for the establishment of Plaid Cymru. Many's the time I called on her at her home in Llandre.

One of those whose company I often enjoyed on bus-trips with the College hockey-team was the poet Alun Lewis, who was to die in Burma in 1944. Alun knew only too well how to put me in my place. 'You know what your trouble is, Gwyn,' he said to me one day while we were lounging on the rail of the balcony in Quad. 'You're too bloody conventional.' I couldn't disagree, though that characteristic can prove useful to someone who doesn't conform to the majority view in the most important matters such as Nationalism and pacifism. Conformity in minor matters is acceptable, even necessary, in someone who is a nonconformist in matters of major importance.

Out of necessity I used to spend many hours every week in the little room belonging to the Law Department. Despite its great reputation, that Department had no need of a larger room, since its students were so few. Elfyn Wigley, Dafydd's father, joined the class in my year with a view to following part of the course. It was perhaps there that he met Myfanwy Battersbie, who later became his wife, for she was a student in the Department at the time. So in the Finals year I was in the same class as both Dafydd Wigley's father and mother. By the time we went into the Honours year there were only five of us in the class. I soon lost touch with two of them, but the other two, Glyn Burrell and Iwan Wallis Jones, became judges. The Professor was Thomas Levi, or Tommy as the students called him, the son of the Thomas Levi who edited *Trysorfa'r Plant*, building up a circulation of forty-four thousand for that splendid children's magazine. Tommy was assisted by three lecturers. Vyrnwy Lewis had been doing research on behalf of Lord Davies of Llandinam and to him was attributed the latter's book, *Force*. Victor Evans was another, a keen Liberal like Professor Levi himself, and a former President of the Oxford Union. I was a neighbour of his in Trefor Road and used to see quite a bit of him. He once took me to a house-party given by the Oxford Group, now known as Moral Rearmament, at the Randolph Hotel in Oxford. This held great appeal for him but not for me. The Department's Senior Lecturer was R.A. Wing who used to entertain us during coffee-breaks in the Union in Laura Place by recounting the amazing exploits of his youth. His pretty girlfriend, whom he later married, used to sit on the floor and lean against his legs, and he would tenderly stroke her back as he went on and on. Only once did I meet Mrs Wing thereafter and that was in Holloway Prison when my daughter Meinir was incarcerated there. Mrs Wing was Governor of the worst of women's prisons.

Professor Levi was a colourful character. He used to fill the College Hall, and other halls throughout the land if it comes to that, whenever he gave his grandiloquent public lectures, to which he gave such titles as 'My Oxford Days'. He was a bachelor, but terribly fond of women. He dressed very well with a silk handkerchief in his breast-pocket and a flower in his lapel. Since he was hard of hearing, he had to use an aid, which was kept in place by a metal band around his head. This handicap affected his voice and the device used to squeak noisily at the slightest movement. He pronounced every 's' as a 'sh', so whenever he talked about 'the three greatesht momentsh of my life: firsht when a lady fainted into my armsh . . . ', the effect would be more hilarious than the words deserved to be. His soft spot for women was famous. When, years afterwards, I would speak in various places, such as Aberdare, I would hear, confidentially of course, that Tommy had been engaged to so-and-so in the town. Once, when I was joint-secretary of the Barry Cymmrodorion, with the dear and beautiful Elinor Williams, later to be Mrs Gwilym Evans, the Professor came to deliver a lecture. Over tea at my home before the lecture, Elinor made an obvious impression on him. Before we set off, he took me aside and, bringing his diary out of his pocket, asked, 'What ish the addresh of Mish Williamsh?'

On the first day of term during our Honours year the five members of the class went to see the Professor with a view to persuading him it would be a pity if he were obliged to come into College to lecture to such a small number of students when there was such great demand for his services up and down the country. If only he would lend us his lecture-notes we should take care to make copies of them. And that's what happened. We paid a girl in town ten pounds to type them out and we didn't have to bother the Professor again for the rest of that year. These lectures had seen better days. Once, in my second year, I was having a chat with the student sitting next to me during the lecture when the Professor turned to me and said with a severe expression, 'Plish, Mr Evansh, do pay a little attenshion. Here I have been up half the night preparing thish lecture for you

. . . .,' and I could see that the pages were brittle and yellow with age!

I happened to be Secretary of *Cymdeithas Dafydd ap Gwilym* at Oxford when we were preparing to celebrate the Society's fiftieth anniversary. Many famous people took part in the festivities and we were looking forward keenly to having Professor Levi with us. But at the dinner, when J.R. Jones, the Arch-incense-burner (one of the arcane titles at the Dafydd), read out a telegram from him and added to the apology the words 'Detained by academic duties', the laughter at such a preposterous idea raised the roof. It was at that dinner, by the way, that W.J. Gruffydd recited part of the *pryddest* by John Roberts of Cardiff that won a prize at one of the Society's eisteddfodau. The first line was '*Mae'n ganol nos ar gloc tragwyddol amser*' ('It is midnight on time's eternal clock'). During the Parliamentary Election in Merioneth in 1945, Professor Levi came to the county to lend his support to the Liberal candidate, Emrys Roberts; he too was one of the Professor's former pupils. He referred to me rather contemptuously: 'Gwynfor Evansh ish only a dreamer,' he said. Fair play to R.E. Jones, who always had a quick and ready answer, for reminding the audience that Joseph had also been called a dreamer and that he had saved his nation.

There was a small band of undergraduates at Aberystwyth to whom I didn't belong, but whose influence was to increase in time, and they were the Nationalists. As far as I could tell, they were to be found only in the Welsh Department and in the Theological College. The activity which brought them to my notice was their selling of *Y Ddraig Goch*, Plaid Cymru's paper, on the streets of the town. I recall four of them in my last year – Gwyndaf Evans, Gwennant Davies, Eic Davies, and Hywel D. Roberts. It was from Hywel that I bought the copy of the newspaper which introduced me to Plaid Cymru. Some time later I bought a pamphlet in yellow covers that I saw outside Jack Edwards's shop, *The Economics of Welsh Self-Government* by Dr D.J. Davies, who had lodged before my time with the lovely family at Ceinfan in Trefor Road. It was this book which convinced me that the Nationalists' policies were economically sound, and I decided to join them.

At the end of my last term I walked home to Barry. I had already done a good deal of walking that year, through the lower part of Montgomeryshire and over the Cardiganshire hills as far as Radnorshire and Breconshire. On one of these hikes we called to ask for a cup of tea at a farmhouse about four or five miles to the west of Cwm Elan. My friend Dilwyn Davies did the asking, in English. The welcome we got from the elderly woman of the house was at first quite surly, but her face lit up when I put the same question in Welsh. She was a monoglot, though she lived within reach of anglicized Elan and Rhaeadr. She must have been one of the last Welsh monoglots in southern Wales. Dilwyn Davies was also my companion on my walk home to Glamorgan. Although he was the son of the minister of Capel Mawr in Bala, he never spoke a word of Welsh to me. He was courting a handsome, Welsh-speaking girl from the Rhondda and later married her. They spoke English together. I got to know them through my cultured fellow-lodger, who was also from Bala, and whose home was quite close to Capel Mawr. He too chose to speak English. But although Dilwyn and I used only English as we made our way south, the journey past the Teifi lakes, through Cwm Irfon, over Epynt and the Brecon Beacons and the hills of Rhondda, down into the Vale of Glamorgan, was thrilling as it was unforgettable. The following day I went to see Miss Cassie Davies, a lecturer at the Barry College and Secretary of the town branch of Plaid Cymru, and joined the Party.

The first thing I did in Oxford was seek out Edwin Pryce Jones, who had come up from College at Bangor. J.E. Jones, the Party's Secretary, had mentioned him in a letter, and had also told Edwin about me, advising us both to contact Harri Williams and Tudno Williams. Our plan was to establish a branch of Plaid Cymru in the University. Since only six members were needed to form a branch in those days, we had no difficulty. There was to be a branch there, or at least a group of Nationalists, ever after, if only intermittently. Many were the journeys I made over the years to Oxford, and to Cambridge, for various kinds of meetings at which the soil required watering.

The heart of Oxford for the Welsh-speaking Welshman was *Cymdeithas Dafydd ap Gwilym*. There I had friends like Edwin and Harri who were of the same mind as me, some of whom, again like me, were learning the language. One of these was Dafydd Jones of Croydon, who belonged to an English-speaking family but who learned Welsh with the help of the Cornishman Caradar's three little books, *Welsh Made Easy*. His problem was in finding someone who could speak the language to him on a regular basis. The only Welsh-speaker he knew was the milkman and every morning at six o'clock, for a whole year, he would get up to have a chat with him. Among the other members of the Dafydd were J.R. Jones, Hywel D. Lewis, Huw Morris Jones, Tudno Williams, Arfor Tegla Davies, and Harri Williams, but I think the liveliest was Gwilym O. Williams, later Archbishop of Wales, with whom I had been to Geneva some years before. The Society's meetings were always very convivial, as were the trips in punts along the river on our way to dine at the

Cherwell Arms. Returning one merry night after such an excursion, G.O. was stepping from one punt to another when they parted and he went headlong into the river. He stood there with the water up to his shoulders and shouting with a broad smile some words that echoed a line from a famous hymn, '*Rwyn hapus yn yr afon*' ('I am happy in the water'.)

I could easily believe that there was a lot in common between our eisteddfod and those of the Gwyneddigion, the cultural society founded among the London Welsh in the eighteenth century. Whether the reader believes it or not, I once won a prize for a *pryddest*, with a long and ribald poem to 'The Haystack'. It was highly praised by the adjudicator, Hywel D. Lewis. The set subject for the *englyn* that year was 'The Landlady', and since I was Harri Williams's fellow-lodger for a term, I was quite familiar with the good woman whom he described in his winning poem:

> '*Un lydan yw'r landledi – a'i bronnau*
> *Fel bryniau Eryri,*
> *A chas iawn yw ei chwys hi*
> *Lond yr awel yn drewi.*'

('The landlady is a broad one, and her breasts are like the mountains of Snowdonia, and her sweat is very nasty as it pollutes the air.')

It was thus that Harri early on demonstrated the literary talent that was to win him the Prose Medal at the National Eisteddfod.

I used to spend many an hour reading books without buying them in Blackwell's splendid shop. While rummaging one day in a kind of cellar there, I came across a small library of Welsh books from the beginning of the century that included the complete *Cyfres y Fil* and a number books, in first editions, that had long been out of print. The shop knew nothing of their worth and I bought them for three pounds. I spent time reading them which should have been given to Law.

Although I usually went to chapel of a Sunday morning at Mansfield College, the Independents' College, attending the Welsh service which followed the English one, I became friendly with a group of Wesleyan students through Arfor Tegla Davies, the writer's son, who died so tragically young. I attended their services and even went with them for a week's missionary work to Dewsbury, an industrial town in Yorkshire, speaking at street-corners, in cinemas, schools, pubs and the occasional chapel. It was on this trip that I discovered what Yorkshire pudding was, for on the Sunday the good woman at whose house I was staying put a large plate of it in front of me. Presuming this to be my lunch, I dug into it conscientiously and soon polished it off, as a compliment to the cook. But oh dear, this was only meant to whet the appetite, and the meal that followed was enough for four.

Two compatriots whom I met at Oxford but didn't get to know well were Pennar Davies, who was a research student at Balliol, the College of the intellectual élite, and George M.Ll. Davies. It was at Balliol that George Davies stayed during his annual visits to the city. The Master of the College, Lord Lindsay, was a close friend of his and he sometimes used to come to see the Welshman in the Rhondda. On his visits to Oxford George Davies used to preach at St. Mary's, the University's church, which was full to overflowing for the students' service on Sunday evenings. I first saw George Davies at close quarters when he was crossing St. Giles, a princely figure in a long cloak.

I didn't walk home from Oxford, but at the end of my last term I travelled back to Wales in the company of my brother Alcwyn in an old Singer car we had bought for fifteen pounds. We did what we intended doing on that journey in a most memorable way, which was to climb Pen-y-Fal, the mountain near Abergavenny known in English as the Sugar Loaf, to see the dawn breaking in majesty over the mountains of Wales.

Chapter 5

War Clouds

For more than two years I served my articles in a solicitor's office in Cardiff, living at home in Barry and so not suffering anything of the poverty and cruel unemployment that was destroying the life of the South Wales Valleys. I was, nevertheless, like everyone else, living under the threatening clouds of war. Part of the heavy irony of this dismal time was that the war, which as a pacifist I was doing my utmost to prevent, was bringing work to Wales. I had seen the ruins of Dowlais while a student at Oxford, when I took a course of study on employment at Cardiff University under the supervision of Professor Marquand, at which I was the only Welshman present. The English students there had had great fun on hearing Marquand dismiss my suggestion that the situation of Wales wouldn't have been so desperate had it been a self-governing country. We went up to Dowlais to see the effects of unemployment. Some ninety per cent of the workers in the iron and coal industries there were out of work. As we passed a small group standing at a street-corner at the bottom of a long hill, I heard one spitting out the words 'bloody foreigners'. Stretching up the grey street there were rows of shops with boarded-up windows. Here once had been a lively, warm-hearted community, with quite a bit of Welsh-language culture. Before the war I had twice been to speak to Bethania's Cultural Society, the chapel where Peter Price and W.T. Gruffydd had been ministers, and later Ap Gerallt who came to us at Tabernacl in Barry. I had been surprised at the size of the audience, although it included few men.

I saw the terrible effects of the Depression in other Valleys, Taff and Rhymney, Rhondda and Cynon, whenever I went there to speak on behalf of Plaid Cymru in open-air meetings. My companions were usually Nationalists from Cardiff – Victor Hampson Jones, Gwyn Daniel, who was mainly responsible for creating the teachers' union *Undeb Cenedlaethol Athrawon Cymru* (now known by its acronym *UCAC*) or Griff Jones; all three have now passed away. We would choose a handy place to hold the meetings, at a street-corner or on a square or tump – our areopagus in Caerphilly was the Twyn – and then we would start spouting. Sometimes a fair-sized crowd would gather; on other occasions there would be only three or four children and a dog for audience. While one of us was speaking, without the aid of a loudspeaker, by the way, the others would be trying to sell our newspapers. Among our regular speakers in the Rhondda were Kitchener Davies and David Davies of Tylorstown. Morris Williams, the husband of Kate Roberts, had recently left the Valley with his wife to run *Y Faner* from Denbigh. David Davies was a stocky, lively man, and completely bald, steely in his devotion to his chapel and Party, and to the cause of peace and the Welsh language. Of course, the unforgettable Kitch was already a nationally-known figure as well as a leader of Welsh cultural life in the Rhondda, where he fought more than one local election in the Party's name. He was like quicksilver, a terrific fighter for all that was true and fine in the desert that London and Capitalism had made of much of our country. His radicalism and eloquence have more than once been described by H.W.J. Edwards, the High Tory Nationalist who lived near him in Trealaw. A privilege that I shall always cherish was to have been able to say a word in tribute to Kitch at his funeral. It is good to think that the Rhondda is not without its witnesses in the present generation and that fighters like Glyn James and Don Morgan, Cennard Davies and Vic Davies, still live and work there.

Many of these open-air meetings were carefully arranged, like the one in Tredegar which was the responsibility of one of Cassie Davies's converts at Barry College. Cassie herself came like a ball of fire to a meeting arranged by Lorraine Davies, another of her students, in Neath. There the heroic Oliver J. Evans had his home; he it was who organized hundreds of these meetings in Mid and West Glamorgan and in southern parts of Carmarthenshire. He would distribute leaflets throughout the district in order to advertize every meeting. At first Oliver, like many another, tended to think that I was too soft – 'gentle' was the kind word he used – to face up to these rowdy meetings, as some of them turned out to be. At Tonypandy, in a meeting at which Kitch and Wynne Samuel were speaking, Oliver was struck in the face by a stone and the blood poured down his face and clothes. But a different view was taken by a close friend of mine who nicknamed me Stalin – the man of steel!

On the outbreak of war, the number of meetings declined sharply, although some were still held in the industrial parts of Carmarthenshire and in the Swansea Valley. In that largely Welsh-speaking valley flourished what strength Plaid Cymru could muster in the South. Wynne Samuel, who was editor of the *Welsh Nation* from 1941 to 1949, was the man responsible for nurturing it; he was the leader there and the most powerful speaker in the Party, I'm sure of that. Soon he would be one of its national leaders. He gathered about him some excellent men and women – Timothy Lewis, Edgar Jones, Llew Davies, Harri Samuel, William Arthur Lewis, and later Wendy Richards and Jac Harris. The men were mostly colliers and tinplate workers. At one notable open-air meeting Wynne Samuel won Trefor Beasley over to Plaid Cymru; Trefor was Secretary of the Llangennech miners' lodge at the time.

I was recently in the Swansea Valley, at a dinner given for Matthew Mulcahy of Clydach, in celebration of his fifty years of work for Plaid Cymru in the Valley. Matthew is of Irish descent and a red-hot Nationalist; he's been in his time a member of the Community, District and County Council, all three. He worked in the Mond nickel works and he has a son and grandson still working there. Every morning before work Matthew would attend mass at the Catholic church. Matthew's religion brings to mind how much Plaid Cymru once suffered on account of its alleged Catholicism. Saunders Lewis's conversion, and that of others such as Catherine Daniel and Victor Hampson Jones, was the cause of it. I once met Saunders in Park Place, in Cardiff, while on my way to a radio discussion with Iorwerth Thomas M.P. that had been arranged by Aneirin Talfan Davies. He told me I was at liberty to say that it was his Catholicism which had driven him from public life. 'Home Rule is Rome Rule' was the slogan that was used against us, and yet in the same breath people could claim that we were 'a bunch of Nonconformists'. In the same way I was called a Tory by Labour councillors in Carmarthenshire and a Communist by Lady Hopkin Morris. We were attacked for being pacifists on the one hand and 'men of violence' on the other.

From John Hughes, an old collier in his eighties who lived near us in Barry, where he had retired to live with his daughter, I learned something of the rich cultural life that had flourished in the Rhondda in the days when the Valleys were Welsh-speaking. According to the Census, some sixty-six per cent of Rhondda people were Welsh-speaking at the beginning of this century, and seventy-two per cent of those in the Cynon Valley. Even in Merthyr Tydfil the figure was nearly sixty per cent, much higher than that in Dyfed today. It was English education that was destroying the language, assisted by war, the bitter anti-Welsh attitudes of the ruling Labour Party, the immigration of English and Irish people, and the enormous exodus of Welsh people into England during the Great Depression. I heard from John Hughes about the choirs and eisteddfodau and how a collier-poet would teach *cynghanedd* (the rules of traditional Welsh prosody) to his butty during meal-breaks underground by writing in chalk on the back of a spade. I spent several days in the Rhondda during the first week of the war, in the company of George M.Ll. Davies, visiting clubs that had been set up by Quakers at Maesyrhaf and Trealaw. It was a pleasure to get to know some of the miners personally while helping George M.Ll. Davies, who used to give unemployed men from the Rhondda a week's holiday in an old brewery at the seaside in the Vale of Glamorgan. Although my main job in the camp was peeling potatoes, it was not without its romance in the circumstances of the time.

The Welsh people were helpless in the face of the social disaster which had overtaken them. The Government's only remedy was to transfer the unemployed to England where industry was crying out for them. After the completely unnecessary Great War which shook Welsh society to its foundations and brought death to its young men in their scores of thousands, Wales was affected even more by a Depression about which it was unable to do anything except pass strongly worded but ultimately futile resolutions, like the one I proposed at the Union of Welsh Independents at Blaenau Ffestiniog in 1938. I called upon the Union to throw its weight behind the campaign to ensure an Economic Plan for Wales, so that 'it might safeguard its survival among the nations of the earth'. These resolutions made it clear that nothing could be expected from London and that the time had come for Wales to make its own economic arrangements. A society was established, known as *Cymdeithas Ginio Difiau*, to which Nationalists contributed the price of a dinner every Thursday so that a meal could be provided at least once a week for those who depended on the soup-kitchens. But we were completely unable to act in any more effective way. All authority over the life of Wales lay in the hands of 'men sitting in Whitehall', as Ernest Bevin once said, and it lies there still.

The handful of Nationalists in those days were considered odd, eccentric people, and their call for a Welsh Economic Plan a foolish dream. What could have been more fanciful than to think it was possible to treat Wales as an economic entity? No attention was paid to them, except to pour scorn. The *Western Mail* was always comparing us with fleas and quoting the old rhyme:

'Big fleas have little fleas
Upon their backs to bite 'em,
And little fleas have lesser fleas
And so ad infinitum.'

With so few Nationalists working for the cause, and without any national consciousness among the people as a whole, the future seemed very bleak. The schools and the cinema were completely English in both language and sentiment, as were the radio, ever increasing in its influence, and the daily papers, the political parties and the local councils. They were all out to nurture an English or British frame of mind. It was little wonder that we kept on hearing that our cause was hopeless. We never saw the Welsh acting or thinking for themselves as Welsh people. Our efforts seemed like those of a mouse scratching at a rock.

I used to preach on a Sunday sometimes, mostly to help out friends in difficulty. One of the chapels I went to was Bronllwyn, the Welsh Independent chapel at Pentyrch, near Cardiff. Its secretary was old William Beer, an Englishman from somewhere in the south of England who had come to Cardiff to look for work at the age of twelve, and then gone to Pentyrch to work in a quarry. That district on the slopes of the Garth mountain, on the edge of the Vale of Glamorgan, and in close proximity to Cardiff, was so thoroughly Welsh-speaking that this Englishman had learned to speak and write the language. By this time only one monthly morning service was held there in Welsh. During the lifetime of William Beer the language had become extinct in Pentyrch. We were appalled to see this happening in the large, heavily populated districts, and yet our hearts lifted when we looked towards the staunch Welshness of the Swansea Valley and Dyfed. Looking westward, the land was indeed bright. But alas, the English flood is now beginning to drown the Welsh character of so many communities.

One of my long walks was with my friend Vernon Williams, from Cardiff, through Pentyrch and over the Garth in the direction of Gilfach Goch, the setting for the stories by J.J. Williams which were published in his book *Straeon y Gilfach Ddu*, I believe. Not far from Gilfach Goch, to our great surprise, we came across a small wooded valley, off the beaten track and strikingly beautiful, winding its way up into the hills of Rhondda. Its name was Cwm Nant yr Arian – the Valley of the Silver Stream. The more I see of the land of Wales the more I am thrilled by its beauty. Except for a few places like the Tumble and Llansamlet, the whole of Wales is beautiful, and even Llansamlet and Glandwr (Landore), which were despoiled for industrial purposes, are being reclaimed now. The Vale of Glamorgan was my favourite place and it has continued to enchant me to this very day. In 1937 the shocking news came that the RAF wanted to take over a huge area of land in the middle of the Vale, including Bethesda'r Fro, the old chapel of John Williams of St. Athan, the hymn-writer, in order to make an aerodrome there. This followed the expropriation of Penyberth in Welsh-speaking Llŷn and the imprisonment of the three Nationalists who had taken action against the bombing school there by setting huts on fire. Few felt as I did about the rape of the English-speaking Vale, and all I did, I'm sorry to say, was to send my first article to *Y Ddraig Goch*.

I used to go on walking tours in other countries too. A year before war broke out, my brother and I went through one of the most beautiful parts of Germany, down the Rhine Valley, with the help of a boat for some of the way, I must confess, sailing past the Lorelei Rock, but then walking through the Black Forest to the border with Switzerland. We stayed at youth hostels, sometimes in towns such as Cologne, Bonn, Coblenz, Mainz, Heidelberg and Freiberg, or else in rural areas such as on the shores of the Titisee. We thus had plenty of opportunity to observe the turmoil of Nazism among young Germans; they were given to singing loudly as they hiked through the countryside in large groups. I wonder how many of them were killed in the war that was soon to engulf Europe?

Ireland, which I visited with George Davies for a conference at Trinity College, Dublin, in 1938, was a much calmer country. This was my introduction to a land I would see a lot of thereafter. I had read a good deal of its history before going. A book that made a deep impression on me was *Young Ireland*, the great tome of Charles Gavan Duffy, which I had bought for threepence at John Evans's secondhand bookshop in Cardiff. George Davies was a fascinating companion to have in Dublin. Two years before, in 1923, he had become the Member of Parliament for the University of Wales and he'd been an intermediary between the London Government and De Valera. So great was Irish confidence in him that he was able to see De Valera in his various hideouts. He showed me the cellar under a Welsh chapel on the quayside where the rebels had kept their arms. We went to see Mrs Erskine Childers, widow of the English leader who had fought on the Irish side and been executed during the heroic but disastrous civil war that followed. George Davies was very fond of the Irish. Among his repertoire of stories there were many which he recounted with an impeccable Irish accent. I remember one in particular about the advice given him by an Irish warder at Dartmoor Prison. The day's work consisted of breaking stones, and on seeing that the prisoner didn't have much idea of how to go about it and was going at it far too hard, the Irishman took pity on him, saying, 'No! No! No! That's not the way at all, sonny. All you 'ave to do is bring the bloody 'ammer up and the Lord God will bring it down!' When George later went to work on the road between

Llanwrda and Bwlch Cefn Sarth, he was so professional with his 'bloody 'ammer' that he was elected president of the hut of sixty navvies.

I came to know George Davies not only through his work among the Rhondda unemployed but also in the pacifist wing of the Peace Movement. I became a council member of the Peace Pledge Union that was founded by Dick Shepherd after he had collected the names of a hundred thousand people who declared that they had renounced war. Although thousands of Welsh people signed this pledge, more might have been expected in a nation on which war had wreaked such awful damage without defending its heritage in the least. But of course, Wales had no freedom as a nation that its people could be called upon to defend. I spoke for the pacifists in the open air as well as indoors, and worked with many true friends such as the Reverend and Mrs R.J. Jones, the parents of the two staunch Nationalists Gwilym and Hywel ap Robert, both of whom have stood as Parliamentary candidates for Plaid Cymru. I shall never forget the brave intercession that Gwilym made from the gallery of the House of Commons on behalf of his constituents in Ebbw Vale at a time when thousands of steel-workers were being thrown out of work.

One of my favourite spots for a peace meeting was King's Square in Barry, outside the hall where the Council met. With an English friend named Wilkinson, a minister with the Independents at a chapel in St. Francis-on-the-hill, that was later turned into a Welsh School, we made a platform out of a cart which we hauled into the middle of the square. Sometimes when we were speaking the Council members would come out of their meeting, my father and Uncle Dudley among them. Fair play to my father, he was wonderfully patient and forgiving. He could understand my pacifism better than my Nationalism, despite the fact that both were harmful to his business, and very much so after the outbreak of war.

Some of the Peace Movement's meetings were very large, like the one in Swansea where the Central Hall, which could hold a thousand people, was filled to overflowing. This hall was later a victim of the blitz. It was there I first had the dangerous feeling of being swept along by the audience; the main speaker was George Lansbury, leader of the Labour Party for a few years. The night Chamberlain announced his accord with Hitler in Munich I was speaking at Seion Chapel in Wrexham, where D.R. Lewis, an early member of Plaid Cymru, was later minister. The large chapel was packed to hear Max Plowman and Vera Brittain, Shirley Williams's mother. That brave old man from Rhos, Dr E.K. Jones, was in the chair. It was about this time that I was invited by Ingli James to stand as a Parliamentary candidate in the name of his political peace movement in a by-election at Caerphilly. In the same year I proposed a motion at Plaid Cymru's Annual Conference in Swansea, committing it to renounce all violence; the motion was seconded by the Reverend J.P. Davies, of blessed memory. It was carried by a huge majority and, although challenged sometimes in the years that followed, it has been solidly upheld ever since. I wonder whether any other Nationalist Party has stuck by such a resolution?

In the previous year, that is 1937, I had gone to Bala for my first Plaid Cymru Conference and Summer School. I also proposed a motion there, this time calling for official status for the Welsh language. I don't know whether it had anything to do with the Language Petition that was to call for the same thing in 1939. With Dafydd Jenkins as its remarkably efficient Secretary, the petition collected 400,000 signatures before the war put a stop to the work. The pacifists were prominent on the field of the National Eisteddfod in Cardiff in 1938, with Annie Jones, subsequently Mrs Annie Humphreys, taking a leading part in our activities. For the first time we had a tent on the festival's Field. There was a special edition of *Peace News* edited by Middleton Murry that carried articles in Welsh, of which two thousand copies were sold. Another reason I have for remembering that particular Eisteddfod was that J.R. Jones, the philosopher, was staying with us for the week. Afterwards we went to his home in Pwllheli where his mother, who had for many years been a widow, kept a small shop that sold *bara brith* – a delicious kind of speckled bread. I realized then from where J.R. Jones derived his intellectual strength, for his mother was a woman of powerful mind. I once heard that she would argue so strongly in favour of the Apostle Paul at Sunday School that she earned the nickname Mrs Paul Jones.

During the week of the National Eisteddfod that was held at Denbigh in the year following I became Secretary of *Heddychwyr Cymru* (The Peacemakers of Wales) in which post I remained throughout the war. The President was George M. Ll. Davies and the Treasurer was Mrs Dan Thomas, who before the year was out would become my mother-in-law. It was this which brought me into contact, soon to be literal, with Rhiannon, whom I saw for the first time at her home in Cardiff during the spring of the year in which the war began. The name of their house was Uwchlyn, for the reason that it stood near Roath Park Lake and also because Mrs Thomas had been born in Cwm Cynllwyd near Llanuwchllyn. I have to confess that my heart lost a beat the moment Rhiannon walked into the room. On seeing her again two months later amid the beauty of

a summer's day at Islaw'r Dref dressed in a very short light frock –
beach wear, no doubt – the boy from Barry fell head over heels in
love! Up to about eighteen months prior to our wedding Rhiannon
and her family had been living in Liverpool, and yet her Welsh was
much better than mine, despite the fact that she had never had a
lesson in the language.

I had to spend several months in London in 1939 to prepare for
my Law exams. My fellow-lodger in Hampstead was Dafydd
Roberts from Aberdare, who did such a fine day's work for Wales,
like his father D.O. Roberts before him. When the examination result
arrived at the beginning of August I was in Amsterdam at an
international Christian conference. That was the only time I heard
the beautifully sung mass of the Greek Orthodox Church. I remember in particular a conversation with a delegate from Latvia who
argued that it was quite impossible for the Latvians to be pacifists
because they had to resist Russia in arms. Soon afterwards Latvia,
together with Lithuania and Estonia, was overrun by Russia in just
two days, and swallowed up as completely as Wales had been by
England. If it hadn't been for that, it is possible that today we could
include these small Baltic nations in a bloc among the civilized and
prosperous peoples of Scandinavia.

On my return to Wales it was evident that war was imminent,
although Lindo, the famous astrologer of *The Daily Express*, was
still forecasting that there would be no war. When Hitler attacked
Poland, with whom Britain had made a pact, war was declared. I
went down to the municipal library to see what the star-gazer had to
say. Across the page in bold type were the words 'Hitler defies the
stars'.

Chapter 6

Llangadog

It was quite a surprise when the Conscientious Objectors' Tribunal granted me unconditional discharge from having to go into the armed forces. Very few were granted complete discharge. Usually, it was conditional upon working on the land or in forestry, or else in the mines or with a Quaker ambulance unit. I see now that it was self-deception to think that I might have been given a long prison sentence under conditions like those that Gwenallt Jones experienced and which he described in his book *Plasau'r Brenin*. I nevertheless had made a few preparations against that contingency. I tried, for example, to commit passages of good literature to memory so that I might keep my sanity when locked up, but I have a terribly poor memory. Anyway, what I chose to do was grow tomatoes – an anticlimax if ever there was one! I thought it would have been unseemly to have become a solicitor at a time when so many of my friends had to go into the forces. My father had formed a family firm that had put up greenhouses on the land of Wernellyn which he had bought at Llangadog seven years before, and it was in that farmhouse I went to live.

I continued to live there after the war because the nature of the work and its location enabled me to travel to all parts of Wales as an itinerant propagandist. The season for this work was between September and May, and during those months there was less pressure on me in the greenhouses than there was between April and September. In winter, however, I would travel home the same night, wherever the meeting happened to be. I had to, because the heating in the greenhouses required attention during the night. Sometimes it would be two or three o'clock in the morning before I came home. For this work I used a poker and other implements, some of them seven foot long, because the water, which flowed through more than three-quarters of a mile of pipes, needed big fires to heat it. An essential part of the work was lifting and clearing out the heavy clinkers that stuck to the iron bars under the fire.

In the Swansea Valley greenhouses are known as *tai gerddi* ('garden houses') and these were the words painted on the covers of the baskets in which our produce was marketed; I got the words, like so much else, from Wynne Samuel. I enjoyed the work immensely, despite the fact that I had never before grown so much as a cabbage. It was all the more pleasant because two of my fellow-workers, Bertie Williams and Gwilym Edwards, had splendid voices – Bertie a tenor's and Gwilym a baritone's. The sound of singing would fill the greenhouses for hours on end, and when women came to work with us in spring and summer we had a first-class mixed choir! Before coming to work for me, Gwilym and Bertie had been earning £1 10 shillings a week – the one in a quarry and the other on a farm. Bertie, too, was a conscientious objector; and for that reason the greenhouses were known locally as Conchies' Corner. Bertie Williams is still with us forty-two years later, but Gwilym Edwards died of lung-cancer, like another two of my workers; all three were heavy smokers. These four were all good men who would do a good day's work without complaint.

The most comical of all the men who worked with us was undoubtedly old Daniels of Pont-ar-Dywi, who was in his late eighties when he retired. He was no ordinary labourer in his younger days. I heard a bit about him from Dr Lewis Evans, the author of a good book on Morgan Llwyd, among many others. Lewis Evans had been brought up in great poverty in the same district as Daniels, not far from Nantgaredig. Daniels was the son of a squireen and he had inherited three farms. But as an only child he had been utterly spoiled by his mother. After a while he developed a permanent thirst. He himself used to tell the story of how he had once gone to see Dr Lawson, an English doctor in Llangadog, complaining about his throat. He opened his mouth wide so that the doctor could look down his throat with the aid of a small light. 'I don't see anything,' said the doctor. 'That's funny,' replied Daniels, 'three farms have gone down there.' Old Daniels was a jolly fellow, despite his tribulations. Having lost his first wife, he married a lovely woman from Yorkshire. By the time I came to know this English lady she had acquired quite a bit of the most rumbustious Welsh. She also joined Plaid Cymru, the final proof of her fine character!

Another comical man with the same name was Daniels the Post, who came from the same district and suffered from the same thirst. This worried his wife terribly, especially since he was often late coming home. One evening he was warned by Mrs Gravelle that his wife was out looking for him. She it was who kept a confectionery and food shop on the village square; she knew everything that was happening thereabouts and everything that was being said. Anyway, when Mrs Daniels returned home after failing to track her husband down, she found him sitting up in bed, as he recounted later, with an umbrella over his head waiting for the storm to break. He was quite a clever chap, was Daniels the Post, and something of a Nationalist. He bought *Y Ddraig Goch* from me for many years. He once tried for a seat on the Llandeilo District Council, publishing an election address which contained only two policy points. The first was to establish a putty factory on Llangadog common, and the second to make a tunnel under the Black Mountain to Brynaman. It was Daniels the Post and his wife who looked after the village's telephone exchange, before everything was centralized. In that capacity they gathered the delicious news of what was going on in the district and then spread it abroad from the information office that was Mrs Gravelle's confectionery shop. It was nearly midnight on 14th January 1942, when just as I was going to bed a message came from Aberystwyth to say that Rhiannon had given birth to a son. That was Alcwyn Deiniol. Six of our seven children are Cardis, since they were born in the Maternity Hospital at Aberystwyth. When I went down to the village early next day I was warmly congratulated by Mrs Gravelle. This wasn't telepathy and the 'phone wasn't bugged in those days: Mrs Daniels the Post had been at it again!

Although there was a streak of hostility towards me in Llangadog, it was a very warm-hearted community. I liked in particular the aristocratic habit in the chapel meetings of calling a man not by his style, as we used to say, not Mr Evans or Mr Jones, but by the name of his farm or house. 'What is Wernellyn's opinion on this?' Glan Sawdde would ask. Mr Jones Glan Sawdde was a brother to Mr Jones Pen-y-bont, the next farm to Wernellyn. The son of Pen-y-bont was Ronald Jones, otherwise known as Keidrych Rhys, who first published the work of Dylan Thomas in his magazine *Wales*. It was undoubtedly Keidrych who advised Dylan Thomas to write to me asking for help in avoiding military call-up. But, prig that I was, I didn't think I ought to help such a fallible and yet unprincipled fellow. Keidrych took his name, by the way, from the river Ceidrych which runs through a lovely little valley at the back of Wernellyn, skirting Garn Goch, a large hill-fort that some believe to have been the main settlement of the Demetae tribe before Carmarthen was built by the Romans about the year 70 A.D. At Dan y Garn was born Mair Davies, one of *Y Diliau*, the folk-group of which my daughter is a member. The Dan y Garn family are staunch Nationalists. The other member of the trio at the outset was Lynwen Jones and I shall refer to her again later.

The Jenkins family had lived at Glan Sawdde earlier in the century. The river Sawdde, by the way, is the subject of a book written by Richard Vaughan, author of the novel *Moulded in Earth*. He was the son of the blacksmith at Llanddeusant, the contiguous parish. The daughter of the Jenkins family of Glan Sawdde married Llywelyn Williams of Brown Hill, on the other side of Tywi, the Member of Parliament for Carmarthenshire, historian and author of *The Making of Modern Wales* and such books as *Gwilym a Benni Bach* and *'Slawer Dydd*, which are stories about the district of Llangadog. One of Jenkins Glan Sawdde's sons became a judge in India and another was Governor of Bengal. Lest anyone conclude that the talent of our community was acknowledged only in India and the far corners of the earth, I should say that we also had poets and musicians who won fame nearer home. A poem written by Dennis Edwards, the cobbler, was chosen for publication in the anthology *Awen Myrddin*. Another poet whose work appeared in the same book was Gwilym Williams, who worked as a road-man. His splendid bardic name was Ap Pelagius and the name of his house was Sbaen ('Spain'), which stood opposite Twrci ('Turkey') on the other bank of Sawdde. Davies Twrci is a staunch Nationalist, while Gwilym Sbaen was a Communist. Another Gwilym, Gwilym Evans of Blaen Crynfe, is also one of our poets, like his father David Evans before him, the author of a volume entitled *Murmuron Crynfe*.

I am neither a literary man nor the son of a writer, but during the war I had to brush up my knowledge of the rules of Welsh prosody in order to be able to adjudicate at local eisteddfodau from time to time. One of these was held at Llanddeusant. There were twenty-seven competitors for the Chair and several poets came over from Cwm Wysg, a highly cultured community next to us, where John Morris-Jones's book *Cerdd Dafod* was to be found in many a home. The Chair was given for a lyric entitled '*Y Geinach*' ('The Hare') and it was won by Gwynfil Rees of Aberaeron. It's a pity that we haven't seen more of his work. He was chaired with due pomp and ceremony according to the ritual of the Gorsedd of Bards, but because there was a shortage of wood, it being war-time, he received only a small chair that was hardly more than a toy.

I have mentioned this eisteddfod because it changed the bigger one held at Llangadog, which still flourishes under the firm leadership of Myfi Morgan, one of the most cultured people in the area. With Marion Davies of Glan Sawdde, she composed an anthem for our singing-festival every year. The Secretary of the Llangadog Eisteddfod, and indeed the driving-force behind everything in the village, was Morgan Beehive, who kept a shop which sold everything but has now closed. He was known as Dampo and he'd been present at Llanddeusant. He was thrilled by the chairing ceremony and everything connected with it, and from then on we had a Chair Eisteddfod at Llangadog, with all the posters printed in Welsh. But Dampo was too fair-minded to mislead the poets. He put two words in brackets under Eisteddfod Llangadog – *Cadair Manddarlun* ('Miniature Chair'). Then he sent copies of the poster to the National Library so that they would be kept for generations to come. The Llangadog Eisteddfod was a big affair: it lasted for two days and two nights, and when I say night I mean all night! It would be considered a failure if it finished before two o'clock in the morning. Mention of the National Library reminds me that Morgan Beehive went there once in the company of none less than Griffith John Williams. The great scholar, with his usual courtesy, had offered to show Dampo around that noble institution. As they passed through the revolving doors into the deafening silence of the main Reading Room where everyone moves as if they are walking on eggs, the silence was shattered by Dampo's tenor voice proclaiming, 'This would be a great place for an eisteddfod!' Dampo was the salt of the Welsh earth. He continued as Secretary of our Eisteddfod until the end of his long life, despite living his last fifteen years in London, where his family had moved in order to run a milk-round. The Llangadog Eisteddfod was unique in having its head office in London!

The southern part of Llangadog parish is Gwynfe, which lies against the Black Mountain. When I went to live there, the culture of Gwynfe was richer than Llangadog's and the intelligence of its people even higher. The cultural life of the community was led by the headmaster, Conwil Jones, and his wife Jennie, both of whom had splendid voices, and by Joseph Evans of Blaencennen and his two gifted sisters. Joseph Evans was Secretary of the chapel known as Capel y Maen for more than fifty years and custodian of the Black Mountain's book of sheep-marks. He was succeeded as district councillor by David Jones of Ysgubor Wern, who hailed from Caeo, another district of rich culture. I could talk about many another, such as David James of Y Bompren; the Ynys Toddeb family, to whom Dr Phil Williams belongs; Morgan Slaymaker, a road-man, and Kitty his wife, an extremely intelligent couple, who are the parents of Owen Slaymaker; then David Thomas of Henfaes, another road-man; Francis the blacksmith, and David Morgan the Post, Rees of Parc Owen; Ifor Rees, the Independent minister who later made his mark with the BBC, and David James, the vicar, were their excellent clergymen. These were all staunch and respected patriots, Nationalists who came together after the war to form a branch of Plaid Cymru at Gwynfe, the only one the Party had in the whole of Carmarthenshire at that time. They deserve to be remembered. As the older, cultured generation disappeared, their place was taken by strangers. Most of the people in Gwynfe now are English, with only a few, such as Heulwen Booth, the granddaughter of Gwynfe's blacksmith in days gone by, left to represent the old culture.

Music was at the very heart of Llangadog's cultural life. Its chief glory was the choir, of which Rhiannon was Secretary for twenty-seven years. It sang almost all the great oratorios, accompanied by its own orchestra. The name in which it gloried was the Cadogian Philharmonic Society, but it was known locally as the Gravelle Choir. Its leader was W.J. Gravelle, a man of rich musical culture who taught seven or eight instruments. He suffered from asthma which kept him awake at night. As I came home in the small hours of the morning through Llangadog's square, I often used to see a light in his bedroom, and assumed that Gravelle was reading music in bed. Rhiannon used to borrow large tomes for him in Cardiff. Gravelle had been a signalman on the railway-line before becoming a full-time musician, with the help of dear Mrs Gravelle and her confectionery shop. He would draw from his choir of splendid voices, basses and tenors, altos and sopranos, a marvellous sound that always brought tears of pleasure to my eyes. Hearing the voices of my neighbours Abraham Jones of Llwyncelyn and his sister Maggie, and Morgan Pen-y-banc and his sons, and Willie Williams of Cefn Coed, an old haulier with the sweetest tenor voice, and scores of others like them, never failed to move me. Listening and watching them sing from the heart always thrilled me to the core. Rhiannon would know that the choir wasn't up to its usual standard if the tears hadn't begun to flow down my cheeks. Even now as I write, my eyes are filling at the thought of 'Baal, we cry to thee' from Elijah and 'Ye nations, offer to the Lord' from Judas Maccabeus, that hymn to the Nationalism of the Maccabees, and scores of other choruses that I could name. I still find a thrill in hearing my people singing the great hymns of Wales, 'its gentle, joyous, vigorous old language sounding on high the virtues of the Meek Lamb'. I find it heartbreaking to think that a day may come when the sounds of 'the gentle language' will be silenced in these valleys. It happened in the ancient kingdom of Ystrad Clud.

Another well-known choir in the district was the Cwm Dwr Children's Choir which was trained by Mrs Cassie Simon, the sister of Mati and Lottie Rees. Her husband, the Llanwrda blacksmith, was its conductor and the choir used to practise in his smithy at Cwm

Dwr. The smith, with his blackboard on the walls chalked up with staves and words, made a deep impression on Thomas Firbank, the author of *I Bought a Mountain*, when I took him there. Firbank wrote a perceptive passage about him in his other book, *A Country of Memorable Honour*. To this splendid choir belonged Lynwen Jones and Mair Davies, the two girls who formed *Y Diliau* with my daughter Meleri, as well as Lynwen's sisters and brother. All the members of this excellent family were singers, the father and mother and sisters and Tomi Charles, the son. Two of the sisters are well-known soloists, though far across the water in Canada, alas. But the voice of their mother Jennie, who is one of the descendants of Joshua Thomas, the historian of the Baptists, still rings out like a bell among us, though she is in her late sixties. I recall seeing Lynwen when she was about seven years old with her head scarcely higher than the balcony-rail, singing *The Hallelujah Chorus* with all her might in the front row of the Gravelle Choir. Someone else who sang with the Cwm Dwr choir from time to time was Gwyn James, the bass, one of the sons of Llety'r Hyddod, who were also Nationalists; his sister Eurwen is Secretary of the local branch of Plaid Cymru. Her mother was in the same year as D.J. Williams at Aberystwyth University College.

We had a different kind of singing from the *Y Ddraig Goch* ('The Red Dragon') party that was founded by Mrs Dorothy Dolben, although all the members of the group also belonged to the Gravelle Choir. It was a happy day for Llangadog when Sid Dolben, a lovely man, came to the village as its stationmaster. I didn't realize it at the time because Mrs Dolben, who had been born the daughter of Watcyn o Feirion at Capel Celyn, the village in Cwm Tryweryn later drowned by Liverpool, was a red-hot member of the Labour Party. She worked hard against me for Labour in the Elections of 1955 and 1959 when she lived at Trawsfynydd. After that the family moved to Abingdon where she founded a branch of the Labour Party, having called at every house in that little town. I tried hard to win her over to the cause of Wales. Often it's more important to win one person than a hundred, if that one is special. This holds true in all spheres of life. It was certainly true of Plaid Cymru in this part of the Tywi Valley. The attempt to form a branch of the Party at Llandovery was a failure until Denley Owen came to transform the situation. Bob and Ann Roberts completely changed things in Llandeilo, and Heddwyn Lewis of Manor Deilo, a lorry-driver, is a tower of strength in the neighbourhood and beyond. So it was with Mrs Dolben. Once she was convinced that Wales must be put first, she threw herself into the work with electric energy. It was she who organized our first Folk

Fair in Llandeilo with its splendid *noson lawen* ('merry evening') that made a profit of £350 when a pound was worth about six times what it's worth today. But her masterpiece was the party known as *Y Ddraig Goch*. As a former member of the choir conducted by Telynores Eryri, she had the experience needed to bring together twenty or so of the district's most talented youngsters, with one or two more mature people like Rhiannon to help out, and form a company that was capable of providing some first-class entertainment. They were in demand throughout South Wales, with the result that Llangadog wasn't able to hear them very often. Their worthy successors in this tradition today are *Côr Telyn Teilo* under their conductor Noel John, who has made such a great contribution to the musical life of this part of the Tywi Valley.

Of course, the district had its share of weakness as well as of strength. One shortcoming to be found generally throughout Carmarthenshire was the fickleness of its people with regard to the Welsh language. Indeed, they never took assertive action on its behalf, which is the only way it can be safeguarded. Every public meeting was held in English, the language used from the stage of every carnival and show. The Young Farmers discussed their business in English and the meetings of the Parish Council were also held in English. To this day English is the medium of instruction at the Secondary School in Llandovery, to which Llangadog children go.

It would have been too much to expect the sympathy of everyone in Llangadog, especially as I had arrived in the village just after the outbreak of war. A small minority were very antipathetic. The surprising thing is that so many were forgiving and kind towards someone so extreme in his ideas as me. Only a few showed their hostility but they were in a fairly advantageous position. The Glasallt family was among the most outstanding in this respect. Mrs Evans of Glasallt, the mother, was a sister of Llywelyn Williams, the former Member of Parliament for Carmarthenshire, but without a smidgen of her brother's magnanimity and robust Welsh character, nor any of his sympathy for conscientious objectors. Llywelyn Williams was a barrister and on many occasions had represented them before tribunals during the First World War. But his unmarried nephews at Glasallt were warmongers, though they kept well away from the field of battle. Their sacrifice was made by producing food for Britain and making a profit out of it – they were great Liberals, of course. Non, the eldest of the two sons who were still at home, and later a deacon in the chapel, went so far as to write a nasty letter about me in *Y Tyst*, our denominational newspaper. I was 'an agitator' who was not to be countenanced, and I was 'perverting the people', he said. His mother was very pompous, too, although perhaps someone as pompous as I shouldn't say so. She was as Tory in her attitudes as Welsh Liberals can be, that's to say, more conservative than the Conservatives. It was little wonder that Nationalists and pacifists upset her. It must be said that I wasn't the family's only *bête noire*, not by a long chalk; our minister Charles Jones, and his wife, also came under the lash. The brother-in-law of Mrs Jones, a minister with the Baptists, came to preach at our chapel one Sunday. As I was leaving the service, I heard Mrs Glasallt Evans say to Mrs Jones, the words falling on the ear like fingers of ice, 'Your sister was more fortunate in her husband than you, wasn't she, Mrs Jones?'

Chapter 7

In Time of War

For five years the monstrosity of world war hung over the country, its personal and social disasters changing the lives of many of its people. I was one of the more fortunate. As Honorary Secretary of *Heddychwyr Cymru*, the Welsh Pacifist Movement, I gave much of my spare time to the movement's work and was able to do so without any great hindrance for the duration of the conflict. Although I had resisted compulsory military service with the rest of Plaid Cymru, I didn't have to suffer imprisonment like A.O.H. Jarman and many others (Chris Rees was jailed for twelve months after the war had ended), nor did I have to face a long series of tribunals, as in the case of J.E. Jones. What I encountered was a lack of understanding of my reasoning: since I claimed to be a Nationalist, why not defend my country against the evil that was threatening it? In vain I argued that my country was Wales and that I was trying to defend it by non-violent means. The methods of modern warfare would do irreparable harm to our national life. By 1939 it was difficult for anyone to claim that there had been moral justification for the war of 1914-18, which did such terrible injury to Wales, though the thousands who had marched to their deaths singing 'Tipperary' had believed they were fighting for the freedom of small nations.

The organizer of the Welsh Pacifist Movement was Richard Bishop, an Englishman and a very colourful character, a Falstaff of a man, large of frame and loud of voice, with a ready tongue and very versatile. George M.Ll. Davies, the movement's President, was a very different sort of man. He had been a bank-manager in Wrexham at the age of twenty-seven, and had he remained with the bank he would doubtless have become a director at an early stage of his career. It was with him that Dan Thomas, my future father-in-law, had begun work as a lad of fifteen, and with him he had joined the Territorials. He was sent to France in 1914, but long before that George Davies had begun keenly to regret joining the Army. He was returned to Parliament for the University of Wales seat in 1923, the only M.P. ever to be elected as a Christian Pacifist. When I got to know him he was working among the unemployed men of the Rhondda and their womenfolk. During the first fortnight of the war I addressed with him about a score of women's groups established by Quakers in clubs for the unemployed of the Valley. George Davies possessed something of his grandmother Fanny's mystical gifts; she was the wife of John Jones of Tal-y-sarn, one of the greatest preachers of the nineteenth century, whose thousand-page biography has been described by Saunders Lewis as the greatest of its kind. He was able to sense the mind and spirit of others in the most sensitive way. For that reason many people came to him seeking moral help in their difficulties and he always gave of himself unstintingly. I once saw him publicly demonstrating his gift in a most unusual manner at a conference of pacifists at the George Hostel in Bangor. He was asked to comply with whatever the audience wanted him to do without anyone's giving him instructions. He went out into the corridor while we, some sixty of us, considered what we should ask him to do. It was decided that he was to walk the length of the hall to the table where the Bible lay and open it at the Book of Isaiah. George then came in, a blindfold was put over his eyes, he was spun around a few times and left facing the wall. He stood still for a moment, then slowly turned around, and walked across the hall towards the stage. He went up on to the platform, crossed to the rostrum, placed his hands on the Bible and opened it. Then he stood quite still. 'I can see that you want me to open the Bible,' he said, 'but I don't know at what Book.'

Part of the work that the Secretary of *Heddychwyr Cymru* was expected to carry out was organizing conferences; another was distributing the excellent newsletters that the President wrote. I'm afraid I earned his rebuke more than once on account of the poor quality of the duplicating. But the most valuable work I did was in publishing a series of thirty-two pamphlets of about thirty pages each, which were sold for threepence. They were printed very cheaply in Denbigh by Gwasg Gee, where Gwilym R. Jones gave generous and invaluable assistance in seeing them through the press. We had decided that the publication of pamphlets would be more practical and effective than a magazine like *Y Deyrnas* which had been published by the pacifists of the First World War. Among the contributors were George Davies, T. Gwynn Jones, Iorwerth Peate, Thomas Parry, Rhys J. Davies M.P., Pennar Davies, J. Gwyn Griffiths, Hywel D. Lewis, Myrddin Lloyd, T. Eurig Davies, Herbert Morgan, and Ben Bowen Thomas. I took responsibility for just one pamphlet,

namely *Tystiolaeth y Plant*, a collection of statements by our generation of pacifists; Waldo Williams's contribution was his famous
poem '*Myfi, Tydi, Efe*'.

Despite being busy in the greenhouses, I still went to Barry every
Sunday up until the fall of France, but when the Panzer tanks raced
in past the Maginot Line and overran France, there was quite a bit
of panic in Wales. It was at this time that the Marxist poet
T.E. Nicholas and many another innocent was imprisoned. The
Barry police said they were considering taking action against me
because of something I had jocularly said to some friends on the way
home from chapel one Sunday evening, something to the effect that
they would soon have to start learning German. I have no idea who
reported this to the police, but anyway, that wasn't all they had
against me. When my father called at the police-station he was shown
a large pile of papers – evidence of what I was supposed to have said
in various places up and down the country. The police used to take
notes at every meeting in those days. Often Sergeant Johnson, a
member at Tabernacl, was one of them. If my Uncle Dudley hadn't
been the town's Mayor, I think it could have been the worse for me.
I didn't spend weekends in Barry after that.

The cumbersome name that was given to the most important
movement working for Wales during the war was *Pwyllgor Diogelu
Diwylliant Cymru* ('Committee for the Safeguarding of the Culture
of Wales'). It had been brought into being as the consequence of a
letter sent to *The Manchester Guardian* by Saunders Lewis and
J.E. Daniel calling for the founding of a non-party national movement that would defend the Welsh people in a way that the Nationalist Party was not able to do in the circumstances of the war – the
influx of evacuees, the transfer of workers, as many women as men,
to work in the industries of the English Midlands, military conscription, and so on. The movement, which was later given the name
Undeb Cymru Fydd ('The Union of the Wales of the Future'), attracted some of our most prominent people and its Council met in
Aberystwyth; it also established county branches like the one in
Carmarthenshire of which I became Secretary. The movement's
effectiveness can be attributed to T.I. Ellis, the son of T.E. Ellis, the
great leader of Welsh life in the late nineteenth century; he was its
exceedingly efficient and committed Secretary, who carried out the
work as a labour of love. Wales was placed heavily in his debt.

One of the movement's early campaigns was an attempt to save
the Epynt mountain and its seven valleys from being taken over by
the War Department. As part of this initiative we held seven or eight
meetings in various parts of the district, at Trecastell and Pontsenni,

at Llanwrtyd and Tirabad, as well as in some of the tiny places up in the hills such as Llandeilo'r-fan and Merthyr Cynog. There was always an uncommonly serious atmosphere whenever a meeting was held at a small school or in the vestry of Pabell Chapel, often by the light of an oil-lamp. My fellow-speaker at every meeting was Dyfnallt, that wild pony of a man from the Black Mountain. Dyfnallt had the reputation of being tight-fisted and keen on money, but that wasn't my experience of him, I must say. He used to come to the meetings on Epynt from Carmarthen in a taxi, at his own expense, calling to pick me up on the way. I always found him generous with his money and his support. We also co-operated in getting rid of Mason, Carmarthenshire's Director of Education, after he had been so impudent as to form a body of military cadets in the county's Secondary Schools and appoint himself Colonel.

The Executive Committe of Plaid Cymru had asked J.E. Jones to go around the Epynt farms, which he did with his usual diligence. I had got to know J.E. on the Party's committees and it was on Epynt that we became good friends. I was to work closely with him for a quarter of a century and more after this, a period when he held Plaid Cymru together as its General Secretary and carefully nurtured its growth by his herculean labours on its behalf. We came close to saving Epynt from destruction, but on the very day that the Government was to have made its final decision, Hitler chose to invade Norway. The War Department quickly grabbed forty thousand acres, the whole mountain and the valleys. The Welsh-speaking community of Epynt was broken up, with the dispersal of some hundreds of its people to other parts of Wales and beyond its borders. Some of the families claimed to have been living in the same place for five centuries. Some of them broke their hearts. The language boundary retreated westward some ten miles, and the anglicization of Pontsenni and Trecastell by a huge military camp was accelerated. When the English army's heavy guns moved in, one of their first targets was Pabell Chapel.

There was an unexpected consequence to the tragedy of Epynt in Llangadog. Two of the mountain's farmers came to live in Llanddeusant, the next parish, where they offended against the war-time regulation which laid it down that farmers had to keep a certain amount of land under the plough. They were brought to stand trial in the little court-room at Llangadog, where they asked to give their evidence in Welsh. Everyone in the court was able to speak the language – the magistrates, the police, and the clerk – yet the official language was English. The two defendants were allowed to speak in Welsh but the clerk said that their evidence would have to be translated into the language of the court. So W.J. Gravelle, our musician, who used to lend his services as translator, was sent for. As a musician he was terrific, but as a translator he wasn't so hot. Anyway, he did his job; the defendants were fined and informed that they would have to pay the translator's fee on their way out. I was astonished. I had no idea that this happened, but later on I heard it was common in Wales. In the days when I'd been articled to a solicitor, I had heard monoglot Arabs and Greeks speaking in court in Barry and in Cardiff. There had to be a translator but nobody dreamt of asking the witness or the defendant to pay the fee; that would have been patently unjust. The only people in Wales who were obliged to pay a translator's fee were the Welsh-speakers themselves. They had to pay for speaking their own language in their own country. The Committee set about righting this wrong. The Llangadog case was joined to the Language Petition that had called before the war for official status for Welsh. Five of us were chosen to meet the Welsh Members of Parliament. We insisted on holding the meeting in Wales and the Welsh Parliamentary Party sent half-a-dozen representatives to meet us. The meeting was held in Cardiff's City Hall, the only time the Members of Parliament had met in Wales up to then. The somewhat unsatisfactory outcome of all this was the Welsh Courts Act. All it did was delete Clause 8 of the Statute of Wales, the Act of Union of 1536, and give the monoglot Welsh-speaker the right to speak his or her language in a court of law without having to pay for the privilege. This right was still refused to any Welsh person who was known to be able to speak English. Several times I was prevented from speaking Welsh in the small court at Llangadog – once by Non Evans of Glasallt. We had to wait until the Welsh Courts Act of 1967 before we had the right to speak our language as a right.

A number of conferences and rallies were organized under the Committee's auspices, none more successful than the one at Colwyn Bay. The hall was full to capacity with representatives from the old kingdom of Gwynedd. I remember asking the Chairman, D.R. Hughes, who it was had been responsible for such a grand turnout. D.R. Hughes was a staunch fellow, and it was he who had ensured the adoption of the Welsh Rule at the National Eisteddfod. It was also his idea to produce *Cofion Cymru*, the little news-letter that the Committe used to send to Welsh men and women in the armed forces. He told me that the meeting had been arranged by a young bank clerk. This was the first time for me to meet Elwyn Roberts, with whom I should work closely over the years, an out-standing organizer who had already founded Plaid Cymru's largest branch at Blaenau Ffestiniog.

I continued working for *Undeb Cymru Fydd* for years after the end
of the war. Its Council's meeting-place was changed from
Aberystwyth to Shrewsbury, which meant that I could travel to it on
the mid-Wales line. One night I slept in the same bed as Bob Owen
of Croesor, or more precisely, I shared a bed with that omniscient
bibliophile, a former quarryman who was given an honorary degree
by the University of Wales. Bob talked non-stop until six in the
morning. Shortly after dawn he turned to me and said it was time for
us to catch some sleep. But within a quarter of an hour he was at it
again, saying, 'D'you know, Gwynfor . . .', and off he went until it
was time for us to get up. Bob Owen was already famous when I first
went to his home in the company of Professor J.R. Jones, whom Bob
used to call John Robet. That was the only time I ever went up the
mountain known as Y Cnicht. Bob's home left an indelible impression on me. He owned one of the country's most amazing libraries,
which consisted of stacks of books and manuscripts in large number.
There were books in the hall, in the bedrooms, even in the pantry;
there were books everywhere. Whenever I went there after a Plaid
Cymru meeting organized by Ifor Owen, the headmaster of Croesor
school at the time, I would find the hospitable Mrs Bob Owen
presiding merrily over her library of a house. Just prior to my first
trip to America, Bob was generous in sharing with me the extent of
his knowledge of Welsh people in the United States. For example, in
addition to telling me about the eighteen men of Welsh descent
among the fifty-three who signed the Declaration of Independence,
he provided me with the names of the fourteen Welsh generals who
fought on the American side in the War of Independence, as well as
the titles of more than sixty Welsh-language journals published in
America during the nineteenth century.

The work of *Undeb Cymru Fydd* overlapped to some extent with
that of the Nationalist Party, but in time of war it was the non-party
movement which could achieve more in safeguarding the culture of
Wales. The best that could be expected was to keep Plaid Cymru in
existence. It was generally thought that the war would destroy it, but
although the Party had opposed the conflict, it came out of the
war-years stronger than ever before. In all, fifteen of its members
were imprisoned for their opposition to the war. I became a member
of the Executive Council of Plaid Cymru in 1937. In the year
following, together with Moses Griffith, the father of R. Geraint
Gruffydd, I represented the Party at a meeting with leaders of the
Scottish National Party in Edinburgh – the first of many visits to
that country. It was at that time I first heard, from the Reverend
James MacKechnie, that in the territory of the Gododdin around

Edinburgh the poet Aneirin had lived and written in the early Welsh of the sixth century.

When I first went to live in Llangadog, the only member of Plaid Cymru I could find between Carmarthen and Rhandirmwyn was John Thomas of Pont Crynfe in Llanddeusant. John had been a weaver but at that time he was a postman and helping his brother run a bus, or perhaps two buses by the middle of the war. They were the 'Thomas Bros' whose names are now to be seen on a dozen or fifteen buses, and their families are still among the most prominent Nationalists in the district. John Thomas was an intelligent man, of short stature, dark complexion and bony frame, a physical type often found in the vicinity of the Black Mountain; Dyfnallt belonged to it. John Thomas was Secretary of the Regional Committee of Carmarthenshire, that's to say, four or five individuals who met on a monthly basis in Carmarthen town – the Party's only organization in the county apart from the branch that Dewi Watkin Powell ran for a while in Llanelli. There were about fifty young people in that branch while Dewi was associated with it. Later on, I founded one in Llangadog with W.J. Gravelle as its Chairman. He was recruited from the Labour Party, more I think by Rhiannon's good looks than by Nationalist arguments! His daughter Mair was also a member, as was Herbert John Lewis, a friend from my early youth who later chaired my County Election meetings, and Francis Williams, a Baptist minister's son. Within a year or two, however, Mair Gravelle joined the WAAFS, her father went back into the Labour Party and the branch fell apart.

In 1940 J.E. Jones managed to put on a one-day Plaid Cymru conference in a small hut at the rear of the *Urdd Gobaith Cymru* ('League of Welsh Youth') offices on Llanbadarn Road in Aberystwyth. It could hold about fifty people comfortably. It was here that we first translated from Welsh into English and it was I who had to serve as translator, giving a synopsis of even the address by J.E. Daniel, the President. The reason for this was that the Party had just acquired a new, English-speaking member of some importance. Nobody knew anything about him but from his dignified, serious manner he seemed to be a man of some consequence, and because he wasn't Welsh-speaking everything had to be translated into English for his sake. A year or two later we discovered that he was a plain-clothes policeman.

By 1943 the Summer School had been resumed and the Annual Conference had grown. The Summer School was one of J.E.'s main platforms and it continued to provide political education over the years as well as serving as an important venue where members of

Plaid Cymru could meet and enjoy themselves socially for a few days. The work carried out by J.E. as the Party's Organizer and Secretary was terrific. He it was who built up the St. David's Day Fund which enabled us to contest seven constituencies at the General Election of 1945, as well as two by-elections in Neath and Caernarfon. He too did most of the work of editing the two monthly papers and seeing them through the press. He made every one of the hundred and more books and pamphlets published by the Party in his time pay for itself. The Summer School and Conference were held that year in Caernarfon, where J.E. was able to keep an eye on things from home, for in those days the Party's offices were in that town. It was usual for members to sleep on straw mattresses on a school floor during the Party's early years, though no one could get to sleep until much before two or three in the morning. Nobody wanted to sleep, anyway, for there was too much fun to be had in the *nosweithiau llawen* that were such a feature of the Summer School. The principal attraction in Caernarfon that year was Bob Roberts, known to everyone as Bob Tai'r Felin, although he couldn't be persuaded to sing until about one o'clock in the morning. Then the voice of the eighty-year-old folk-singer would ring out through the building like a bell.

A lecture was delivered at Caernarfon by Douglas Young, the brilliant Chairman of the Scottish National Party, who was given a year in prison for his opposition to the war. He had become a great hero in Scotland and London was afraid that Scottish Nationalism would muster around him. Many Scots looked upon him as the saviour of their country. When I walked through the centre of Glasgow with him – he was well over six feet tall, with a black beard and wearing a kilt and cloak – I noticed that many people greeted him as if they knew him and agreed with what he stood for. But Douglas Young had an Achilles' heel: even while he was President of the S.N.P. he continued to be a member of the Labour Party and when obliged to choose between the two, he chose Labour. From that moment on his influence in Scotland waned until it disappeared altogether.

Another major personality of the national movement in Scotland was the great poet Hugh MacDiarmid. His real name was Christopher Murray Grieve and he was a good friend, a staunch Nationalist, and yet a most peculiar fellow. I was the guest speaker at a St. Andrew's Night dinner given by the S.N.P. at the North British Hotel in Edinburgh in 1944. There were about four hundred people present and Douglas Young was in the chair. After dinner there were various items by some talented performers, and at the end of the evening Douglas Young called upon 'the poet Grieve' to propose a vote of thanks. Hugh MacDiarmid stood in the doorway of the bar where he had spent most of the evening, wearing his overalls and his hands grimy from the Clydeside engineering works where he was employed at the time. What we had from him was a vehement attack on the performers who had taken part in the concert. All we had heard and seen, he said, had been 'kailyard stuff', by which he meant culture that was worthy only of the parish pump. Douglas Young kept his head under the table all the while, muttering, 'What a man, what a man!' On another occasion I was co-speaker with Hugh MacDiarmid in a debate on the national question in the Cambridge Union. The distinguished broadcaster Ludovic Kennedy was the third speaker on our side. On the other, one of the speakers was Leo Abse and another Nicholas Fairburn, who has just lost his place in the Cabinet. Like Abse, Fairburn was fond of wearing fancy clothes and, again like him, he was a British National-ist fiercely opposed to freedom for his own nation. The debate was broadcast live. We felt as if the audience was coming our way until Hugh MacDiarmid spoke third and last. At once there was hostility that was more than audible. The poet didn't put forward a single reasonable argument in favour of political freedom for Scotland and Wales. From first to last, amid a cacophony of hooting and hissing, his speech was little more than a bitter and fierce attack on the English. We lost the debate but Hugh MacDiarmid didn't care a sausage; he had made his point. I think it was in Cambridge he told me that, before the First World War, he had worked for a local paper in Monmouthshire, at the time of the anti-Semitic riots there. In his personal dealings I found Christopher Grieve to be a most mild-mannered man. I am grateful for the kindness the veteran Nationalist has shown me over the years.

I have another reason for remembering the Caernarfon Confer-ence, because it was there I became Plaid Cymru's Vice-President. J.E. Daniel, a lovely man of rare brilliance, had to resign from the Presidency. At the previous meeting of the Executive Council he had taken me aside to explain his reasons. He urged me to accept the Presidency but I was unable, mainly on account of my father who had been suffering greatly because of me. The words 'spy' and 'traitor' and 'fifth columnist' had been painted on his vans and the windows of his shops. A warehouse had been burned and the police had seen people trying to set fire to another. Abi Williams was elected as President, a staunch, unbending man and a powerful speaker who within a few years was to suffer bitterly for his convictions.

By this time I was doing a lot of travelling up and down the country. This was to be the pattern of my life for the next quarter of a century and more. My car would regularly clock up between thirty and thirty-five thousand miles a year, mostly on Party business. I'm sure I must have travelled well over a million miles along the roads of our little country! The car I had during the war, and for a long time afterwards, had seen better days. I spent many a night in it after breaking down on the way home. I always used to heave a deep sigh of relief on arriving within ten miles of Llangadog, for even if the car packed up then I knew I could have walked it from that distance. Petrol was rationed during the war and there were only enough coupons for journeys that were absolutely necessary. But I had a good friend who kept a shop and pump-station at Ffairfach, namely Wynford Morgan, the brother of Eirwyn, the former Principal of the Bangor Baptists' College, and he would make sure that I had enough petrol and coupons.

Whenever I could manage it without upsetting anybody, I used to set off immediately after meetings and buy chips on the way home. It was thus I became something of an authority on the chipshops of Wales, about which I once threatened to write a book. One night I stopped to buy chips at a shop near the railway at Gwaun Cae Gurwen, and on coming out, eating the chips from a newspaper, I found a policeman standing near the car and complaining that there wasn't enough light at the vehicle's rear. At the time only a small light at the front of the car was allowed but there had to be enough light at the rear so that the number-plate was visible. To prove his point he took me about twenty yards back from the vehicle. 'Can you read that?' he asked. 'Yes,' I replied, 'ETX 240.' 'Aaw, go on, you knew it,' he said, and jotted down the details in his little book. As a consequence, I received a summons to appear at the small court at Pontardawe, the one where Cen Puw had to pay for a translator in 1969. I wrote a letter in Welsh to explain why I couldn't attend and asked Wynne Samuel to keep an eye on the case. Wynne was working part-time for a local newspaper, and since he wasn't able to be in court either, he enquired of another correspondent what had happened in my case. The latter flicked through his notes and said, 'Oh yes, some little farmer chap from Llangadog didn't have any English, so they let him off with 3s 6d costs.'

The Party's Annual Conference and Summer School were held at Lampeter in 1944. There the food inspectors paid us a visit. These were the days when food was rationed as well as petrol – two ounces of cheese a week and so on. I used to supply the tomatoes, which were otherwise hard to come by. But what had attracted the attention of the inspectors were two fine cheeses, which were obviously breaking the regulations. They asked where the cheeses had come from. It was Dr D.J. Davies who offered an explanation. 'We squeezed everyone's two-ounce ration together,' he said, 'and put them on a wooden armchair, and then got Eic Davies to sit down heavily on them.' Eic weighed eighteen stone! As was our custom in those days, the members of the Summer School went to the service in the local chapel on Sunday morning. The well-known preacher at Lampeter was the Reverend John Green. He assumed that all the respectable-looking strangers whom he saw in the congregation that morning were English visitors, and for the sake of our immortal souls he turned to English for most of the service. 'How Green was my John,' cracked Dafydd Miles as we made our way out at the close of service.

By the Conference held at Llangollen in 1945, just five days before the bomb was dropped on Hiroshima, the Party had contested seven seats at a General Election. In the town of the International Eisteddfod on the first day of August, I was elected President of Plaid Cymru.

Chapter 8

With the Small Nations

After the war the Breton Nationalist Party was ruined as a result of persecution of its members. A very small group of them had been guilty of collaborating with the Germans and even fighting for them in a military unit named after Father Perrot, a priest and Nationalist who had been murdered by members of the Resistance, almost certainly Communists. What the great majority of Nationalists had done was to take advantage of the German occupation to promote the language and culture of Britanny, which since the days of Napoleon France had been trying to suppress, and to further the movement that had been working for self-government. The French education system is so completely centralized in Paris that it's said the Education Minister can tell at any given hour what is being taught in all the schools of the land. It was this system which had completely proscribed the Breton language from all state schools, even as a subject. There had been a slight slackening after the Germans occupied the country. But as the occupiers were being driven out the French Establishment, and especially the Communists, with the support of the greater part of the people, it must be said, seized their opportunity and began trying to destroy Breton Nationalism altogether. Dozens were murdered, others executed, and hundreds and perhaps thousands were imprisoned, many for life. A number escaped with their lives to Wales. My wife Rhiannon and I gave sanctuary to a dozen of them at various times at Wernellyn.

> *'Brython i aros gyda Brython,*
> *Er i bedair canrif ar ddeg gerdded dros y dwr.'*

('Briton came to stay with Briton, though fourteen centuries had walked across the water.')

They came to Wales under false names. Bob Horel was in fact

Robert Divroad, whose daughter has recently finished her course at Aberystwyth. Once, when Rhiannon went on holiday to Britanny and stayed in the homes of some of the refugees or their friends and relatives, she returned with an old man who, like the others, was under sentence of death but who had been hiding in the hay-lofts of remote farms. We knew him as Monsieur le Meliner but we heard later that his real name was Motineau. He was with us for six months and he placed quite a strain on our French because he hadn't a word of English and we knew no Breton. Whenever I took him for a trip to some meeting or other, the words that always came to his lips as he gazed at our hills and mountains were '*Ah, les montagnes, les montagnes!*'. Britanny is, after all, quite a flat country.

The only prominent Breton to stay with us was Dr Moger, the alias of Yann Fouéré, the leader of the Breton Nationalist movement. While he was with us he wrote a book on the history of Breton Nationalism which was published by Plaid Cymru, one of the many things we did for Britanny. Yann's wife Marie Madeleine and their three children came over a little while later and stayed with us for nine months. Erwann, the eldest son, partly repaid their debt by helping Plaid Cymru in Brussels, where he works with the European Community. Yann Fouéré's stay in Wales was rudely interrupted by an application from the French Government to extradite him to France. If that had been allowed to happen, he would probably have been executed. He was suddenly arrested by the police and imprisoned in Birmingham. I spent most of that day on the telephone. I had a lot of help from two people in particular – Rhys Hopkin Morris, the M.P. for Carmarthen, and Cyril O. Jones, the patriotic solicitor from Wrexham. Because the latter was highly respected in the Labour Party he had some influence with Chuter Ede, the Home Secretary at the time, who was surprisingly very supportive. In this way Yann was saved from being taken back to France, though he wasn't allowed to return to Wales. He made a new home in Ireland, near Galway, where he built up a lobster business. We in Wales weren't allowed to give shelter to our Breton cousins but the Irish were. A good number of Bretons gathered there, including Alan Heussaf, the Secretary of the Celtic League and editor of its magazine, *Carn*. Another Breton who found refuge in Ireland was Roparz Hemon, the great scholar who was to work for the Institute of Celtic Studies in Dublin for the rest of his life. His trial attracted a lot of attention and we in Wales put heavy pressure on the French authorities for his release. Dewi Watkin Powell went across to Rennes as an observer on behalf of *Y Faner* and about the same time the National Eisteddfod sent a strong deputation to Britanny, under the leadership of W.J. Gruffydd, to report on the situation there. It was thus, Roparz Hemon said, his life was saved.

Someone who kept in close contact with Britanny and who is a friend of Per Denez, the leader of the national movement today, is Delwyn Phillips, who spent most of his life in Birmingham before retiring to Aberystwyth, where he was soon appointed Secretary of the Plaid Cymru branch. Delwyn had been the main pillar of the Welsh Societies in that dismal English town: he was Secretary of the Cymmrodorion and the Brythoniaid, Secretary of the Plaid Cymru branch, Secretary of the Independent chapel in Wheeler Street, and the organizer of Welsh classes and lectures galore under the aegis of the University. One of his protégés was Roy Lewis, who used to be on the Party's staff. Delwyn worked wonderfully well, and now his mantle has passed to his son Rhys ap Delwyn, who came to Llandeilo as a dentist. Right-hand man to Delwyn was Jac Jones, a shop-steward in industry whose dream it was to return to live in Wales in a cottage in the Preselau hills. On retiring, he settled near Efail-fach to keep a small guest-house. He and Mrs Jones are there to this day, stalwarts of the chapel, Plaid Cymru and other good causes. For ten years he was the Party's Treasurer in the Carmarthen constituency.

During the year I am speaking about, the first after the war's end, I was the Welsh Secretary of the Celtic Congress that met in Dublin. De Valera was Prime Minsiter of Ireland at the time, and that explains the gift of two thousand pounds from his Government towards the cost of the Congress. How much would that be in today's money, I wonder? Even the expenses of the delegates were paid, something unheard of in the Nationalist movement in Wales, for Plaid Cymru never paid anyone their expenses. I chose the sixteen Welsh delegates with great care. One of them was the poet R.S. Thomas; I note this fact because it was in Dublin that he told me he hoped to write in Welsh, his second language. Saunders Lewis delivered a magnificent lecture, as usual. We were given an official reception by the Irish Government in Phoenix Park at which five or six hundred people were present. As I had other duties, I was late arriving at the large pavilion where the refreshments were being served. When I arrived I was called over by my good friend Frank Gallagher, the Minister of Information (if that's the right title), to join a small group clustered around Mr and Mrs De Valera. On seeing that I was without food, Mrs De Valera insisted on going to fetch me some, making her way through the crowd to the long counter and returning in a moment with a full plate of refreshments and a cup of tea. I doubt whether Mrs Winston Churchill would have behaved thus in a similar situation. After the buffet we went for a stroll in the great park, where I had an experience that I had never had before and have never had since, namely feeling the arm of a Government Minister and the Speaker of the Dail resting lightly on my shoulders as we walked.

I was again in Dublin, this time as Chairman of the Celtic League, a post I was to hold for ten years, some twenty years later, in 1966, during the fiftieth anniversary celebrations of the Easter Rising of 1916. In November 1980 I addressed a rally of the Gaelic League from a platform outside the famous General Post Office that had been the headquarters of Connolly and Pearse during the rebellion. Although I admire the sacrifice of those heroes, I think the Rising was a disastrous mistake, for it led to the Civil War from which the country took fifty years to recover. I noticed in 1966 that the celebratory flags were confined to O'Connell Street and that only Fianna Fail took part. My sympathies were with Fianna Fail. I was once invited by this party to address a meeting it had arranged at the National University in Dublin. The topic was confederalism for the countries of these islands, which is part of Plaid Cymru's constitutional policy. Tom Mullins, who was for many years Secretary of Fianna Fail, was a personal friend of J.E. Jones and myself, and he used to come regularly to Plaid Cymru's Summer School and Annual Conference. We had many a good turn done us by De Valera. For example, when he came to Cardiff at the beginning of his world tour, it was Plaid Cymru which officially welcomed him. We gave a dinner at the Park Hotel which hundreds attended – the Lord Lieutenant and High Sheriff, the Lord Mayor and Members of Parliament, and leaders of business and industry, and so forth. But it was the President of Plaid Cymru who spoke first to welcome the great Irishman. On another occasion in Cardiff I shared a platform with him at a meeting of the Anti-Partition League, and was a speaker with him at a dinner given by that organization. Many's the time I addressed the annual dinner of the League, as one of its chief guests. Just before my first trip to America I received a letter from De Valera to hand to Mr Boland, the Irish Ambassador to the United Nations, asking him to call a meeting of the national deputations so that I could address them on the question of Wales. Mr Boland promised to arrange it by the time I got back from my tour of the States, but on my return the meeting didn't take place. Conor Cruise O'Brien had intervened to prevent it. I called on De Valera several times when he was *Taoiseach*, or Prime Minister, and always had a warm and courteous welcome from him. He enquired in detail about what was happening in Wales. Despite the fact that the memory of Lloyd George was something of a stumbling-block, he remembered George M.Ll. Davies with pleasure. We never chatted without his mentioning our respective languages, always distinguishing between the P Celts and the Q Celts – the Welsh and Bretons, and the Gaels of Ireland and Scotland.

In his attitude to the Irish language De Valera was similar to Thomas Davis, the leader of Young Ireland, but they are a very small minority who take that standpoint these days. As in Wales, there is a distorted psychology among many Irish intellectuals and the middle-class which perhaps has its origins in an inferiority complex. It manifested itself in the contrast between two appearances I made on 'The Late Night Show', the most popular television programme in Ireland. The first time, when I spoke about politics in Wales, was an exceptionally pleasant experience, with the terrific singers known as the Clancy Brothers adding to the enjoyment. On the second occasion the topic for discussion was the importance of the Irish language. The interviewer was more hostile than anyone I had ever encountered in Wales and the whole programme was designed to belittle the language. When I was last in Dublin, I found that the Irish language campaigners were quite gloomy about the situation. The *Gaeltacht*, those areas in the west where the language is supposed to be strong, is still on the wane, the parents tending to speak more and more English to their children. In Dublin itself British attitudes are on the increase among the middle-classes and intelligentsia. It seems certain that the language would have disappeared altogether if it hadn't been for the Irish Government but even it has lost all enthusiasm for trying to revive it. It must be said that it made quite a bit of effort in the years after the creation of the Free State, whereas the Catholic Church was always less sympathetic. The Church has been a bastion of the national spirit and identity, as it is in Poland today, but it was the bane of the language. But perhaps I shouldn't be speaking of 'the Church' in Ireland; Saunders Lewis once chided me for speaking thus. We had been talking about the firm support given by Archbishop McGrath, the Catholic Archbishop of Wales, for the Welsh language. When I commented on the difference between this and the attitude of the Church in Ireland, Saunders said it wasn't possible to speak of a Church in Ireland, only of bishops. He went on to explain who it was became bishops. In an Irish family, he said, it was the son who wasn't much use on the farm or fit for any other work who would enter the priesthood. If he were to show any exceptional talent as an administrator, he would be elevated to a bishopric. It was in the Orders, he said, that the best priests were to be found, and I must say that it was there, particularly among the Capuchins, that I found the most impressives ones I ever met.

There were also Cornish members of the Celtic League, the little political movement for which J.E. Jones worked so hard, publishing with the help of Dr Noelle Davies an excellent annual magazine. I went to Cornwall on two occasions to speak in a short series of meetings held by Mebyon Kernow, the Cornish Nationalist Party which has contested local elections and one or two at a Parliamentary level. During the second visit I saw three short plays performed in the Cornish language.

I was often in Scotland from 1938 onwards, about a dozen times in all, speaking at the Nationalist Party's Annual Conference. On one of these trips, when the Conference was at Inverness, Myfi Morgan organized a busful of Welsh Nationalists to visit the conference on the Saturday that I was due to speak. Among their number was the musical family from Carreg Folgam in Llangadog, whose party was known as *Seiniau Trichrug*. About fifty Welsh people were given a place of honour on the stage and, at the end of my speech, the audience rose to their feet to sing '*Hen Wlad fy Nhadau*'. I had never heard such rousing singing in Scotland before.

I saw the S.N.P. growing from a much lesser party than Plaid Cymru. Our example helped to inspire them to become the big party which won eleven Parliamentary seats in 1974. Continuous schism had kept the S.N.P. a very small party for decades. It had contested only five of Scotland's seventy-two seats in 1959, at a time when Plaid Cymru was fighting twenty of the thirty-six in a country less than half the size of Scotland. The same weakness was to be found in Britany. By 1964 the situation had improved and the S.N.P. doubled its vote from Election to Election up to and including the Elections of 1974. Of course, the oil discovered in the North Sea helped. Compared with Wales, moreover, Scotland has some obvious advantages. There was a Scottish state until 1707. The country has its own legal system, ancient Universities which are thoroughly Scottish in character, its own Established Church and five morning newspapers with wide circulations. The country hasn't suffered as much as Wales from immigration. It is farther away from London and it isn't divided, as Wales sometimes is, by language issues. On the other hand, there is no Scottish language strong enough to link the people with their past and therefore no great national literature in it, nor is its history as inspiring as that of Wales – except, of course, to the Scots. Plaid Cymru had a more complete philosophy than the S.N.P. and its emphasis on the civilization and spiritual values of Wales was healthier than the heavy stress that the S.N.P. laid on economics. Plaid Cymru's victory at the Carmarthen by-election in July 1966 was a great encouragement to the S.N.P., inspiring it to win Hamilton in November 1967 and thus send Winnie Ewing to

Westminster. It was during a series of large meetings in Scotland soon after Carmarthen that I first met Winnie Ewing, on a trip to Aberdeen, where she spoke alongside me. She had just joined the S.N.P. At a meeting in Glasgow held in the McLellan Galleries, a large hall in the city-centre, Margaret Bain was converted to the S.N.P., as she has often said, and she too became a Member of Parliament some seven years later.

The last time I was in the McLellan Galleries was at the beginning of September 1980 when we were in the middle of our campaign for a Welsh television channel. I had flown from Rhoose Airport in Cardiff. As I went to catch the 'plane, I asked how long the journey would take, and was told, or so I thought, an hour and ten minutes. After an hour and ten minutes the 'plane landed and I alighted from it, with everyone else, or so I thought. Dr Robert McIntyre, the S.N.P.'s President, was supposed to meet me, but there was no sign of him. It was now half-past six and the meeting was due to begin at a half-past seven. I assumed that he had been held up by the traffic and, after waiting for ten minutes or so, I went into the cafeteria to have a coffee, popping out every so often to see whether he had turned up. By ten minutes past seven I was beginning to grow anxious: there was still no sign of Robert. So I went to the taxi-rank and asked the first cabbie how much he would charge to take me to the McLellan Galleries. 'Where?', he asked. 'The McLellan Galleries, in the centre of Glasgow,' I said. He thumbed through a small book, and looking up at me a little surprised, said, 'It's 210 miles.' I was in Leeds Airport! I rushed back into the building and up to the desk of the company with which I was flying. I asked the time of the next 'plane to Glasgow. There wasn't one that evening. Was there one going to Edinburgh, then? Yes, there was, it was on the runway that very minute; it had been held up for some reason or other but it was about to take off. Could I go on it? The stewardess asked the captain. Yes, I could, thank heavens. But I had a ticket to Glasgow and with a different company. The girl said she would have to ask Cardiff. The Edinburgh 'plane was held up while she telephoned Rhoose. With the help of a young man standing near by, the negotiations were completed satisfactorily, but I would have to pay £14. I had only £8 in cash. Could I pay by cheque? She would have to ask Cardiff again. Fortunately, Cardiff was still on the 'phone. But it was agreed, and I made out a cheque which I gave to the stewardess, whereupon she burst out laughing; no, she was beside herself with laughter. 'What's the matter?', asked a voice on the line from Cardiff. 'Ho, ho, . . . Ha, ha,' the Leeds girl was choking. 'The cheque . . . He, he, he . . . is written . . . Ha, ha, ha, . . . in Welsh. . . . Ho, ho, ho!' She had never seen anything so funny in all her life. It occurred to me how much Leeds had degenerated since the days when it was the heart of the Welsh kingdom of Elfed. The girls of the seventh century wouldn't have giggled over a cheque written in Welsh. It was now a quarter to eight and a thousand people had been waiting for me in Glasgow since half-past seven. I begged the young man who was standing at the girl's side to 'phone the McLellan Galleries, ask for Mr Billy Wolfe and inform him that I was catching the 'plane that would arrive in Edinburgh at nine o'clock.

I ran for the 'plane carrying my bag and a heavy parcel of books that Dafydd Williams, the Party's Secretary, had asked me to sell. I sat down in the only empty seat, drawing breath like a man with asthma, but at last I was leaving the old kingdom of Elfed for the land of the Gododdin. 'I know you, don't I?', said the man in the next seat as my breathing began to subside, and he mentioned my name and said I could put the parcel down by his feet. Taking it for granted that he was a Scottish Nationalist, I began sharing my troubles with him, but he wasn't a Nationalist at all. He was a businessman on his way home from Norwich. He had seen me on television and recognized me. His surname was Davies but he knew of no Welsh blood in his veins, and so unlike Delwyn Williams M.P., he was unable to take pride in his Welshness. But he proved to be a very likeable chap. He lived, he said, a few miles from the centre of Glasgow and would take me in his car from Edinburgh to within three miles of the McLellan Galleries, where I could take a taxi. In the end he took me at eighty miles an hour to within sight of the place. By now it was a quarter to ten. I could see people standing outside the hall having a smoke. Billy Wolfe had received the wonderful young man's message from the airport in Leeds. When I went up on to the stage after an interview with the press and radio, the packed audience was on its feet and in great fettle. The clock outside was striking ten.

The small nations of Europe, several of them under the paw of a foreign government, have made a unique contribution to civilization, and they have the potential to make an even greater one. Following the example of J.E. Jones, I kept in touch with a good number of them, and not only the Celtic nations, mainly by means of the society of which the Dane Scadergaard was Secretary. One of its conferences was held in Cardiff and representatives from these small nations were often invited to Plaid Cymru's Annual Conference. With the advent of the European Community, a number of them opened an office in Brussels. The strongest and richest among these were the Flemings. Their National Party, the Volksunie, maintained close links with Wales. It published an attractive booklet on the history of Wales, a free translation of the brochure published by *The South Wales Echo*, and they are about to bring out another on the history of the campaign for a Welsh television channel.

I visited several other of these small nations, such as Corsica, Catalonia, and Euskadi, or the Basque Country, as it is known in English. Two things made a deep impression on me in Euzkadi: first, the complexity of the co-operative societies created by the National- ists, particularly at Mondragon where none of the 18,000 employees lost their jobs, and secondly, the way in which manual workers and others contributed to the cost of establishing their daily newspaper, which cost nearly two million pounds, as well as to their clubs, the Batsoci. Dafydd Williams and I were given a terrific welcome at one of these clubs in Bilbao. They are not drinking-clubs, though there are bars in them, of course. They provide all kinds of activity, such as music, drama, literature, photography, and so on, and they also have excellent facilities for preparing food. Dafydd and I sat down to a splendid dinner with forty others. That club had been built at a cost of £150,000 and there was another half-built in the next munici- pality which cost £250,000. They owned fifty of these clubs through- out the country and were aiming at putting up eighty. I asked the organizer of the Nationalist Party how they went about raising these huge sums. 'We don't organize anything,' he replied. 'We simply go to see our supporters and look them straight in the eye and say we should like them to contribute a thousand pounds, and we always get it.' It's hard to imagine the Welsh responding like this. There are well-off people in Wales who consider a hundred pounds to be generous. But then we haven't been under Franco. In Euzkadi about twenty-two per cent of the population speak the Basque language. Jean-Paul Sartre has written, 'If they succeed in destroying his language, the Basque will become an abstract man, as they wish him to be. He will then speak Spanish, which is not and never was his language. The speaking of his own language is a revolutionary act.' Unlike in Euzkadi, the strength of the language in Catalonia is astonishing. It is claimed that about six million speak Catalan. After being banned from the schools and official life for years under Franco, it is once again blossoming as the language of the schools and university. When I addressed a large rally of the Catalan Nationalist Party in Barcelona, with a crowd of seven thousand filling the colourful stadium, I spoke in Welsh only, and was trans- lated into Catalan only. Not a word of English or Spanish was heard. The translator was Esyllt Lawrence, a Welsh Nationalist who is married to a Catalan Nationalist.

Chapter 9

Land and Society

The philosopher J.R. Jones held the view that it is as a result of interpenetration between a people and its land and language that a nation is formed. Every nation certainly has its territory that has been hallowed by the lives and graves of its men and women and by the dust of its saints down the ages. In the mind of the Nationalist all is sacred. It was this conviction which was challenged by Iorwerth Thomas, the Labour M.P. for Rhondda West, who at the time of great struggle for the land of Wales proclaimed in a radio discussion with me that 'Land is land'. For him it was only earth, while for us it was our mother-country. The Welsh nation has been maintained by the land of Wales all down the centuries and in our own day it continues to nourish our society. It wasn't for economic reasons in the first instance that Plaid Cymru placed such heavy emphasis on agriculture and the family farm, but for social reasons. A prosperous agricultural economy must be secured, and within it the smaller units of land, because the families who work them are the very backbone of Welsh-speaking society. Because we are aware of the importance of territory in the making of a nation, we fight hard to defend it, and because rural society is so essential to our health as a nation, we work for its well-being, calling for and sometimes creating, by means of our Party members, rural and often co-operative ventures. It was this thinking which prompted the successful campaign – one of the most successful ever – to obtain electricity supplies for rural areas. As a Member of Parliament, it was fitting that I should have switched on the power in a small ceremony at the last of the Welsh farms to receive electricity from the public grid. That was at Nant-yr-ast, a hill-farm on the slopes of the mountain of the same name at Blaenau Cothi, which looks out towards the mountain of Craig Twrch in Ceredigion. As a small boy I sometimes used to spend the day at Blaen Twrch, which was farmed by the Williamses, who were cousins of mine, and there I once saw an enormous cauldron boiling over a peat fire under an open chimney. This was the country of Joshua Thomas, the historian. Just before going to Nant-yr-ast, I had called at Cwm Pedol, his former home, and had spoken about him in a small Baptist chapel on the occasion of the two hundred and fiftieth anniversary of his birth.

By the end of the war the War Department owned hundreds of thousands of acres of the land of Wales. In reply to a Parliamentary question, Clement Attlee, the Prime Minister of the day, said the Government held 500,940 acres of Welsh land, that is three times as much as in Scotland which is four times the size, and fifteen times as much as in Northern Ireland. Most of it was upland, although Castle Martin was as good agricultural land as any in the Vale of Glamorgan. Since it looked as if the Government intended keeping this land for itself after the war was over, Plaid Cymru and *Undeb Cymru Fydd* set about organizing a campaign to thwart it. On one Saturday the *Undeb* organized five conferences. The two at which I spoke, at Maenclochog and Llandeilo, were full to overflowing and quite exciting. The best men of the Preselau, a highly cultured district, had come together that day under the leadership of Titus Lewis and Parry Roberts. The Reverend Parry Roberts, who was known to all as *Parry bach*, was a giant among Baptist ministers, a kind of bishop in the district, where his name is fragrant still. He arranged to buy a cottage on the Preselau hills so that he would have to be physically evicted by the War Department. His sons are still working in that tradition. Ithel Parry Roberts and his wife Jean are the Nationalist leaders at Hendy-gwyn (Whitland).

In the beautiful countryside which lies between Llangadog and Epynt, the War Department had been using a large tract of the Black Mountain. At the suggestion of Keidrych Rhys, the poet and journalist, the Party organized a mid-winter meeting on the shore of Llyn y Fan under the cliff of Cadair Arthur. The procession, which made its way, with flags waving, up the mountain road towards the lake, received a good deal of publicity, including several pages in *Picture Post*, a very popular illustrated magazine of the day. Keidrych was to do us several good turns of this kind. He it was in 1949 who arranged publicity for the huge rally at Machynlleth, the town where Glyndwr's Parliament House stands, the first of a long series of such events that J.E. Jones was to organize. He, too, was responsible for the press conference we held at the Piccadilly Hotel in the centre of London during our campaign against the radio ban which prevented Plaid Cymru from making party political broadcasts.

The War Department had a military range of ten thousand acres near Trawsfynydd. They found this insufficient for their purposes,

and in the early 'fifties it was announced that they intended adding
another ten thousand to what they already held. Plaid Cymru opposed this move, not only by the usual means but this time acting
directly in a manner which might have resulted in the protesters'
being sent to prison. For two whole days we lay siege to the camp by
sitting down on the roads which led to and from it. On the two nights
prior to the sit-downs, J.E. Jones and I both slept at Bryn Llefrith.
Early each morning we held sessions for the instruction of the
protesters in the finer points of our non-violent methods. Each of us
was to sit calmly in his place without striking back in the event of his
being struck, and if he were removed he was to return to his place
immediately. In a photograph taken during the second sit-down, I
notice that D.J. Williams and Dan Thomas are to the fore, one each
side of me, and that Waldo Williams is sitting next to Llwyd o'r Bryn.
I believe that everyone who appears in this photo continued to work
for Plaid Cymru for many years thereafter. We prevented every lorry,
every truck, and all kinds of vehicles from going into or coming out
of the camp. The work of the army came to a complete halt. On the
second day the police and military were expecting us, and so we took
up our positions before dawn, coming in from the Abergeirw side
under the direction of staunch Nationalists from that area. Chief
Constable Jones-Williams, who was a fellow-deacon of Dr R. Tudur
Jones, one of the group, was there throughout the day. The camp
was in constant touch with the army's headquarters at Shrewsbury.
The intimidating tactics used against us on the first day weren't
repeated on the second. We weren't subjected to any kind of force.
A number of techniques for removing us were considered by the
police and the soldiers but they were vetoed by the Chief Constable.
Preparations were made for the hose-pipes from a fire engine to be
turned on us but that idea, too, was rejected. Every now and again
throughout the day I was called to discuss the situation with the Chief
Constable and the camp's Commandant. At one point a soldier came
up to us and, after saluting the Commandant, asked whether he
could bring a food-lorry through. 'Better ask him,' said the Commandant, pointing to the Chief Constable. The soldier then saluted
the head copper and asked the same question again. 'Better ask him,'
said the latter, referring to me. I was then saluted by the soldier – the
only time I have ever had that experience – and he asked me for
authorization. I made sure it was only food that was in his lorry and
then wrote out my permission in Welsh on a piece of paper. He
looked at it. 'Cor blimey,' he exclaimed. 'Bloody Russian!' The
following day this incident made the front page of *The News
Chronicle*. As a postscript to this episode, I should add that a public

inquiry was held at Dolgellau under the chairmanship of Sir Wyn Wheldon. I gave evidence on behalf of Plaid Cymru, of course, and the War Department was refused permission to grab more land.

There was an interesting repercussion to the Trawsfynydd sit-downs in England. It was from them that Michael Scott and Bertrand Russell got the idea of taking similar action at the time of the first campaign against the nuclear bomb. The Committee of a Hundred was formed for precisely this purpose. That was my first contact with Michael Scott, with whom I was to find myself some years later in Cambodia, trying to enter Hanoi in North Vietnam.

It wasn't only the War Department which evicted farming families from their land and emptied it of its people; that was also done by the Forestry Commission, which in 1949 announced its intention of bringing a million acres of Welsh land under forestry. If that had happened, one fifth of the land of Wales would have been planted with conifers, and forestry would have taken the place of traditional sheep-farming. The Commission's first step was to attempt the compulsory purchase of forty thousand acres of land at the head of the Tywi Valley where the boundaries of Ceredigion, Breconshire, and Carmarthenshire meet. If they had succeeded in this aim it's possible that they would have acquired the million acres they wanted. In order to prepare evidence for opposition to this scheme, I spent a day in the company of J.B. Evans, the founder of the Farmers' Union of Wales, walking through the Blaenau Cothi forest which extends from near Pont-ar-Gothi as far as Rhydcymerau, the native district of D.J. Williams. The area was described by Gwenallt in one of his more hard-hitting poems as 'Trees where once was community, forest where farms had been'.

> 'Ac ar golfenni, fel ar groesau,
> Ysgerbydau beirdd, blaenoriaid, gweinidogion ac athrawon
> Ysgol Sul
> Yn gwynnu yn yr haul,
> Ac yn cael eu golchi gan y glaw a'u sychu gan y gwynt.'

('And on branches, as if on crosses, the skeletons of poets, deacons, ministers and Sunday School teachers, bleaching in the sun, washed by the rain and dried by the wind.')

I made a record of this journey and drew some conclusions in an article and pamphlet. The Upper Tywi campaign was first mooted at a meeting at Y Fannog, a farm high up on the mountain where the Tywi is hardly more than a trickling stream. Present in the kitchen but confined to her bed by illness was the woman of the

house. The most important incident that happened during the campaign was a rally organized by Wynne Samuel at a beautiful spot
within sight of Twm Siôn Cati's cave, where the Doethie runs into
Tywi. A huge crowd had turned up and the meeting was lively. One
of the speakers was Jennie Eirian Davies, that most eloquent of
women. But it was her good looks that made the deepest impression
on Emlyn Jones, an affluent old bachelor who kept sheep on the
Tregaron side of the mountain. 'Are you married?' he shouted from
the crowd. 'Yes, I am,' said Jennie. 'Dammit,' said Emlyn, 'or I'd
throw my cap in.' One of those present who hadn't been invited was
Hopkin Morris, the Member of Parliament for Carmarthen. He was
asked to step up on to the platform to speak, and that was how he
came to represent the local farmers as a barrister at the subsequent
inquiry in Llandovery. Ever after, the thing that was always said of
him was that he had fought for the farmers of the Upper Tywi
Valley. The battle was eventually won. The farmers presented me
with a colourful certificate that expressed 'the deep gratitude they
owe to Gwynfor Evans, Esq., County Councillor, the President of
Plaid Cymru, for the great help and support which enabled them to
defeat the attempt of the Forestry Commission to deprive them of
their land by Compulsory Purchase, 1949-1952'. Soon afterwards,
some of them sold their farms to the Commission for a good price.
Among the farms that were sold was Talar Wen.

A happy consequence of the rally in the Upper Tywi valley was
the winning of Dr D.H. Davies, an Ammanford doctor, to the cause
of Plaid Cymru. I have already mentioned how one person can make
a big difference to the work for Wales, and the Doc, as he was known
to us, was a good example. He went home from the meeting having
decided to establish a branch of Plaid Cymru at Ammanford, where
all our efforts had hitherto been in vain. He worked like a Trojan,
and in a little while he was on the 'phone telling me the branch had
twenty members. The next time he rang he was able to report there
were fifty. Thereafter the messages came regularly. 'We've passed the
70 mark . . . the 100 mark . . . the 150 mark', up to two hundred.
They fought elections and put five members on the town council.
Doc is still on the Dinefwr Council, where one of my sons, Dafydd
Prys, is a fellow-councillor, and he is still working staunchly for the
cause.

I suppose our efforts over many years to win recognition for
Monmouthshire as an integral part of Wales should be considered
as one of our most successful campaigns on behalf of Welsh territor-
ial integrity. The expression that had been used ever since the Statute
of Wales of 1536, by which the county had been placed under the

jurisdiction of Oxford, had been 'Wales and Monmouthshire', as if the county wasn't a part of our country at all. Its ambiguous status was a cause for constant concern in Wales. We held meetings in Newport and other towns in order to enlighten people about the Welsh character of the county, which had been Welsh in language, apart from a strip along its eastern boundary, up until the middle of the nineteenth century. We published three excellent pamphlets by Dafydd Jenkins, Griffith John Williams, and D.J. Davies. I never knew a more splendid couple than Dr D.J. Davies and Dr Noelle Davies, on whom I often called; Dr Ceinwen Davies lived with them at Pant-y-beiliau in Gilwern. Dai Cefn-mwng, as he was known, had been a collier in the anthracite coal-mines for eight years. He had been obliged to leave the mines because of a serious accident underground and so was able to travel the world. He had been a labour union organizer in the United States, a mineral prospector in Mexico and China, and a middleweight boxing champion in the American Navy. He became a Welsh Nationalist at a folk high school at Elsinore in Denmark, where the Director told him to return to Wales and work for his own nation. His exact words, according to D.J. Davies, were: 'Your country is ruled by England. Your duty, young man, is plain. You must go back to Wales and work to make her free.' The young Welshman had protested that there was no hope of success, because England was so powerful and Wales so weak. I shall never forget Nielsen's reply: 'The path of duty is plain before you and you must tread that path. That is the important thing for a human being, not whether you succeed or fail, but to do what is morally right.' D.J. had been an active Marxist in Ammanford and had fought the class war. At the Danish folk high school he had seen, like Robert Owen before him (a Welshman highly respected in Denmark), that the aim of all politics should be social harmony, and that by winning national freedom these conditions could be created in Wales. There he met Dr Noelle, a lecturer at the school, an Irishwoman whose exceptional brilliance tended to be concealed by her gentle manner. It was she who put her husband's books on to paper as he dictated them. She also wrote a number of books under her own name, the best-known of which was *Education for Life*, a work that owed much to the ideas of the Danish patriot Grundtvig, among others. Her book on Grundtvig, a great prophet and the founder of the first folk high school, was published by Plaid Cymru. A good number of Denmark's young men and women passed through the fifty schools that he established. Only two subjects were taught at the first generation of these schools – the history of Denmark and the literature of Denmark. They were therefore quite

different from the schools of Wales, where Welsh history and literature were ignored at that time. And it was on that basis the country's
co-operative system was built. There were no examinations and the
taking of notes was forbidden. They depended entirely on the oral
method. At my request, Dr Noelle wrote an excellent book about
James Connolly, the Irish Socialist and Nationalist; it was published
by Plaid Cymru and has been out of print these many years. It was
Connolly who said on his way to execution that British Socialists
would not understand why he was there – 'They will forget that I am
an Irishman'. It was to his nation that he gave his first allegiance.
How many Labour union men in Wales give their first allegiance to
Wales?

D.J. Davies was Plaid Cymru's principal economist. His book
Can Wales Afford Self-government? gave us confidence that we
weren't talking through our hats about self-government. He formulated a co-operative policy so firmly based that it continues, with
workers' control an essential part of it, to the present day. I also
asked him to outline the practical application of his political philosophy, the result being *Towards an Economic Democracy*, a book the
Party published in the mid-'fifties. These two people, D.J. Davies
and his wife Noelle, had a powerful influence on me, second only to
Saunders Lewis.

Furthermore, D.J. Davies was the leader of the campaign to make
Monmouthshire an acknowledged part of Wales. It was Plaid
Cymru's success in the Carmarthenshire by-election of 1966 that
enabled us to finish this particular job. At that time the Beeching
Commission was considering the system of legal administration in
England and Wales. Dewi Watkin Powell, who was later made a
judge, knew it was sitting and it was he who prepared the strongly-
worded memorandum which we presented on the legal system as it
affected Wales. He came with me twice to see the Commission's
Secretary, an Irishman who was warmly disposed towards us. As a
matter of fact, consideration of the status of Wales had already taken
place and the time for giving evidence had passed. The Commission
had decided that Wales would be split up, the South to be administered from Bristol and the North from either Liverpool or Chester.
But as a result of the pressure we brought to bear, and with the recent
upsurge of Nationalism behind us, the decision was smartly changed.
On the third visit the Secretary informed me that the Commission
had decided, 'against our better judgement', as the Report puts it,
that Wales was to be administered as an entity from Cardiff and that
Monmouthshire was henceforth to be part of it. From this point on,
as a result of the growth of Nationalism and the continuing

campaigns of Plaid Cymru in favour of a united Wales, there was no more talk of carving the country up whenever its economic life was considered. This was a victory of great importance. The present generation knows little of how the concept of Wales as an economic entity used to be jeered at. It was scorned, for example, by Aneurin Bevan, but Plaid Cymru persisted in arguing that the national unit should be the basis for all political and economic arrangements. This was confirmed in the economic field with the establishment of the Welsh Economic Development Agency, for which we had long campaigned.

Chapter 10

County Councillor

When I used to think before the war about the weak position Plaid Cymru was in, I drew some comfort from the thought that it had one member at least on a County Council, and that was the Reverend Fred Jones, Dafydd Iwan's grandfather, who sat on the Cardiganshire Council, although not in the Party's name. I didn't know of anyone else. It was much the same situation when I was elected to the Carmarthenshire Council in 1949. The only other Council member elected on the Party's ticket was Wynne Samuel, and he was on the Pontardawe District Council. I stood for the first time in 1946, in the Llangadog ward which included Llansadwrn and Gwynfe. At that election I lost by one vote after two recounts, and yet I was carried from the count to the village square on the shoulders of strong men, as if I were the victor, and there I had to address a large crowd at one o'clock in the morning. I was later told by T.J. Evans, the Council's Treasurer, that the chief officers had stayed up awaiting the result in the County Offices. I was elected without opposition in 1949 and remained a member for the next quarter of a century. It wasn't work that I enjoyed very much. Every time I went to a Council meeting I would have a pain in my stomach, and I had the same sensation whenever I had to speak or ask a question at Westminster. For most of the time I was a Councillor or Member of Parliament I was in a minority of one, and had to put up with the hostility and sometimes the malice of the majority.

I happened to join the Council at a moment when the Labour Party found power in their hands for the first time. I knew about the good and necessary work the party had done over the previous fifty years, but it had become a degenerate party in Carmarthenshire, at least from what I saw of it on the Council. 'We are the masters now,' said Douglas Hughes at the inaugural meeting, and they demonstrated it by rubbing the noses of the feeble Independents in the mud. Douglas Hughes was a good man of considerable standing, but a bully nevertheless, rather like a Tammany Hall boss. There was a tender side to his character but it was the worst side that he showed me in public. Although members of his party were pleasant enough as individuals, as a gang they were malicious in their anti-Welsh attitudes. Neither Douglas Hughes nor the Labour Party knew how to deal with a Nationalist, though they knew only too well how to treat a Tory or a conservative Liberal. The usual slogans and the most barren clichés would do for them. The easiest thing was to call everyone who opposed the Labour Party a Tory, and so I was labelled a Tory, despite the fact that I was more radical than any of them. Better that, I suppose, than being called a Fascist, as Merlin Rees and Ivor Richards referred to me when first I went into Parliament. But not only was I a Tory in their eyes, as a Nationalist I was a narrow Tory. That's what every Nationalist is in the view of Labourites, while they of course are internationalists of broad outlook. Without being at all aware of their own British Nationalism, they despise Welsh Nationalism and oppose any attempt to win for Wales a place in international life. They persisted in claiming that they alone were internationalists. The essence of their internationalism was to bury the Welsh nation as a peripheral region within England. Although their internationalism extended no further than London, their naive belief that Welsh nationality was a regrettable barrier on the road to internationalism provided them with some sort of moral basis for their lack of patience towards the Welsh language and the idea that Wales should live as a nation. It was 'narrowness' to worry about this small nation of ours and its language. 'I believe in one language for the world – Esperanto,' said the longest-serving member of the County Council, a Welsh-speaker from Llansadwrn. 'That's the sort of Socialist I am.' They hate the notion of allegiance to Wales: they give it instead to Great Britain and their own social class. In a letter to the *Western Mail*, Dr Alan Williams, scourge of Nationalists in the Carmarthen constituency, went on, 'I am a creature of the universe.' Robin Oakey has described this phoney internationalism as 'belonging to the most primitive period of Socialism, to a tradition known to historians as naive cosmopolitanism, which was characteristic of Socialist movements in every country in their early days'. It often came to Wales via Ruskin College and the London Labour College.

With the passing of the years the anti-Welsh prejudice of the Labour Party increased. At times it was unbelievable; for example, I was invited by the Workers' Education Association to give a lecture on the history of Wales at a course for teachers to be held at the Education Committee's centre at Glan-y-fferi (Ferryside). At one of its meetings a Labour member got to his feet to complain most bitterly that the premises of the County Council were to be used for political purposes by 'a certain party'. Despite the fact that these lectures had nothing whatsoever to do with politics, and although I was the only Nationalist speaker, the W.E.A. was obliged to cancel the course. Another example was the splendid courses for sixth-form pupils that were held at Cilgwyn in Newcastle Emlyn by such inspired Schools Inspectors as Cassie Davies and J.D. Powell. They encouraged scores of young people to persevere in their study of the history and literature of Wales. But the Labour Party was deeply perturbed. Douglas Hughes rose to his feet at a meeting of the Education Committe to proclaim that the courses at Cilgwyn were 'a breeding-ground for Nationalists' and that they were being abused by 'the members of a certain party' to indoctrinate the pupils in political Nationalism. Unless the lecturers were removed, he said, the County Council would withhold its support for the courses and refuse permission for children from the county to attend them. The Labour Party had its way and some of the country's most brilliant lecturers and writers were consequently replaced.

Despite all this, the Labourites were very keen not to appear excessively anti-Welsh, and this gave us an opportunity of winning a small victory from time to time. The first, in 1949, was to correct the corrupted forms of place-names that over the years had appeared on roads leading into towns and villages. Llangadock was corrected to Llangadog, Mothfey to Myddfai, Llangendeirne to Llangyndeirn, Llandilo to Llandeilo (Lord Dynevor complained bitterly about this one), Llanelly to Llanelli, Llandebie to Llandybie, Minke to Meinciau, and Llangunnor to Llangynnwr – although the Church in Wales still sticks to the barbarous spelling. In those instances where the anglicized form was too widespread, such as Carmarthen, Whitland, Llandovery, and Kidwelly, the correct Welsh form was also shown – Caerfyrddin, Hendy-gwyn, Llanymddyfri, and Cydweli. In the year following it was agreed to put up every sign on the County Council's buildings in Welsh as well as in English and to use both languages on all vehicles. When I first entered Westminster, I persuaded the police authority to put the word *Heddlu* on the side of their vehicles, and in time several other authorities made the same improvements.

With only one exception, every Labour member of the County Council was a Welsh-speaker. They always conversed with one another in Welsh, and yet, when on their feet at Council or Committee meetings, they spoke exclusively in English, except when quoting a verse or two by Irlwyn, a local poet, as they were wont to do from time to time. English, the sole language of officialdom, was also the only language of public life. Because they weren't in the habit of discussing public affairs through the medium of Welsh, and having read almost nothing in the language, they spoke a form of Welsh (with the exception of four or five chapel-goers among them), which was poor and quite inadequate, rather like the language of children in their early 'teens. Whenever I spoke in Welsh, as I often did, I had to give a synopsis in English, 'for the sake of our English friends'. Over the years I tried in vain to persuade the Council to appoint a translator, and towards the end of my stint I succeeded in getting them to experiment with instantaneous translation. Hywel Jones came down with equipment from Aberystwyth University College, but during a three-hour meeting I was the only one to speak in Welsh. The Chairman was an Independent and 'a good Welshman', and a solicitor to boot, but not a word of Welsh escaped his lips on that occasion.

The Labour Party used to decide everything in advance at meetings of the caucus. It was impossible to change any of its decisions in debate. Although it was good and necessary to have a group of party members on the Council, it was a bad custom which obliged each member to vote in exactly the same way. Sometimes, such as when they decided not to join the Association of Welsh Local Authorities, because a majority of one in the caucus was against, it meant that the view of nearly three-quarters of the Council was not acted upon. It wasn't possible for Labour to justify the iron grip of the caucus by claiming that there was a wide gap between their policies and those of the Independents. There was no such gap; in fact, there was no difference at all. I never saw a motion divide them, except for a few that I myself put up from time to time. Too puny to stand up to them, the Independents hid behind the skirts of the Labourites. I could give countless examples of this, but I shall note just a few. Labour decided to close twenty-nine schools in rural areas. They had some respectable enough educational reasons for doing so, but the two main arguments they had against rural schools were that they were too small and that they were Welsh-medium. I fought hard against the closures and held meetings in more than one of the affected districts. The madness was checked in the end, not because of any campaigning by the Independents, for there wasn't any, but because the Welsh Department of the Ministry of Education withheld its approval. I had gone to see Sir Ben Bowen Thomas, the influential head of the Welsh Department, and had won his support. Just one more example: the BBC once visited the school at Rhydcymerau in order to show how Welsh-medium education was run in a small rural school. They made a lovely film that reflected the excellence of the school's work. But the BBC had gone there without first asking permission of the Education Committee. The Labour Party was extremely annoyed. It was decided to close the school. When I opposed this move, it was said that the only reason I wanted to keep the school open was that D.J. Williams, the veteran Nationalist and writer, had been a pupil there.

The most important qualification for getting a headmaster's job was membership of the Labour Party. 'Other things being equal, we appoint Socialists,' was what they said quite openly. If a candidate was secretary of a branch or ward, that was a further advantage. Because of this, we made some disastrous appointments that did immeasurable harm to the educational standards and Welsh character of the primary schools. Many a school suffered at the hands of a lumpish, un-Welsh and sometimes anti-Welsh headmaster. I attacked this policy vigorously, once accusing the Labour Party of corruption in an article published on the front page of *The Carmarthen Journal*. At the next meeting of the Council, Douglas Hughes rose immediately to announce that they were going to bring a case of libel against me unless I withdrew the charge and apologized in the same newspaper. My refusal to do so was perfectly safe because they wouldn't have dared take the matter to court. The Independents' attitude to the appointments was always spineless; they co-operated with the Labourites in the hope of getting their man in occasionally.

It was the same with the reorganization of local government. The Civil Service, usually working through boundary commissions, had been behind these plans from about 1947 onwards. Their aim was to centralize power in order to be able to expedite bureaucratic control over local authorities. Aneurin Bevan was the Minister responsible in 1947 when the commission of the day announced recommendations which would have reduced the number of Welsh counties to five or six. We in Plaid Cymru opposed them, arguing that to play about with the county boundaries was irrelevant to the real need. What we knew was needed was to strengthen the counties' powers and reform their structures in a way which would ensure adequate funding. We sent a letter to the local councils and were asssured of their keen support at the time. My pamphlet, *Yr Her i Siroedd Cymru* ('The Challenge to the Welsh Counties'), was published in both Welsh and English, with a section on the status of Monmouthshire, and this was adopted as the basis of its case by the Association of Welsh Local Authorities, which purchased two thousand copies. The report, however, was buried by Aneurin Bevan. But the matter was raised twice again when the District Councils came to be incorporated with the County Councils. It was last raised in 1968, when the Labour Government made very similar recommendations to those implemented by the Conservatives in 1971. The three south-western counties were to be replaced by Dyfed and the three north-western by Gwynedd. The number of really powerful councils in Wales was reduced to a quarter. The two main arguments that were put forward for this centralization was that the larger councils would be cheaper and more efficient. We argued that the opposite would be the case. I came back from London to a meeting that was to discuss the matter in Carmarthen. Despite the fact that the clerk and the Labour Party, which was now in a minority, were strongly in favour of the plan, I managed to persuade the Independents to throw it out. But I was unable to be present at the Council meeting itself when the the the report of the Local Government Committee was discussed, and at that meeting it was decided by quite a large majority to accept the plan. Once again the Independents had given proof of their lack of backbone.

The same thing was to be observed during the discussion of West Glamorgan's scheme for the drowning of the Gwendraeth Fach and the supplying of water to Swansea and its environs – a scheme devised by Mr Crann, an Englishman who was that city's Chief Executive and is now second in the hierarchy of the Welsh Water Authority in Brecon. The Carmarthenshire Council agreed to oppose the scheme, but another plan had to be found in its stead. The Labour Party put forward a wholly impractical scheme for building a dam across the river Cleddau above Milford Haven, and it was to this that the Independents lent their support. I proposed a completely different scheme, namely the utilization of a long valley in the Upper Tywi area with which I had become familiar during the campaign against the Forestry Commission, and to run the water down the Valley as is done in Tryweryn, and collect it between Llandeilo and Carmarthen for pumping to Swansea. This scheme didn't entail the drowning of a single farm, nor the eviction of anyone at all. The only cause for concern was that the scheme might disturb the nests of some rare birds and drown some rare plants, and thus cause anxiety to David Davies, the naturalist from Rhandirmwyn, a man for whom I have the highest regard. After my scheme's rejection by the County Council, I outlined it in an article in *The South Wales Evening Post*, and it was subsequently accepted. The Gwendraeth Fach was saved and the lovely Llyn Brianne reservoir was created instead.

An extraordinarily interesting situation was caused by the County Election of 1958: twenty-nine members of the Labour Party were

elected, twenty-nine Independents, and two Nationalists. To add to
the interest, the two Nationalists bore the same name, or nearly so –
Gwynfor S. Evans of Y Betws, and myself. We two held the balance
of power, and so were in a very influential position, at least during
the first weeks when eleven aldermen and I don't know how many
Committees and all their chairmen were appointed. It was clear from
the start that we couldn't support Labour, which had been so hostile
to all manifestations of Welshness. So we decided to lend our support
to the Independents, but without informing them immediately. First
of all, we would have to squeeze as much out of them as possible, as
did the three Nationalist M.Ps. during the last Labour Government
at Westminster. We reached agreement on policies for the roads,
social services, and Welsh-medium education. After agreeing all this,
we gave the Independents the smallest majority possible by letting
them have six aldermanic seats while Labour had five. But this was
enough to decide the constitution of the Committees and their
Chairmen when they were subsequently returned to power. Labour
had taken the great majority of seats on every Committee, as well as
the chairmanship of every one, without exception. We came to an
arrangement which reflected the Council's make-up. We gave the
Independents a majority of one on every Committee and ensured
that they and the Labourites would take the chair in turns: whenever
there was an Independent chairman, a Labourite would be vice-
chairman and he would take the chair in the year following. Also,
one from each side would be elevated in turn to the chairmanship of
the Council. Something like this continued over the years that followed, but when the Labour Party eventually regained its majority,
I was thrown out of every one of the sub-committees on which I had
previously sat. At the time of the by-election of 1966, which sent me
to Westminster, I wasn't considered worthy of being a member of
any of the County Council's Committees, except for two on which
every member sat, namely the Education and the Roads and Bridges
Committees.

Quite a bit was achieved as a result of the understanding we had
reached with the Independents. In the field of education,
T.J.R. Jones was appointed Language Organizer, the best officer we
had; yet the Labourites got rid of him later on because he was too
enthusiastic about the Welsh language. It was also agreed to establish
bilingual Comprehensive Schools in Carmarthen and Llanelli, and
Welsh-medium primary schools in Carmarthen, Llandeilo, and
Llandovery. The Welsh-medium schools of Carmarthen and
Llandeilo have done much to improve the situation of the language
among the children of those two towns. In a survey that was made

of the county's schools in 1950 it was revealed that only twelve children were able to speak the language in Llandeilo. For years now there have been about a hundred in the Welsh School. Incidentally, another survey, in 1936, had shown that eighty-four per cent of the county's children were Welsh-speaking. Today the average has dropped to under thirty per cent. At Llandovery there is only a Welsh unit in the English primary school, the reason being the fierce opposition on the part of the English school's headmaster, and of a gang who have gathered around him. The consequence is that only about fifty children receive their education through the medium of Welsh in that town. The battle for bilingual Comprehensive Schools went on for another twenty years before it met with success. I managed several times to persuade the Education Committee to support the principle of establishing such schools, but the Director of Education and the headmaster and governors of Carmarthen Grammar School were determined to prevent it, and of course the Labour Party was in full sympathy with them. There was a determined and energetic campaign in favour of the idea of bilingual education in the town of Carmarthen itself, but we failed to get the Education Committee to set a date for its opening. In the end that was achieved by the Dyfed Council and the subsequent success of Ysgol Bro Myrddin has fully justified the effort. In Llanelli, too, Ysgol y Strade is a resounding success.

The experience of Carmarthen and many another place shows how essential it is that the campaign for Welsh-medium education should go on among parents and friends of the cause outside the Education Committees. The only county which out of conviction pursued a policy of establishing Welsh primary schools and bilingual secondary schools within the reach of every pupil who wished to attend them was the old county of Flintshire, where the Director of Education, Dr Haydn Williams, with the assistance of Mr Moses Jones, gave such a splendid lead. The Carmarthenshire Education Committee was very far from following such a policy, and the language's situation in many districts is precarious as a consequence. At Ammanford, for example, we tried to convert one of the two primary schools into a Welsh-medium school during the 'fifties. At the time there were two first-class headmasters – John Thomas and John Evans, both of them wholly behind the scheme. John Evans had exceptional ability as a teacher of Welsh as a second language and published proposals to that end. He wished to become headmaster of an English school in order to show how children could be given the chance to become Welsh-speaking before the age of eleven. But the Labourites objected vehemently. They said such a scheme would be 'apartheid'. As a consequence of our failure, the proportion of Welsh-speaking children in the town has fallen from about half to less than a fifth. A further Welsh-medium school has now been added to the two English schools; it is small but it's growing under its capable headmaster, Randall Isaacs.

I have referred to roads as part of the pact we made with the Independents. I have always believed that roads and railways have an essential part to play in an economy's infrastructure. The roads and railways of Wales were the subject of the first Debate on the Adjournment which I was given at Westminster; this is given to individual Members at the end of the day's business, often in the early hours of the morning. I played an energetic role on the County's Roads Committee. That was the only committee I was to chair, in 1973. On account of the emphasis I placed on good roads, I was given the nickname Gwynfor Dual Carriageways, and that did me some good in the Parliamentary by-election. In much the same way I gave priority to railways. At the beginning of the 'sixties I had a spot of good luck. With the help of Sid Dolben, Llangadog's stationmaster, I got hold of a confidential document containing statistics about the financial situation of British Railways. Two long articles of mine were published in the *Western Mail* on consecutive days which I had based on the unchallenged figures in this document. They proved that the most profitable region in the entire British Railways network at the time was that of Cardiff, which went as far as Aberystwyth and Craven Arms. Some eighty-four per cent of the income was attributable to the carrying of goods. British Railways never published its income from this source; only its income from passenger transport was known. Since this was only sixteen per cent of the total in the Cardiff Region, they had always been able to 'prove' that the railways of Wales were being run at a heavy loss. Furthermore, Beeching's cuts were more draconian in Wales than they were anywhere else. But British Railways' confidential figures showed that in 1962 the Cardiff Region had made an overall profit of £13 million. If Wales had had control of its own railways, it wouldn't have had to suffer so many of Beeching's drastic cuts.

Another campaign that was to last years was the one for the line which runs via Llangadog through the heart of Wales. This line would have been closed if it hadn't been for the intervention of Keith Joseph when he was Minister for Welsh Affairs. Relations between us had grown warmer after I wrote to him, on his appointment, to wish him well. I said I was sure that he, as a Jew loyal to his own people, would understand Welsh people who were loyal to theirs, and that he would have some sympathy for them. I went to see him about two matters: the first was about the need for an Economic Authority for Wales (I also went to see Edward Heath on the same errand when he was responsible for regional policy), and the second was about the mid-Wales line that British Railways was proposing to close down completely. Joseph asked to see maps of Wales; he opened them and spread them out before us, tracing the path of the railway-line. Then he went to see Ernest Marples, the Minister for Transport. The result of all this was that the line was kept as a light railway. Plaid Cymru also impressed the importance of the mid-Wales line on the mind of the Welsh Office. Richard Marsh, the Labour Government's Minister for Transport, talked about closing it when George Thomas was Secretary of State for Wales and I was Member of Parliament for Carmarthen. Marsh was later to tell the story of when the matter came before Cabinet. 'But Prime Minister,' said George Thomas, 'this line runs through six marginal constituencies.' In fact, it ran through three, but Carmarthen was one of them. The railway-workers acknowledged our lead by asking me to be one of two speakers who addressed the conference which packed the Temple of Peace in Cardiff, where the movement known as Transport 2000 was launched. I kept in contact with Keith Joseph for years after that. After I entered Parliament, he asked me to meet him occasionally and he would report back to Edward Heath on our meetings.

I said it was the Roads Committee which was the only one I chaired out of all the County Council's Committees. I was for four years Vice-chairman of the Libraries and Museums Committee, one of the Education Committee's sub-committees. But when the time came for me to take the chair, the Labour Party proposed three years in succession that the Labour member who was already in office should remain there. I nevertheless managed to do one or two things that were worthwhile. For years I had been wanting to see the library and the museum, together with a picture-gallery, brought together under one roof, in place of the slum buildings we used for these purposes. This attempt had been unsuccessful, but a new building was now found for the library and the museum was moved to an ideal spot in the old Bishop's Palace at Abergwili. It would not have found a home there if it had not been for Archbishop Gwilym O. Williams. I had persuaded the committee to buy the Palace after lengthy discussion, and we had agreed a price with the Church in Wales but hadn't signed the contract, when the news came like a bolt from the blue that it was about to be sold for a higher price to Slater Walker, who would turn it into flats. I was able to 'phone the Archbishop and write to him quite frankly because we had been friends since our schooldays, and he intervened in a forthright manner despite the fact that he really had nothing to do with Church buildings. We then came to a second agreement, but once more the Church's firm reneged on the contract, and once again I had to speak to the Archbishop. He again intervened and this time it was conclusive. Success such as this justifies the long and boring work of committees. Today the historic Palace of Abergwili houses one of the country's best museums, with a splendid collection of relics from Ancient Egypt as well as Welsh treasures from the Roman period on.

Alun R. Edwards, the trail-blazing Librarian of Cardiganshire, had secured for his county a mobile library service of which I was particularly envious. I tried to persuade our Committee to establish something on similar lines. Neither the Librarian nor the Committee was very enthusiastic, but in the end it was agreed there would be an experiment with just one small vehicle. This met with such success that we then decided to have a van fitted out for the purpose, then a second and a third. The Librarian was greatly taken with this success – the best thing the Library had ever done, he said. One result that pleased me was that many more Welsh books were borrowed from the mobile libraries than from the stationary ones.

I used my status as Member of Parliament to help the town of Carmarthen in several ways. With the help of Peter Hughes Griffiths, the marvellous Plaid Cymru organizer of the 'seventies, I called three public meetings to consider establishing in the town an old age pensioners' centre, a theatre and a leisure centre with a concert hall, a swimming-pool, and a running-track. Three committees were formed and they worked very well, with Henry Wilkinson chairing the recreation centre committee and Dr Margaret Evans the theatre committee, both of them Nationalists. As a consequence, we acquired a convenient facility for old people in the middle of town, a first-class leisure centre at Johnstown on the outskirts, and a part-time theatre at the Lyric Cinema.

A matter of very great importance on which a small group of us worked for six months before raising it on the County Council was that of silicosis and pneumoconiosis. Plaid Cymru had always been concerned about these diseases and their effects on the working men of Wales. Towards the end of the 'forties it published a pamphlet on the subject, *Silicosis and the Welsh Miner*, by D.J. Davies, who was himself a former collier. These terrible diseases are more common in the anthracite coal areas than anywhere else, and anthracite is almost wholly confined to Carmarthenshire. It was an awful sight to see ex-miners, old in appearance despite their years, fighting for breath as they climbed the slightest hill, the walls of their lungs having been turned as hard as iron by the coal-dust; or else, when the disease had become terminal, seeing them lying pale in their beds and having to reach every now and then for relief from the oxygen at their sides. When they died, the Coal Board's doctors hardly ever admitted that they had been killed by pneumoconiosis: the cause of death was usually given as pneumonia, bronchitis, or disease of the heart. The aim was to avoid paying widows the compensation that would have been due had their husbands died of pneumoconiosis. This injustice was widespread throughout the anthracite coalfield. When I was a Member of Parliament, I had more widows coming to see me about this than about any other matter, and usually I knew that there was almost nothing I could do to help them. One of the great victories achieved by Dafydd Wigley and Dafydd Elis Thomas during the last six months of the Labour Government was to pass a Bill to help quarrymen suffering from silicosis and their widows. I never saw the Miners' Union nor the Labour Party fighting seriously for the victims. Any Labour Government could have ensured justice for them, but it never did. Why? Mainly because it put a greater price on the nationalized industry and therefore on the Government itself. Our most lively member in this respect was Dr D.H. Davies from Ammanford and he was the king-pin of our committee, which also consisted of another specialist, two insurance experts, two Coal Board officials, and a collier. Of course, my fellow-councillor, Gwynfor S. Evans, was also a member; his own father had died of pneumoconiosis. Doc Davies went through all the Miners' Union records that referred to silicosis. The result of the committee's work was a ten-point charter dealing with every aspect of the problem, including of course ways of preventing the disease in the first place. Our aim was to get the County Council, the health authority at that time, to take action. I put the charter on the agenda of the next Council meeting for discussion. It took up nearly four pages. When the time came, I rose to present it to my fellow-members. Immediately, Douglas Hughes was on his feet asking the Independent Chairman, whom he had seen beforehand, to rule that the motion was out of order, and that's precisely what the Chairman did. I protested that this was crazy. Was not the Council a health authority? Had it not passed resolutions in previous years about the atomic bomb, about the Suez crisis, and other matters which were quite irrelevant to its work as a Council? But I couldn't move them. The Chairman shouted at me to sit down but I kept at it, with the other Gwynfor Evans on his feet beside me shouting for all he was worth, and half the Labour Party bawling back at us. It was pandemonium. The Chairman walked out shouting that the meeting was at an end.

The Labourites had done a good day's work. No Nationalist or anyone else for that matter was able to discuss pneumoconiosis in the chamber of the County Council thereafter.

Among those who were incensed by all this and by his party's other antics was the most sensible and intelligent man who served on the Council during my time as a member – Jac Llewelyn Evans from Llanelli, a former member of the Independent Labour Party, who often intervened with a calm and wise comment when the rest of his party were doing their worst against me. Before long he left the Council. The next time I saw him was in the meeting at which Pennar Davies was adopted as Plaid Cymru candidate for Llanelli: he had joined our Party. I attended his memorial meeting and said a few words about him, together with James Griffiths. The main part of the meeting took the form of a lecture by a speaker from the University's Extra-Mural Department on the radical tradition in Wales. After tracing the tradition through the nineteenth century and the early days of the Labour Party, he said, in the hearing of the Member for Llanelli, that its custodian today is Plaid Cymru.

Chapter 11

Radio and Television

A good way of becoming acquainted with the riches of Welsh culture is to be, as I was for fifteen years, a Parliamentary candidate in Merioneth. It was the district known as Penllyn that made the most lasting impression on me. I listened in astonishment to the talents of its people – poets, singers, and harpists who took part in gatherings known as *nosweithiau llawen* at places such as Llanuwchllyn and Y Parc. I heard there the singing of *penillion*, to the accompaniment of the harp, the like of which I had never heard before. One of the most popular competitions was to see who could recite the most *englynion* from memory; an *englyn* is an epigrammatic quatrain which is composed according to the strict rules of Welsh prosody. Although contestants were not allowed to repeat an *englyn* that had already been recited, nor more than one out of a chain, the competition would go on for some while. It was evident that hundreds of these verses had been committed to memory by these country people. I wasn't at all surprised to hear Ioan Bowen Rees, the Chief Executive of Gwynedd County Council, say that it was the *nosweithiau llawen* of Llanuwchllyn that had made a Nationalist of him when he was in the army. Like me, Ioan is related to a splendid family who live in Cwm Cynllwyd. That is the valley where O.M. Edwards was born. Mrs Dan Thomas, my mother-in-law and the finest of women, was the daughter of Blaen-cwm, the topmost farm in the valley. From the war years on, I had ample opportunity for wonder at the talent of country poets in scores of districts and to be thrilled by the great gifts to be found in communities which have only a very small number of people living in them. Where the Welsh language is alive the seams of our tradition yield great treasure. I soon learned to see the enormous difference in quality between the culture of a Welsh-speaking county such as Merioneth and an English-speaking one like Radnorshire, or between the Welsh-speaking and English-speaking parts of the same county, as in Montgomery or Pembrokeshire. Intellectual life was much poorer in the areas where the Welsh language had been lost. They might have been in another country altogether: the people there had little interest in the things of the mind, rarely reading or engaging in discussion with one another.

The popular culture of Wales is a wonderfully intellectual culture, and I don't know of its counterpart anywhere else. The *noson lawen*, an informal entertainment as uniquely Welsh as the eisteddfod, was in its heyday during the war and for a quarter of a century thereafter, and it still hasn't quite died out, despite television. Sometimes it would be held in houses that were big enough to hold a hundred people or more, many sitting on the floor or stairs. For one evening the home of some Nationalist would be like that of the gentry, patrons of the poets, the story-teller, and the musician. I would be invited to some of these occasions in order that I might put over a political message in the midst of the merriment. I was once at Cernioge Mawr near Cerrig-y-drudion, a staging-post for the Royal Mail coaches on their way to Holyhead. I have more than one reason for recalling that evening. The weather was rough and in the darkness, as I made my way towards the house, I stumbled into the water of a ditch. There happened to be present that evening a Calvinistic Methodist missionary who was serving in the Khasia Hills of northeast India – the Reverend Sam Davies, the brother of J.P. Davies, the early pacifist and Nationalist. He talked about how they were intent on creating a nation there, a Christian nation. Their national anthem is to this day sung in Lushai to the tune of '*Hen Wlad fy Nhadau*' . The master of ceremonies that night was Llwyd o'r Bryn, a highly cultured farmer and the very best of his kind. I was to hear Llwyd leading scores of *nosweithiau llawen*, and he was the main source of many of the stories I told up and down the country.

On my travels I was to make many a good friend, such as R.E. Jones, Elwyn Roberts, R.E. Holland, and O.M. Roberts, who took me by surprise because they thought exactly as I did. It was then I realized there was more than politics holding Plaid Cymru together. The Party was a society of people who were united in their way of thinking, although to call it a philosophy would have been an exaggeration. Some of my journeys in the years just after the war were fruitless. I once went to Rhyl, only to be told that the meeting's organizer had postponed it without informing me. On another occasion I made a special effort to get to Llanegryn through ice and snow and found that the organizers had taken it for granted that I wouldn't turn up. That trip cost me dearly: I was prevented by the weather from going home that night and, when I eventually got back, I discovered that the greenhouse pipes had frozen; a lot of them had to be broken up in order to save the others. But some of the journeys bore fruit in abundance. Twenty or twenty-five or thirty new members could be gained at meetings which had been properly organized. A series of exceptionally successful meetings was arranged in the lower part of Cardiganshire by Dafydd Orwig, that marvellous organizer. Dafydd would go and stay in a district for three or four days and visit all the homes thereabouts. This was how he got to know the people. He found out who would be likely to join Plaid Cymru and who would be prepared to take on a job with the local branch. He would then arrange big meetings, at which my job was to spread a little light and warmth, and win over new members. In this way about a dozen new branches were formed in the space of a few months.

Our opponents used to say that we Nationalists played on people's emotions. My contention was that we didn't play on them enough. Our speeches tended to rely too much on reason and facts. It was our opponents who were shamelessly emotional; for example, Jim Griffiths with his hand on heart and a sob in his voice going on about the dangers of his days underground. In fact, he worked underground for about a year, as D.J. Davies was fond of reminding us. D.J. had worked with him, and for him, at the White House, the Labour Party's centre in Ammanford. Of course, if you are trying to win people over to your point of view and want them to take action, an appeal must be made to their hearts as well as to their minds. You will never succeed unless you are able to arouse your audience's emotions. Their reason must be nourished and their spirits awakened. I would try to achieve this by devoting the first twenty minutes of my speech to warming up the audience's feelings about Wales. Having won their sympathy, I would then go on to develop an economic and political thesis. It was in that order I usually spoke. I was surprised some couldn't see that nothing effective could be done about improving the economy without acting politically, and that a balanced economy couldn't be created until the people of Wales had political control of their own country. I used to make much use of that splendid book by E.D. Simon, *The Smaller Democracies*. The four or five Scandinavian countries among those that the author had studied are the nearest to being models for Wales. One of Simon's main conclusions was that the chief reason for the success of these countries was their size. I had always put a strong emphasis on size: it was an integral part of the argument for the decentralization of power within Wales itself, and I stressed the advantage of being small. Although size is of course comparative, it is obvious that Britain with its fifty-five million inhabitants is in a different category from Norway, Denmark, Sweden, and Finland with their four or five million. Wales is to be listed with the small countries, being less than five per cent of the population of Britain. The tendency throughout the present century has been to believe that the bigger the country or industry, school or college, or constituency or local council, or whatever, the better. I often came up against the argument that Wales was too small to be self-governing. This point of view, together with the claim that Wales is too poor and weak, was the most common objection I came across, and it still influences people. In opposing it, I maintained that a self-governing Wales would have no greater advantage than that it is a small country. I still believe that Great Britain is a dangerous anachronism and that it is high time for the British state, like others of its kind, to be broken up.

I fought my first election in the summer of 1945, with high hopes, just as Lewis Valentine had in Plaid Cymru's first Parliamentary election in 1929. Although we had quite a few more voters than 'the gallant six hundred' who supported him, it was no encouragement to come bottom of the poll with just over two thousand votes. It was too much of a blow for some of my supporters in Merioneth and, after the count, some of the tearful women had to be cheered up – a job that often fell to me. It was no fault of the organizers, who couldn't have been better, for my agent was none less than Elwyn Roberts himself, who came from Abergynolwyn in Merioneth. His assistant was Marion Eames of Dolgellau, who was to become a fine novelist; she was later appointed the county's organizer, and a splendid one she made, too. She was my agent at the Election of 1950 when the result for us was just as miserable. In the year following, a lack of finance prevented us from contesting Merioneth, but we transferred our votes almost completely to Labour, in order to elect T.W. Jones (later Lord Maelor) and unseat Emrys Roberts, the Liberal. Plaid Cymru fought four seats that year and its total vote was some ten thousand. Gwilym Lloyd George drew attention to this figure at Westminster as proof that it was all over for the Party. Among those who gave up a whole week to work for Plaid Cymru at the 1945 Election was Meredith Edwards, the actor, who stayed at the same guest-house as me; he has continued to work hard for Wales and the Party ever since. Another member who put in a great deal of time at every election in Merioneth was Arthur Thomas of Llanfair Caereinion, a tower of the Party's strength in Montgomeryshire. I received great kindness and generosity from many friends in every part of the constituency. I recall their friendship now with gratitude and not without some nostalgia.

The immediate post-war years were quite gloomy ones for Plaid

Cymru, although it was now, unlike the S.N.P., in a stronger position than it had been before the war. It mustered enough strength at the General Election of 1945 to fight seven seats in addition to the two by-elections it contested, and this showing compared well with the 1935 Election, when the only seat it fought was Caernarfon. But the Party's progress in the post-war period was slight. My parents, like many others, couldn't understand what I was doing with a movement that seemed so hopeless. 'Why can't you be like other people, Gwynfor?', my mother used to ask. 'Why can't you be a Liberal?' My father, too, had heard in his business that no one else was working for Plaid Cymru. I knew differently, of course. I knew about the work of stalwart Nationalists in various parts of the country, and about the heroic efforts of J.E. Jones and Wynne Samuel on our staff. But it was true that our progress was slow, and when I found Dr Gwenan Jones a bit low-spirited on this account in 1946, the great news I had to cheer her up was that we had just formed a branch at Gwynfe, the only one in the whole of Carmarthenshire at that time.

No doubt our lack of progress had a lot to do with the growth and formation of the Republican Movement which at this time began to gather its energies around its monthly newspaper. For two or three years its members remained within Plaid Cymru, but at the Annual Conference in Dyffryn Ardudwy in 1949, after failing to carry their motion that the Party should adopt a more Republican stance, they left us. A few years later they gave up trying to sustain an independent movement and split into three factions: some, like Harri Webb and Cliff Bere, came back into the ranks of Plaid Cymru, others such as Huw Davies left party politics altogether for a while and the rest, led by Gwilym Prys Davies, went into the Labour Party. The loss of Gwilym Prys Davies was a particularly heavy blow to us. He had in him the making of a national leader. I used to feed him with political literature when he was in the navy. The Principal of the University College at Aberystwyth when Gwilym was a student there was Ifor L. Evans, who believed that he would prove to be the saviour of Wales. Our paths were to meet next in 1966, at the by-election in Carmarthen, where he was the Labour candidate.

In 1950 I had some heartening success at the Court of the University of Wales, which I had been using as a forum for the airing of important matters such as the Welsh language, the place of Welsh History in the curriculum, Welsh-language radio, and in particular a Broadcasting Corporation for Wales. It was the question of a Welsh-medium College, for which Saunders Lewis had been arguing for some while, that I raised at a meeting of the Court at Aberystwyth in that year. The motion that the Court should consider the propriety of establishing a Welsh College was carried by an overwhelming majority. In my judgement the gracious buildings of St. David's College at Lampeter would have been ideal for this purpose. A committee was formed which was to consider this matter for four years under the chairmanship of Ifor L. Evans, and after his death, that of Sir Emrys Evans, the Principal of the University College of Bangor, an uncompromising opponent of the idea. What disappointed me was that I had no support from any of the committee's members, who included Alwyn D. Rees and T.I. Ellis. Alwyn was not converted to the Nationalist cause, any more than my friend J.R. Jones, until the 'sixties, when he became the influential editor of the monthly magazine *Barn*, but he and Tom Ellis argued strongly for the use of Welsh as a medium of instruction in subjects other than Welsh at the Colleges that already existed, and that was the recommendation of the majority report which was adopted by the Court. A sum of money was earmarked for the appointment of staff who would lecture in a limited number of subjects through the medium of Welsh, such as History, Philosophy, Music, and Art. For all practical purposes, it was only at Aberystwyth and Bangor that this was to happen, and there wasn't much development of the policy over the next generation, despite the fact that a growing number of undergraduates had received their secondary education in Welsh. The main initiative was the establishement of College hostels where Welsh was the official language. Yet in Cardiff, where most Welsh-speaking students are, no Welsh hostel is provided. After meeting Saunders Lewis and Griffith John Williams at the Park Hotel, I wrote a report as a minority of one in favour of a Welsh College. It is good to note that the matter is being raised again these days.

I mentioned my using the University Court to promote the aim of creating a Broadcasting Corporation for Wales. The creation of Welsh institutions has always been one of Plaid Cymru's aims. This consideration was particularly important with regard to radio because it was the most powerful of the mass-media up to the 'sixties, when television became more common. It's not easy to realize today how potent it was. At the National Eisteddfod in Llandybie in 1944 I gave a lecture entitled 'Radio in Wales' under the aegis of *Undeb Cymru Fydd*; it was published in both Welsh and English and, according to T. I. Ellis, it sold some ten thousand copies. The cover was designed by my brother-in-law, Dewi Prys Thomas, who usually did the striking jackets for the Party's publications; he also drew some of the most hard-hitting cartoons we ever published. Dewi was later appointed Principal of the Welsh School of Architecture in Cardiff. He made it into a magnificent national institution which, thanks to him, is more Welsh in character than any of our University Colleges. It is strange how little recognition this huge achievement has received.

Be that as it may, the main argument in my lecture 'Radio in Wales' was that there was need to place this exceedingly powerful medium under Welsh control within an independent corporation. From the start it was Plaid Cymru which led the campaign for a Welsh radio service and for the acknowledgement of Wales as a national entity. During the early 'thirties there were no Welsh programmes whatsoever. Radio in Wales was ruled from Bristol by an Englishman by the name of Appleton. The BBC had re-created what it was pleased to call 'the Kingdom of Arthur'. It took years of work under the leadership of Saunders Lewis to get programmes in Welsh and to secure regional status for Wales. When Nationalists demanded a service in the Welsh language, E.R. Appleton responded on the BBC's behalf. His reply was typical of the British Establishment's attitude towards Wales in the inter-war years before Welsh Nationalism became a power in the land: 'Wales, of its own choice, is a part of the British Commonwealth of Nations, whose official language is English. When His Majesty's Government decided to establish a Corporation for the important task of broadcasting it was natural that the official language should alone be used . . . To use the ancient languages regularly – Welsh, Irish, Gaelic and Manx – would be either to serve propaganda purposes or to disregard the needs of the greatest number in the interests of those who use the languages for aesthetic and sentimental reasons rather than for practical purposes . . . If the extremists, who want to force the Welsh language on the listeners of the region, should get their way, the official language would lose its grip.' Eventually, regional status was won for Wales in broadcasting. This was the regime inherited by Sir Hopkin Morris when he was appointed Regional Director for Wales. He had led the effort to get Welsh-language programmes on the wireless during the war. At the outset we were given nothing at all, but in a little while we had twenty minutes a day in the Welsh language, quite a bit less than the splendid service of ten hours a day that we now receive from Radio Cymru and Radio Wales. We argued that there would be no justice until we ruled ourselves in the field of radio broadcasting. We continued to work for a corporation during the post-war years. I argued our case before a full meeting of the Welsh Parliamentary Party chaired by Sir Henry Morris Jones. I presented it to two Royal Commissions which were considering broadcasting arrangements, the first under Beveridge and the second under Pilkington. As a consequence, although we didn't get a Welsh

Broadcasting Corporation, we did win a kind of federal set-up, with control over radio in Wales and later BBC television in Wales, at least nominally, in the hands of the Broadcasting Council, but in fact in the hands of the Corporation's chief executives in Wales. Over the years there has had to be an ongoing battle to bring about improvements in the Welsh service and to prevent a falling away. For example, early in the 'fifties, the small Welsh-language service was transferred to a very weak wave-band on which few people could hear the transmissions clearly. In fighting against this change, we formed a Listeners' Association which was organized by J.E. Jones. Its Chairman was the Reverend Roger Hughes, a highly respected man. About two hundred people undertook to refuse to pay their radio licences. Several were taken before the courts, including myself who appeared at Llangadog, where the Chairman of the Magistrates, Non Evans of Glasallt, shut me up when I tried to speak in Welsh.

When the Welsh Advisory Committee of the BBC was appointed in 1946, the most worthwhile thing I did as a member was to ensure a bilingual rule in its discussions, its minutes, its agenda and in all its correspondence. After the creation of the Broadcasting Council towards the end of the 'fifties, I was also a member of that until I resigned because Mrs Rachel Jones, the English-speaking wife of the Dean of Brecon, was appointed to its chair. This was a crazy Tory appointment, for she was unable to understand a good part of the programmes for which she was nominally responsible. I endeavoured to persuade other Council members to resign too, but Professor Huw Morris Jones was the only one to do so. I didn't expect Sir David Llewellyn to resign, for he had no sympathy for the Welsh language and was the only Welsh M.P. to have voted in favour of Liverpool's Bill for the drowning of Cwm Tryweryn. It was he who said of the Nationalists that their only motive was to make good their failure in life, 'to make up on the swings what they lost on the roundabouts'. It would have been worth my belonging to the Broadcasting Council if only to secure a series of lectures on the History of Wales which were subsequently published in two volumes as *Wales Through the Ages*. It was mainly with a view to publication that I had pressed for them.

It was David Llewellyn who caused a fuss about an alleged excess of items about Plaid Cymru on the radio news. There was a scandal at about this time involving public land at Crichel Down in the south of England which had been sold to land-developers at a ridiculously low price. David Llewellyn, by profession a journalist, claimed that the Welsh news bulletins put out by the BBC were 'a scandal, dripping with Welsh Nationalist propaganda', in comparison with which 'Crichel Down pales into insignificance'. Some Labour and Tory M.Ps. leapt to his assistance, including Ness Edwards, Postmaster General at the time, and therefore the Minister responsible for radio in the Labour Government. They kicked up a fine old rumpus, and despite the fact that the committee set up by the Government under the chairmanship of a high-ranking civil servant and knight by the name of Ince found that there was no basis whatsoever for the accusation (his committee in fact concluded that Plaid Cymru was getting less than its share of news), the BBC was alarmed. Ifan Pugh, the head of the News Department, had to resign, and from then on the Party was given even fewer items in the Welsh news, and nothing at all of course in bulletins from London. The British political parties went to enormous trouble over the years to gag Plaid Cymru on the media and to prevent the broadcasting of news about the Party as far as they were able. Since a political party depends on being able to communicate with the people, it has always been important to them, just as it still is today, to keep Plaid Cymru out of the news as much as possible and to prevent it from putting its policies before the public. Our inability to communicate was the main obstacle to our growth. When the Labour Party first came to prominence towards the end of the last century and the beginning of this, and also in the heyday of Irish Nationalism, the principal means of communication was the platform and the public meeting. Then all parties were equal in opportunity. But the pre-eminence of the public platform declined when the wireless and the London newspapers came into their own. For many years now the mass media, like everything else, have been centralized in London, which has a tighter control over our lives than anything that was possible in days gone by. Because they know this, the British parties are determined to exclude us from presenting Plaid Cymru's policies on the air, and so they have succeeded in keeping us out of news bulletins broadcast from London, even at Election times.

The attitude of all parties became clear during the campaign to win for Plaid Cymru the right to broadcast on the radio in Wales. Because it was so important, we pressed long and hard for this right. I gathered together our case in two pamphlets – *The Political Broadcasts Ban in Wales* and, after the advent of television, *The Wicked Ban*. I discussed the matter twice with the Conservative Postmaster General, Dr Charles Hill (later Lord Hill), who had made a name for himself during the war as 'the radio doctor'. In association with the Scottish National Party and the party known as Commonwealth, we held a rally to further the cause at Trafalgar Square in London. Only a few hundred turned up, though we had a fair bit of publicity.

The next time I was to speak there, at a rally organized by the Campaign for Nuclear Disarmament, a crowd of a hundred thousand filled the Square. Perhaps I should say of Commonwealth, in passing, that it was a Socialist party that had been created during the war. Its policies were strikingly similar to those of Plaid Cymru. Its first leader was Sir Richard Acland and towards the end of the war it had two Members of Parliament. We worked closely together for many years. It was I who wrote the Welsh part of the book *Our Three Nations* that we published jointly with the S.N.P.

The Beveridge Commission announced that it was in favour of Plaid Cymru's right to broadcast and the Broadcasting Council was consequently spurred, under the chairmanship of Lord MacDonald of Gwaunysgor, who had been a member of the Labour Government, into taking action. It decided to arrange two series of political broadcasts in Wales by each of the parties a year, talks of a quarter of an hour each, one to be in Welsh and the other in English, on behalf of the four parties which fought the required number of seats in Wales. This meant that at last Plaid Cymru would have broadcasting time and so the British parties would be obliged to formulate Welsh policies. Neither the Tories nor Labour had any kind of policy for Wales at the time. We were summoned to a meeting of representatives of the four parties on 28th January 1955 in order to take a decision on the timetabling of the talks, but on 20th January the BBC sent out a letter cancelling the meeting. By then the Labour Party had put its great machine into action. In February, representatives of the Broadcasting Council for Wales were summoned to appear at Westminster before a powerful committee of twenty-seven delegates of the three British parties. Among the Labour Party's delegates were Clement Attlee, Herbert Morrison, and Morgan Phillips, the party's Secretary. Members of the Tory shadow-cabinet were also present. It was a matter of great importance to them that they should prevent permission being given for Plaid Cymru to present its policies on radio to the people of Wales. At that meeting, the Broadcasting Council was ordered to withdraw its decision. I was later told by Lord MacDonald that he was ashamed of his party that day. The Labour members, he said, particularly Herbert Morrison, had done most of the talking. Of course, it was Labour which had most to fear from the growth of Plaid Cymru. The representatives of the Broadcasting Council returned to reconsider their decision in the light of the order made by the party leaders. They unanimously agreed to reiterate their resolve. There was no precedent for what happened next, nor did it ever happen again. The Postmaster General announced his intention of using a veto banning the Welsh broadcasts. Although the BBC itself had banned broadcasts, as in the case of Saunders Lewis's radio talk about Welsh Nationalism, this was the only time the Government ever threatened to use its powers of censorship. The gagging of Plaid Cymru was that important in its view. The headline in the *Times* report was 'Mr Attlee Concurs'.

This policy continues to the present day, albeit in moderated form. The British parties deny that they have anything to do with the allocation of time on radio and television – and it's television that counts now – but this isn't true. I was present at one of the meetings of the parties' representatives at Westminster which had been called to discuss party political broadcasts and how to allocate them. It is at election time that the gagging is most harmful to Plaid Cymru because these days General Elections are fought largely on the television screen. Although the London papers have their significance, it is the London news-bulletins going out several times a day that are all-important. It is they which carry weight politically. Over eighteen days of the last General Election there was not so much as a single reference to Plaid Cymru by London. Quite literally, we were not in the picture. The three British parties had items in every London bulletin on radio and television and in every issue of every London newspaper. For the vast majority of viewers and listeners and readers, only they were in the field, and nothing was done to make up for this in the broadcasts from Wales either. Plaid Cymru had its share in these broadcasts, but the Liberals also had just as big a share, in addition to the huge coverage they received from London. The wonder is that Plaid Cymru has won the support it has.

Because Plaid Cymru had little opportunity of presenting its policies on the radio, some members set up what was known as a pirate radio. We ran this illegal operation, trying always to avoid the attention of the police, in the late 'fifties and early 'sixties. It broadcast after the close-down of BBC television programmes at about eleven o'clock. Harri Webb and the actor Ray Smith often took part, broadcasting from the attic of Garth Newydd in Merthyr Tydfil. The operation took a serious turn one night in the Swansea area while we were transmitting from the home of Aneurin Rhys Hughes, who now holds an important job in Brussels. For one thing there was no television in the house, so we were relying on a 'phone-call to tell us when the BBC was about to close down. But there was no 'phone in the house either. There was, however, a 'phone-box just outside, and it was arranged that the call would be taken there. Dr Gareth Evans went out to the kiosk to wait for the vital call. But there had been a misunderstanding about the precise timing. The BBC went on much longer than scheduled. After Gareth had been out there for quite a while, he spotted a policeman walking up and down on the pavement. The officer then opened the kiosk door and asked Gareth sharply what he was doing, whereupon the latter put his hand over his heart and said with great gravity, 'Affairs of the heart.'

By the mid-'fifties it had become evident that television would cause revolutionary change in communication systems and that the effects would be seen in much wider fields than the political one. It was threatening to undermine the cultural heritage of Wales and weaken the Welsh language to a terrible extent. Where there was a television set in a Welsh-speaking home more English was often heard on the box than Welsh on the hearth. The situation called for some positive action to safeguard our cultural inheritance. We were aware of the importance of having Welsh programmes in the English language, without which it wouldn't be possible to nurture a national consciousness among English-speakers. But what demanded most of our attention was the threat to the Welsh language and its culture. We worked hardest at getting programmes in Welsh, first of all on the BBC and later from the independent company known as Television Wales and the West. Because our success in this respect had proved so modest and the crisis was so large and increasing all the time, it was decided, under the leadership of Dr Haydn Williams, to set up an independent Welsh company, namely Teledu Cymru. Dr Williams was the chief benefactor of Wales in the field of formal education. It was he who had persuaded the Flintshire Education Committee to allow parents the opportunity of giving their children a Welsh-medium education if they so wished. He had set up Welsh primary schools within the reach of everyone, and was also the pioneer of the bilingual Comprehensive Schools, as Ysgol Glan Clwyd and Ysgol Maes Garmon bear witness to this day. Furthermore, he had secured the appointment to the County of fifty Welsh-speaking teachers straight from college on an annual basis.

It was one thing to form a company, quite another to get permission from the Independent Broadcasting Authority for it to operate. We received help from an unexpected quarter – from an Austrian who was head of the Economics and Political Sciences Department at the University of Puerto Rico, namely Leopold Kohr. He had first come to my attention in a review in *The Observer* of his seminal book, *The Breakdown of Nations*. The reviewer had attacked the book mercilessly, but fortunately, had quoted several sentences and a long paragraph which gave the essence of Kohr's argument in favour of small units, of which he was the great prophet. I recognized immediately that he was speaking our language and wrote to him in Puerto Rico, enclosing a copy of my pamphlet, *Welsh Nationalist Aims*, which had been published a little earlier in Hyderabad, India. This was about 1954 and it led to a regular correspondence between us. Two or three years later I arranged for the Professor of Economics at Swansea University College to exchange places with Leopold for a year; I was a member of the College Council at the time. As soon as he arrived, he became the centre of a circle of friends in Swansea. It was at a party in his house that I met Kingsley Amis, the novelist. Leopold had a rare gift for making friends and they were so numerous that they formed a network throughout the world. In a little while he went to Aberystwyth to join Alwyn D. Rees's staff in the University College's Extra-Mural Department; he made his home in Baker Street in the centre of town where he was within three minutes of everything he needed. He and Alwyn became bosom pals. Today Kohr's ideas about the essential importance of size have become well-known, and with the publication of *Small is Beautiful* by E.F. Schumacher, they became famous and influential. Schumacher acknowledged that Kohr had been his mentor. At my request, Leopold summed up his ideas about Wales in his book *Is Wales Viable?*. His books had a wide circulation in English, German, Italian, Spanish, and Japanese, and one, *Cymru Fach*, was published in Welsh by Y Lolfa. More recently, the prophet has been honoured in his own country with the presentation of the Salzburg Golden Ring, an award that has only ever been made twice before. The British Ambassador came to Vienna for the ceremony. Wonderful Salzburg, the capital of a province that was independent for centuries but which now belongs to a federal Austria – that's Leopold Kohr's city. He was born in a nearby village, Obendorf, where the carol 'Stille Nacht' was composed. I spoke this year at an international conference in his honour at Salzburg, on the theme 'Smallness as a Principle of Survival'.

This is how Leopold Kohr helped us with our campaign for a television company. One of his many friends was the gracious Australian Sir Robert Fraser, Secretary of the Independent Television Authority. We went to ask him for his help. The greatest problem was that TWW and Granada were sharing most of the territory of Wales between them, and in 1958 the Conservative Government was zealously protecting their interests. The scheme we had for years been advocating was that we should have a single company serving the whole of Wales. This would generate an income of about £3 million. But such a scheme had been impractical, ever since the independent companies had been formed, for TWW had incorporated the whole of Wales with Bristol and part of south-western England. All Robert Fraser could suggest was a company that depended on one piece of virgin territory, that is to say a region that was not served by any other company. This could only have been Cardiganshire, and the Welsh company would have to compete with TWW and Granada for viewers in the rest of the country. But at least this presented us with an opportunity. After the failure of Teledu Cymru, I wrote to Robert Fraser thus: 'In the midst of the bitter disappointment . . . the selfless and generous sympathy you have given from the start stands out as the finest thing in our experience of Independent Television. You could not have done more.' I shouldn't have remembered this point if it had not been for a letter I received a fortnight ago from Bernard Sendall, who is writing the history of Independent Television, asking for permission to quote from it. We were told that we could expect an income of about £750,000 in the first year, but the Government insisted on imposing a completely unreasonable condition, namely that we should have to produce ten hours of programmes weekly. TWW had produced only seven hours and Westward, which had four times our capital and income, only two. It was this condition which obliged us to put up expensive studios. For three years several of us worked hard to make a success of the company. Dr Haydn Williams carried out some terrific work, despite the fact that he was still Flintshire's Director of Education. In fact, he was to kill himself with the work. A sub-committee of three was responsible for publishing a magazine, the only time up to then there had been a Welsh television magazine. We used to meet in the office of Eric Thomas, the publisher of *Y Cymro*, at the Caxton Press in Oswestry. If the company had flourished, it would have been our intention to invest the profit from the magazine in the publishing of Welsh books. Teledu Cymru was conceived as a trust that wasn't going to make anybody a fortune. It was written into its articles that no more than fifteen per cent of the interest on the invested capital would be paid out. A good deal of that capital came from Nationalists, much of it through Elwyn Roberts.

For ten months in 1962-63 Teledu Cymru produced seven hours a week of good-quality Welsh-language programmes. The staff were committed and capable. Many of them went on to make names for themselves in broadcasting. It was our boast that we had the best news department in Wales, under the direction of John Roberts Williams, and that our children's programmes were more attractive than those of the BBC and TWW. A lot of new talent was discovered. It's surprising how many entertaining programmes were produced for as little as sixty pounds, a ridiculously small sum even in those days. The programmes were very popular among those who received them. But the snag was that they didn't reach many people. The company's income depended completely on the number of sets that could receive the signal. Each set was worth four pounds. The responsibility for putting up transmitters and getting programmes to the people rested with the Independent Television Authority. But the number who could receive the signal proved to be disastrously disappointing. Finding the cost of an aerial was a major difficulty for many potential viewers. But an even greater problem was that large numbers of homes received their programmes via rediffusion companies. Almost none of these took advantage of our programmes, because of pressure from TWW, which had shares in many of them. By far the greatest difficulty was that it was impossible for many densely populated areas to receive the signal at all. The final disappointment was Moel Famau. Although we had hoped for a set-count of sixty thousand from that transmitter, we got only twenty thousand. Sixty thousand was our total in the whole of Wales and that produced an income of £240,000. We were working within a budget of £450,000, which was remarkably low. We had to give up the venture.

A lot of nonsense has been written about the lack of business acumen and broadcasting experience on the part of Teledu Cymru's Board. There was only one reason for the company's failure: the signal didn't reach enough people. The Government didn't raise a finger to help us. But a lot of good came of the effort. When the company was taken over by TWW it was obliged to put out the seven hours of Welsh-language programmes which had been broadcast by Teledu Cymru. That's what its successor, HTV, broadcasts today in 1982, and not a minute more. The BBC was also encouraged to increase its Welsh output, so that twelve hours a week of Welsh programmes would be broadcast between them, at all times of the day and night, of course. This will continue to be the situation until S4C comes on the air on 1st November this year.

The campaign for more hours in Welsh and more programmes for children continued throughout the 'sixties after the failure of the Teledu Cymru experiment, though without much success except in the case of children's programmes. Besides their scarcity, the spread of hours in Welsh, very few of them at peak-viewing times, made them ineffective. For this reason Plaid Cymru supported the resolute campaign of *Cymdeithas yr Iaith* for a Welsh television service at peak-hours on the fourth channel that was unused at that time. The Welsh Language Society's campaign is one of the proudest chapters in the history of modern Wales. In an attempt to promote it, I published a pamphlet setting out the basis for the Society's action and drawing on the experience of other countries such as Switzerland, Norway, and Iceland, just as I used to do when arguing in favour of creating a broadcasting corporation for Wales. I managed to persuade the Court of the University of Wales to set up a committee to consider the question. At that meeting I sat next to Bishop Mullins, who has learned to speak Welsh so well. He told me, when I complained that Plaid Cymru was not receiving the support of people living in Wales who were of Irish descent, that he believed the young people were coming over to us. No one spoke to better effect at that meeting than Dafydd Iwan.

Under the chairmanship of Sir Goronwy Daniel, and with the help of scientists with expertise, the committee did some research into the technical aspect of things as well as into the financial and political, such as the relationship between the Welsh-language service and the BBC, HTV, and the Government. It also looked into the common allegation that there wasn't enough talent among the Welsh-speaking Welsh to sustain a satisfactory service. It was proved that there would be no difficulty in finding the talent to maintain a service of twenty-five hours a week. The difficulty was not a dearth of talent but a lack of money. It was also proved that there was no technical difficulty in using the spare fourth channel. The University committee then published an influential report that boosted the confidence of those of us who had been working for a Welsh-language service on the fourth channel. The greatest feat would be to get the Government to take action, and for that we had to wait another eight years.

Chapter 12

Welsh Independents

Although I am not by nature very religious, there has never been a time since I began to think for myself when Jesus was not my Lord and Master: I am not speaking of the great mystery. I have been guilty of some reckless things which, fortunately for me, have been kept from human gaze, and yet through it all no one has challenged the place of Jesus in my mind as the Way and the Truth. Among all the great ones of earth it is He, who was born of a lowly, unremarkable family, who followed the carpenter's craft with neither the advantage of a good education nor a high place in society, who was sent to preach among the poor and to topple the great ones from their pedestals, who came into collision with the establishment of the day, and who was despised and killed as a transgressor – He is the incomparable one. Jesus Christ is the face of God. He contains the whole of Christianity. For me, it is He who gives meaning to life, just as his Resurrection gives life to His church. As His follower I have the privilege of being counted among Christians, and in their company I have come into contact with many of the best people, the richest in their humanity, that I have ever known – scores of them ministers of the Gospel, the salt of our Welsh earth.

I have always been a member of a chapel and, for more than a generation I took charge of a Sunday School class. Hilda Ethall is fond of reminding me that I had the privilege of teaching her as one of a class of Barry College girls in 1937-39. Some two years later I should meet Huw, who became her husband, in a small group of conscientious objectors who used to meet at Miss Wilson's café in Llandovery. Huw was working in forestry at the time, as were most of the lads who met in Llandovery – Brynmor Thomas of Aberystwyth among them. One of the things that I take pride in is that my Sunday School classes at Llangadog produced three ministers. Ronald Williams of Caernarfon was a carpenter with my father before going into the ministry. His father, too, the Reverend Alwyn

Williams, my own minister, had been a carpenter until he was nearly forty. Before he went into 'the awesome office' of the ministry, Gareth Thomas worked in a bank and had a good job in London, while his father, Llew Thomas, worked on the road for the County Council. One of my own sons, Guto Prys, did a bit of everything before coming to his final decision – a law course, selling encyclopaedias, labouring on the Llyn Brianne dam, teaching in the Malvinas, and working on buses, in greenhouses, and in a library. His father grew tomatoes for a living. All three of my pupils were lucky enough to sit at the feet of Pennar Davies, the polymathic poet, and the other splendid teachers of the Independents' Memorial College in Swansea. The Welsh Independents are indeed fortunate in having two such great men as Pennar Davies and R. Tudur Jones as Principals of their Theological Colleges in Swansea and Bangor.

I have received more honours than I deserve from my fellow-Independents. I was elected as the Union's Chairman – the title is now President – in 1953. The Bible was presented to me by the outgoing Chairman, W.T. Gruffydd, a friend and neighbour, a valiant Anglesey man, a poet, thinker, powerful preacher, and an extremely warm personality. He died this year at the age of 96. I handed on the Bible in turn to another friend, R.J. Jones, the father of Hywel and Gwilym ap Robert. I greatly admired R.J.; I was much taken with the way he held his head in the pulpit and with the zest of his delivery, the sort of ardour and positiveness that is found in particular among preachers from the Preselau, men such as Thomas Rees, Lewis the Tumble (as he was known), Ben Owen of blessed memory, T.E. Nicholas and many another. None gave me more support than R.J. and his wife. I once had the great pleasure of driving them, together with Pennar Davies, to the Independents' World Conference at St. Andrews in Scotland. I remember nothing at all of the Conference but the long journey through the Lake District and the mountains of Scotland is still vivid in my mind. On the shores of Ullswater R.J. recounted for us how his life had once been saved by deep breathing. He had been in a very feeble condition, so much so that it was thought his life was in danger. A number of doctors had failed to do anything for him, but he heard from a friend about someone in Bristol whose methods were quite unorthodox. Without much hope of a cure, R.J. went to see him. This doctor didn't treat his body, nor did he advise him to go on any special diet, nor did he give him any medicine. His only advice was that R.J. should go out into the fresh air several times a day, or stand before an open door or window, and breathe in so deeply that he could expel the air from his lungs with a sound half-way between a roar and a whinny. R.J. gave us a demonstration on the very spot. His terrifying neighing sounded far out across the lake. Pennar and I insisted on giving it a try, and there we were, the two of us, on the shores of Ullswater, drawing air into our bellies and then whinnying, except that the sound we two novices made was as nothing compared with R.J.'s magisterial roars. I don't know whether Pennar's bellowing ever grew more accomplished in the course of time. I'm sorry to say that we escaped from the Conference for one day and went deep into the mountains of Scotland, which are sometimes as beautiful as those of Snowdonia. On the mountain road between Aberfeldy and Kinloch Rannoch we spotted the words Freedom for Scotland boldly painted on a large boulder. With voices raised to a shout, we went up to the stone. R.J. took off his hat and with his wife representing the women of Wales, we sang '*Hen Wlad fy Nhadau*'. Romantic fools, perhaps, but one must sometimes allow a moment of happy release from reality. At Kinloch Rannoch Pennar and I took off our shoes and socks and ventured into the cold waters of the lake, so that we could say with the poet, 'We twae hae paddled i' the burn'. On the way back to St. Andrews, we spotted a fine old tavern in the shadow of the grim castle of Wemyss (pronounced Weems) that was advertising a late dinner. There we ate a duck with a sweet orange sauce that was so delicious yet another bond was forged between us. Whenever we met thereafter the memory of that Wemyss duck would always bind us ever closer.

It was at Pen-y-groes in Carmarthenshire, a mining village famous for its silver band, that as the Union's Chairman I delivered an address to congregations gathered in two chapels – the service was also broadcast to Calfaria, the Baptist chapel. The first man to have spoken from the Union's chair had been Gwilym Hiraethog, on the subject of Satan. I didn't take my lead from him. I spoke about Christianity and Welsh society, developing a line of thought I had often followed over the years. I was heartened by the presence there of my Uncle Idris, my father's brother, a preacher of the first water who had spent most of his life in London, more's the pity. In 1913, in Swansea, his father had delivered the Union's sermon on the text of 'A New Heaven and a New Earth'. With this, says R. Tudur Jones in his magisterial history of the Union, 'Social Preaching came to its maturity'. I stand in the tradition of my grandfather.

One of the responsibilites of the Union's Chairman was to preside over the meetings of its Council and Executive Committee. It was at that time Curig Davies, the Secretary with so many fertile ideas, had the vision of a printing-press and a new home for the Union which in due course he turned into a reality. I was a sort of Aaron to this

Moses of a man. My job was to persuade a committee, the Council and the Annual Conference that Curig's vision was workable. I had to stay on as Chairman of the Press and Buildings Committee for another six years in order to get both these schemes up and running. Curig's memorial are the John Penry Press and Tŷ John Penry in St. Helen's Road, Swansea, both of which have been of immense benefit to the Union. The man who is commemorated in the names of these buildings wasn't present at the official opening. When a reporter from *The South Wales Evening Post* asked that morning whether he could interview Mr John Penry, we had to admit that he wasn't there, at least not in the flesh. He had been in another place for several centuries, having been executed in 1593.

For ten years I was the Union's Treasurer. In this capacity I preceded Emrys Evans and came after Brinley Richards, the last of the literary men of old Welsh-speaking Glamorgan whose culture is described with such rich scholarship by Griffith John Williams in his great book, *Traddodiad Llenyddol Morgannwg*. A slab of indigenous Welsh wit and culture, Brinley Richards left the coal-face while still young to take up law. Born in Nant-y-ffyllon, he spent his entire life in the service of Wales and his beloved Tir Iarll. He was on the Maesteg Council for forty years. He was put by Labour, the ruling party, on only one committee – the Pigeons Committee. He watched the drastic rundown of his community without losing any of his spirit or enthusiasm. I often had the impression that it was his inexhaustible store of knowledge about his native district and its characters which kept him going. He would relate their feats and practical jokes, their poems and sayings, with the unfailing mastery of the true story-teller. On the day of his funeral I gave a lift to Roy Isaac, the brother of Norah Isaac, the district's most famous daughter, and as we went past chapel after chapel he recited for us the number of their congregations – ten, fifteen, twenty, one with only five members, some already closed down. He could remember a time when there had been twenty-one ministers in the Welsh chapels of Maesteg. Today there's only one. It's all bingo and clubs now. But there is an excellent Welsh School in Maesteg, so the district is not dead yet.

I worked closely with Trebor Lloyd Evans during these years. He was Secretary of the Union of Welsh Independents, a genial kindred spirit, a piece of Penllyn's rich culture, a nephew of Llwyd o'r Bryn, a hard worker for *Urdd Gobaith Cymru* and one of the founders of the Welsh School at Lon-las in Swansea. He was a tower of strength to the John Penry Press, which published several of his excellent books. There is a long tradition of cultural and political activity among the Welsh Independents. Many of us are glad, as Llewelyn

Williams used to say, to be nonconformist in politics as well as in our religion – Independents denominationally and independent in political thought and action. It seemed appropriate to many that the Union's Chairman was at the same time President of Plaid Cymru, both receiving and handing out the knocks in the political field.

Chapter 13

Among Friends

Within a year of my being elected Chairman of the Welsh Independents, I was contesting Merioneth again for Plaid Cymru, and in the year following I stood at a by-election in Aberdare where we took second place and beat the Tory candidate, Raymond Gower, later M.P. for my home town of Barry, into third place.

The first time Plaid Cymru contested Carmarthen was at the General Election of 1955. This decision caused some consternation among supporters of Sir Rhys Hopkin Morris, the Liberal M.P. I received a deputation led by J.B. Evans, who was later to be the Conservative candidate in the constituency, which tried to bring pressure to bear on me to withdraw our candidate, as if I were able to do that. They were afraid that our intervention might have had the effect of losing the seat for Hopkin Morris. In vain I tried to placate them by saying that the Liberals of Carmarthenshire were too conservative to vote for Plaid Cymru and it was from the Labourites that we would draw our support. That is precisely what happened: former Labour supporters were at the core of our 3,500 votes and Hopkin Morris was returned with an even bigger majority. Hopkin Morris had the reputation of being a great radical but he managed to conceal his radicalism while he was M.P. for Carmarthen, thanks to Tory support. On a platform he would create the impression that he was a man who would fight to his last breath for principles, particularly that of Freedom. People would praise his grand-sounding speeches to the skies, but if they were then asked what exactly he'd said, they would scratch their heads and couldn't remember any of it, except that he was in favour of Freedom. He was, of course, as keen about Freedom as Mrs Thatcher is today. But if anyone spoke up in favour of Freedom for Wales, as I did in more than one debate with him at the Guild Hall in Carmarthen, Hopkin always contended it would put our poor nation under the control of the wild people of Glamorgan and Gwent. He would nevertheless answer questions fully and in a masterly fashion. I never had much idea what these answers meant but to the audience they were always convincing. There was a move at Westminster in the early 'fifties, led by Nigel Birch, the Conservative Member for one of the Flintshire seats, to make Hopkin Morris Speaker of the House of Commons. I used to come across him at debates in the county, which were quite popular in those days. The campaign came to nothing, however, and Hopkin Morris was put on the Panel of the House's Chairmen.

Plaid Cymru's candidate at the 1955 Election was Jennie Eirian Davies from Brynaman; it was to be a rehearsal for her magnificent effort in the by-election two years later. Because the Liberal Party had taken such a long time to find a candidate after Hopkin Morris's death, Plaid Cymru's campaign was painfully long drawn out. I must have spoken with Jennie in at least a hundred meetings and I knew that her commitment exhausted her energies for a while. Despite the strain, she never once failed to give a substantial and polished performance. These meetings did much to prepare the ground for the seeds of Nationalism. They also gave thousands an opportunity of hearing Jennie's beautiful accent and her powerful oratory. I always think the women of Carmarthenshire have the loveliest of Welsh accents. There's no need to say that Jennie was a first-class candidate; she was a woman of principle and conviction, popular with both the voters and the press. Her sharp wit always had great appeal. 'Who will look after the kids if you're elected?', some bitter Liberal asked at one meeting. 'Hopkin Morris!' replied Jennie. She even won the support of some of the farmers. Two farmers met in Carmarthen Mart and began talking about the electoral race. One of them asked, 'Who's your horse?', to which the other replied, 'I haven't got a horse, I've got a mare.'

It must be borne in mind that in those days people came to public meetings. Often I spoke at a hundred meetings during Election campaigns in Merioneth, a dozen of them on the eve of poll, and they would all be packed out. This meant that a substantial number of the electors had come to hear the candidate. The meetings weren't always peaceful because there was a lot of heckling in those days. I think it must have been during the 1955 campaign that I called at the school in Llandderfel. As I got out of the car on the common in front of the school, I could hear a commotion coming from the meeting. Inside it was pandemonium. Tudur Jones was sitting calmly at a table in front of the audience. When I sat down he handed me a piece of paper and on which he had written 'Don't say anything about Lloyd George'. It was dangerous to criticize the great Welshman in a bastion of Liberalism like Llandderfel. When Tudur dared to do just that, a stout fellow in the back row leapt to his feet and shouted, 'Three cheers for Lloyd George, boys!' In fact they gave more than three and Tudur was not allowed to say any more. My mentioning of Tudur now brings to mind the tremendous contribution he has made as College Principal, scholar, theologian and preacher, and as a journalist. He is one of the century's outstanding Welshmen. He has left his mark on our country and his influence is sure to last for a long time yet and increase on account of his writing. A genial companion and a hearty laugher, he carries his learning lightly. He has been one of Plaid Cymru's most important thinkers, a Parliamentary candidate, for five years the Party's Vice-President and for twenty-three the editor of one or other of its newspapers. For six months he edited the *Welsh Nation* as a weekly. On the front page of the first number he carried a picture of Marilyn Monroe, who had recently been in the news because of some connection she was supposed to have had with Wales. Someone had referred to Wales in her presence and she had asked, 'Where is Wales?' When Dyfnallt heard about this he enquired, 'Who is Marilyn Monroe?'

One of the great privileges I have had from working for Plaid Cymru is the friendship of men and women of quality – for instance, Waldo Williams, whom I used to meet often at The Bristol Trader, the home in Fishguard of his great friend D.J. Williams, where Cassie Davies spent a lot of time when she was a Schools Inspector in Pembrokeshire; she refers to this connection in her book *Hwb i'r Galon*, which reflects so well the virtue and vivacity of her life. I happened to be in the house when Waldo called there on his way back from a cycling trip through Ireland. He recited for us the *cywydd* he had composed while riding along on his bike. I wonder what became of that poem, for it isn't included in his book, *Dail Pren*. I had an extraordinary privilege when Waldo was sent to prison for refusing to pay his income-tax as a protest against the Government's spending on weapons of war. Every stick of his furniture had been sold and he'd been sleeping on the bare floorboards. In Swansea Gaol he was permitted just one visitor a week and I was one of the few who were allowed to see him. I had carefully prepared a list of things I wanted to discuss with him, so that no second would be wasted, for Waldo could be a bit taciturn at times. But there was no need to worry. In the bare little room with a policeman within a yard of us, it was Waldo who did all the talking. He talked about his life among the gypsies of Pembrokeshire. I am only sorry that I didn't have a tape-recorder with me. The meeting held in commemoration of the poet at Crymych was a superb example of the unique nature of the folk-culture of Wales, the kind of meeting that Cassie Davies used to arrange so splendidly. The hall of Ysgol y Preselau was full to overflowing. The meeting began at two o'clock, with people reciting Waldo's work, and singing in twos, threes, and fours, or else in small choirs, singing to the harp or to the accompaniment of fiddle or piano, reminiscing about the poet, discussing and chatting about him from the stage; it was a most civilized meeting. I had to leave at six o'clock in order to attend another meeting, but no one else budged. Waldo's memorial meeting went on and on without losing any of its vitality – where else but in Wales would you find a phenomenon such as this?

Perhaps the most remarkable of all my friends was D.J. Williams himself. For thirty years or more I enjoyed his hospitality, and that of Siân his wife, Wil Ifan's sister, at The Bristol Trader. D.J. *was* Plaid Cymru in Fishguard. It was he who used to distribute *Y Ddraig Goch*, the Party's newspaper, collecting a hundred subscriptions every year. He also wrote to the local press. He it was who collected money and organized meetings of all kinds, whether brains trusts, debates, *nosweithiau llawen*, or plays; some thought this a waste of time for so fine a writer. Whatever the nature of the meeting, I had to be there, for there always had to be a guest-speaker who would say a few words on behalf of the cause, even during the interval of a play. Whenever I had a speaking engagement in the town, D.J. would insist that I turned up three hours early so that I could be taken around a dozen homes to be introduced to the families who lived there. He used to contend that they wouldn't dare not come to the meeting after having had the privilege of being introduced to the guest-speaker. During the long years of our friendship I heard D.J. telling hundreds of stories about people and incidents and various sayings he had come across over the years. He had an eye for seeing the peculiarities of a person's character as well as the ups and downs of his own life; he also had an ear for the vivid word or expression; the imagination to place everything in its context against the background of his own fine humanity; a sense of humour to see the funny side of things and the seriousness to deal with the more sombre side; the artistry to choose his words unerringly; a richness of idiom and vocabulary to dress them in fitting language; and an instinct for remembering everything clearly. There must have been thousands of incidents and anecdotes etched on his memory, and he could call them up whenever he wanted to. The stock of his stories was as varied as life itself, and some were pretty ribald. He once confided in me that he could tell his most bawdy stories only to two people – Saunders Lewis and me. What a pair! He put only a small selection of this inexhaustible treasury on paper. It grieves me to think that his stories were recounted to a creature so prosaic as myself, for they have by now been consigned to oblivion, like so much of our folk-culture.

When the Carmarthen by-election was coming up, I wrote to D.J., who had been suffering from a heart condition for some years, to tell him not to come over. I might just as well have spoken to the wall. He came, of course, and stayed for a long while, walking hundreds of miles from farm to farm in northern Carmarthenshire in order to visit the families of 'The Old Faces' whom he had described so memorably in his books. His last visit to his 'square mile' was on Sunday evening, 4th January 1970. He greatly appreciated the honour of returning to Rhydcymerau to chair a concert that had been arranged for the benefit of the National Eisteddfod at Ammanford by his old friend D.O. Davies, a member of the family who had lived in The Cart and Horses, the public house that has such a prominent place in D.J.'s autobiography, and who was also Chairman of the Eisteddfod's Finance Committee. The chapel was packed. At the end of the concert's first half, D.J. came forward to address the audience, who were delighted at this – indeed, some of them were rolling with laughter at what the old master had to say. After about five or six minutes of this hilarity, he changed key and began to speak seriously about our responsibility for the maintenance of the values and culture of our country. He spoke about the chapel's great characters when he was a boy, about their prayers and the things they had held dear, about their culture and godliness. He referred to each of them by name, pointing his finger at the pews one by one as he described them. The long dead were with us again in spirit that evening, he said, a cloud of invisible witnessess who were all about us, and indeed we felt their presence just as much as the speaker. He then returned to his seat, having put us in a sober frame of mind and at the same time exciting us. He sat down in his corner with his arm resting on the pine ledge between him and the next pew. He was then seized by a great shudder and his arm began twitching. And then he died, sprawled the length of the pew, with his head on my raincoat. D.J. had himself joined the cloud of witnesses. The circle of his life had run from Rhydcymerau via the coalmines of Y Betws and Ferndale, through the Universities of Wales and Oxford, through the schools of Fishguard and Wormwood Scrubs, and back again to Rhydcymerau. When I got home that evening and told my wife Rhiannon what had happened, she couldn't bear the thought of D.J.'s body lying in the cold darkness of the mortuary at Carmarthen, and insisted on bringing him back to our home at Talar Wen, where he lay for three days in a coffin in my study. A song that our daughter Meinir wrote about this time was published in the volume commemorating D.J., *Y Cawr o Rydcymerau*. The service was held in our home before the funeral. On a cold January day more mourners stood outside the chapel at Rhydcymerau than were able to get inside. No one who was present at the service will ever forget it: the gravity of Cassie Davies, the verses of Dafydd Iwan who found them hard to sing, the testimony of Stanley Lewis, D.J.'s minister, and the tribute paid by Lewis Valentine, with whom D.J. had caused the Fire in Llŷn. Stanley talked about how he had once been canvassing with D.J. at Sanclêr (St. Clears) during the by-election, he on one side of the street and D.J. on the other. He had noticed that D.J. was leaning in pain against a wall, for he was suffering from angina. Stanley ran over to him and tried to coax him to go home at once in his car, but D.J. wasn't having any of it. 'What?', he asked, 'with the life of Wales in the balance? Nothing of the sort.' They went on canvassing until nine o'clock that evening. Lewis Valentine said he had been in D.J.'s company some eighteen months before and D.J. had told him he thought he had three more years to live. 'What are you going to do?', asked Val. 'Work like a Trojan,' replied D.J.

On being returned to Westminster in October 1974 I received a gift from D.O. Davies, the friend who had organized the concert in the course of which D.J. had died. He was a bank-manager in Ammanford, and it was with him that D.J. had stayed the night before; the two had been very close friends. D.O. was the last to have been born at The Cart and Horses in Rhydcymerau – the wittiest of the silver-tongued Jenkinses, indeed, the wittiest of all the Party's members. He was a peerless story-teller, an unsurpassed letter-writer, an unfailing friend, and a patriot who once spent a week in gaol for the sake of the Welsh language. He was also a friend of Dan Thomas, my father-in-law, another bank-manager of the same temperament; these two were the only Welshmen to have served as Presidents of the Bankworkers' Union. The gift I received from D.O. was D.J.'s own copy of Waldo's poems, *Dail Pren*, with his name inside the cover. I should like to end this chapter by quoting from a letter sent to me by D.O. with the book because it sheds light on the way D.J. lived, and on D.O. himself, for that matter. 'When Dafy John of Abernant came to open Penrhiw (the Plaid Cymru office in Carmarthen) and stayed with us just before presiding at the concert in Rhydcymerau, where he was to die, he was as usual travelling light. His books were heavier than his clothes and effects. After the funeral, Emlyn Miles called at our house and was kind enough to give me the books. There was, too, a small pad of Basildon Bond notepaper and a copy of the magazine *Taliesin* for Christmas 1969. "I'm always

telling you, Oswald," he would say, "about something or other you
ought to get and read, and this is one – you must take *Taliesin*." Also
there were William Barclay's *The Mind of St. Paul*, in its Fontana
edition, and *God Calling* by Two Listeners and edited by A.J. Russell.
I was told by J.E. Jones on the way to the funeral at Rhydcymerau
that D.J. was in the habit of giving a copy of this book to each of his
friends who was made a deacon. The message for 4th January, the
day on which D.J. died, was 'Do not plan. All is well. Wonderful
things are happening. Do not limit God at all . . . '. And lastly, *Dail
Pren*. Between its pages there was a letter from Wil Ifan and a
translation of the poem '*Medi*', and in D.J.'s own handwriting the
words, "*Safwn yn y bwlch*" ('Let us stand in the breach'). This book,
somehow, is the most valuable of all those in my possession, and
that's why it is fitting that I should give it to you, wishing you all the
best in your new and important mission . . .' The letter ends with
references to places dear to both Waldo and D.J. and alludes to
Waldo's great poem. '*Preseli*': 'May Y Garn Goch, Y Mynydd Du,
the Brecon Beacons, Foel Drigarn, Carn Gyfryw, Tal Mynydd, Banc
Llywele, Penrhiw, the Square Mile, back you in all independence of
judgement.'

Chapter 14

London

At the beginning of his letter D.O. Davies had referred to the opening of Penrhiw, 'the Old Farm House' immortalized by D. J. Williams in his book *Hen Dŷ Ffarm*. The name was given to Plaid Cymru's office in Carmarthen, which was opened by D.J. on the day before he died. The office was named after D.J.'s old home because, when the Party was in financial straits in 1964, he had sold Penrhiw and given us what he had received for it, without holding back so much as the solicitor's fees. The Party had been given only one such gift before (although Mrs Griffith John Williams later left us in her will her house at Gwaelod-y-Garth), and that was the family home of Judge Sir Alun Pugh in Llannon. He decided to make us the gift after I had met him at The Farmers' Club, one of London's most exclusive gentlemen's clubs. I had addressed a very select dining-club attended by London Welshmen on the subject of Nationalism that evening. Five of the fifteen people present had been enthused enough to ask me to go into the bar afterwards to discuss what they might do to help Plaid Cymru. Among the five were Sir David Hughes Parry and Llefelys Davies, the head of the Milk Marketing Board. But it was only Alun Pugh who did any-thing. He had been a friend of J.E. Jones ever since J.E. had formed a branch of Plaid Cymru in London in 1929-30; the dramatist John Gwilym Jones had been its Secretary. Alun Pugh was also one of the four able barristers who drafted the constitution of a Free Wales. The other three were Arthur Price, T. Huws Davies, and Vincent Lloyd Jones. Like Gerald Morgan, who was later to be-come headmaster of Ysgol Penweddig in Aberystwyth, Alun Pugh had been born and brought up in Brighton. He had learned Welsh from the three booklets known as *Welsh Made Easy*, the work of Caradar the Cornishman. It was he who persuaded me to join the Reform Club in Pall Mall, which I used as convenient lodgings that were cheap in those days and within a quarter of an hour's walk from Westminster, past St. James's Park with its comic water-fowl. I was to remain a member for three years.

Three of the four trustees of the famous Reform Club were Welsh-speaking Welshmen – Alun Pugh, Gwilym Lloyd George, and Lord Justice Morris, who had made his home there. One of the funniest members was Lord Arwyn, a Welsh-speaker from Y Glais in the Swansea Valley, the greatest authority in Britain on explosives. There was no better food to be had anywhere than at this Club and many's the time I dined there in the company of friends. One of the most memorable occasions was when Lord Hailsham came to discuss a Parliament for Wales, of which he was in favour, with Dewi Watkin Powell, later to become a judge, and myself. Another time, Dewi was accompanied by the actor Meredith Edwards. I put this on record only because of what happened on that occasion. After dinner, the three of us were having coffee in the gallery which is above the large and impressive marble hall. Everyone was expected to keep his voice down, so sober-sided was this place, but it was difficult for three Welshmen to keep to this rule while Dewi competed with Meredith in the telling of stories about characters in the Welsh capital and acting out some of the scenes in Cardiff dialect. As is well-known, Cardiff has its own way of speaking in English, which is promoted by the genial members of the Cardiff Language Society. The accent is to be heard at its purest whenever Owen John Thomas, one of Plaid Cymru's stalwarts in the city, opens his mouth in English. Anyway, things got a bit out of hand that evening in the midst of the Reform Club's dignified hush. The hall started to resound with our laughter. On the gallery on the other side of the hall we could see a man sitting by himself and staring pointedly at us. We were afraid that he might have been thinking of complaining about our behaviour to the Club's officials. But in a little while he came over to us and asked with great respect in a quiet voice whether he might sit near us. He said he hadn't enjoyed anything so much as our laughter for many years. He sat beside us, an audience of one, listening intently to the noise we three were making but without understanding a word of what was being said.

On my return to Westminster in 1974 I stayed for a few months with the two Dafydds – Dafydd Wigley and Dafydd Elis Thomas – at a cheap hotel in south London. The Reform Club had become unreasonably expensive; I couldn't afford to belong to it, let alone stay there. For the next three years Dafydd Elis Thomas and I shared a convenient flat in Chelsea which we acquired at a low rent through the kindness of Brian Morgan Edwards; its only disadvantage was that we had to climb sixty-six steps to get to it. I couldn't have had a finer flat-mate than Dafydd. We had many discussions during which I had an opportunity of fully appreciating his intellectual brilliance and gentle nature. We ate most of our meals at Westminster, where the prices are kept low by means of subsidies from the tax-payers. We ran into some trouble within about a fortnight of the Election in 1974, after the three of us, the two Dafydds and myself, had been at a celebration of the Welsh Office's first ten years which was being held at Lancaster House. There wasn't much food to be had there, although there was more than enough drink. So we went back, in high spirits, to dine at Westminster. In the Members' dining-room, a very sober place, the two Dafydds displayed their friendly personalities, and their release from the shackles of convention and class, by taking on their laps the young woman who waited on us. At dinner next evening when she came to take our orders, she said to me, 'You was in an awful state last night, wasn't you, Mr Evans?' I had to put up with tribulations like that only too often. Twice in the bar where M.Ps. are allowed to take their friends, but where only they can order drinks, the man or woman behind the counter asked me, 'Are you a Member here, sir?'

I mentioned the meetings that D.J. Williams used to arrange in Fishguard. I would often have four or five a week in all parts of Wales, mainly with a view to building up the strength of Plaid Cymru. We also organized all kinds of campaigns. One which lasted for decades under various guises was the campaign for an Economic Development Authority for Wales. This was at the heart of our short-term strategy. Since it was obvious that Wales wasn't going to have a Parliament for a long while yet, we had to have institutions which, though less powerful, would contribute to the reinforcement of the nation's economic life. A Development Authority had been the main plank of our electoral programme in 1945, and it was about this policy that I used to speak for the most part. When Dr Thomas Jones, for many years the grey eminence of Welsh life, together with Ben Bowen Thomas, the Warden of Coleg Harlech, came to our Election meeting at Harlech, he praised this policy as something that seemed to him highly practical. By the 'fifties it had developed along the lines of the Tennessee Valley Authority, which had done miracles in restoring life to large parts of seven of the American States, a region the size of England. The Authority considered the region's economic and cultural life as essential parts of what it called 'a seamless web'. The T.V.A.'s ambitious scheme was based on electric power, and that's what our scheme for Wales proposed, too. We were fortunate enough to have the assistance of an expert on electricity in the person of C.F. Matthews, a committed English-speaking

Nationalist who lived in Newbury in England. When the only committee with any clout came to consider the organization of the
electricity industry throughout Britain – the Herbert Committee – it
held one session in Cardiff specifically to listen to our evidence in
favour of establishing an Electricity Board for Wales with powers
sufficient to develop the industry. It took us a whole day to put our
evidence before the Committee; I presented the case but it was C.F.
Matthews who had prepared the material, and that we gained high
praise in the Herbert Report and from the Chairman himself was due
almost entirely to him.

We made a good deal of effort during these years to get Welsh
boards for the nationalized industries and services. Who can deny
that Wales would have been better off if only we had succeeded?
Although we had some partial success with water and gas, our
effectiveness was checked for various reasons. We met with no
success at all with the railways, the consequences of which I have
already touched upon, nor with coal or steel or the docks. This year
the Welsh docks have once again made a substantial profit and yet
that profit is to be invested in their English counterparts while they
have to make do with second-hand equipment. The Englishmen now
being appointed to look after them won't stick up for them like
Welshmen would. Had we succeeded in getting a Welsh Docks
Board, it's possible that Port Talbot would have been developed into
a major European port. It has all the necessary conditions – deep
water not far off-shore, plenty of room for large ships to manoeuvre
– it faces the open sea, without any of the dangers of the over-busy
channel between England and France, and it has the potential advantage of a land-bridge to industry in South Wales and the English
Midlands.

The coalmines of Wales started to be closed on an increasing scale
at the beginning of the 'sixties under a Tory Government. This policy
was pursued mercilessly by subsequent Labour Governments, which
closed Welsh pits at the rate of one every seven weeks, on average,
during the period from 1964 to 1970. By then oil had become king.
In 1962, the Cwmllynfell pit, where three hundred men worked and
on which the whole village depended, was closed. This was done
despite the fact that there was plenty of coal left in the ground, and
best quality coal at that. Fortunately, the Chairman of the pit's lodge
was Isaac Stephens, a Nationalist. By his efforts, and under the
leadership of Wynne Samuel, the miners gathered in the village hall
to hear Wynne and Trefor Morgan and myself setting out a co-
operative scheme which would have put the pit squarely in the
ownership and under the control of the workers. We had two

meetings attended by the men and two with the lodge, the pit's executive committee. The miners took warmly to our scheme for the formation of a workers' co-operative. It was Wynne who was mainly responsible for drafting the expenditure and income accounts and for finding a market for the coal in the greenhouses of the Netherlands, where there was more of a demand for the red seam anthracite than could be satisfied. There's no doubt but that the workers would have been better off under this scheme and yet it was bitterly opposed by each one of the four great powers – the Tory Government and the Coal Board, of course, but also more ferociously by the Labour Party and the Miners' Union which is associated with that party. The Labour Party objected to our proposal regarding pneumoconiosis for the same reason as did the Labourites of Carmarthenshire, namely that it would harm their nostrum of centralized nationalization. Despite knowing that the schemes in both cases would be for the benefit of the miners, they turned their brass faces to them in the name of state control. Jim Griffiths insisted that the success of the co-operative principle at Cwmllynfell would have meant the end of the Coal Board. The workers showed their determination by planning a stay-down strike. When the Coal Board heard about this plan, it announced that it would close a pit of similar size in the neighbourhood and ask the men of Cwmllynfell to name it. They didn't need the coal, they said, but more than that, they didn't want to see a co-operative venture working in the coalfield. In this way they killed off the most promising scheme that the coal industry in Wales had seen at that time.

Chapter 15

Cwm Tryweryn

Except for the campaign in favour of a Parliament for Wales, Tryweryn was the most important of all our battles. It was used like all the rest in an attempt to awaken Welsh consciousness and commitment to the nation. Plaid Cymru has carried out this essential work, which no other party has attempted, not only by means of conventional electoral politics but also by unceasing effort in trying to create national public bodies, many of them in the economic sector. Each of these campaigns has contributed something to the creation of an independent Welsh way of thinking and to the nurturing, in some, of a loyalty to Wales. This militant Welshness over many years has kindled fire and pride in Welsh breasts, and in a great number of parents who speak no Welsh a determination to send their children to Welsh-medium schools. What would the condition of Wales be like today without the work of this small minority? What would be the fortunes of the language? Would we have any of the institutions that we now have? Would any of the developments we have seen since the war have taken place? How much life would there be left in the nation? It's a grave mistake to measure the success of Plaid Cymru in electoral terms alone. As well as being a political party, it's a national movement that revivifies the nation as it works from within it, gathering together those who dearly wish to ensure a national future for Wales. That is the most fundamental difference between Plaid Cymru and the British parties.

The Tryweryn campaign was a classic example of the way we work. The first the people of Capel Celyn and its Valley knew of the plan to drown their homes was when they read in *The Liverpool Daily Post*, towards the end of 1955, about Liverpool's decision to create a reservoir in Cwm Tryweryn. Previous to that, they'd been told that Liverpool was intending to make a dam at Dolanog which would have put the home of Ann Griffiths, the hymn-writer, under water. But that was only a ruse to draw the fire of the Welsh and then make a show of yielding to pressure by moving to another valley where the Corporation would have had twice as much water at lower cost. That Valley was Cwm Tryweryn in the heart of cultured Penllyn. Liverpool didn't bother to consult the people who lived in the valley, nor did they approach the Penllyn and Merioneth Councils. As Gwenallt wrote,

> 'Cyfododd y Goliath pres yn Lerpwl
> i waradwyddo ac ysbeilio'r werin
> gan gasglu'r afonydd at ei gilydd i gyd
> i foddi'r gymdeithas yn Nhryweryn.'

('The Goliath of money arose in Liverpool to shame and despoil the common people by gathering together the waters and drowning the community of Tryweryn.')

The Party immediately formed a Defence Committee of people from the area with Dafydd Roberts of Caefadog as its Chairman. The power behind the Committee was its able and totally committed Secretary, Elizabeth Watcyn Jones, who had been born and brought up at the Post Office in Capel Celyn; she was the daughter of Watcyn o Feirion and a good example, like her sister Dorothy Dolben, and her father, of the Valley's culture. As Mrs Mrowiec (she married a Pole), Elizabeth published a fine book about her husband's country, *Teithio Pwyl*, which is a valuable introduction to the life and problems of that troubled land. As Plaid Cymru's candidate in Merioneth, I attended meetings of the Committe, which were held in Bala. The first thing was to organize protest meetings locally and in Liverpool, where the Secretary worked heroically to alert the city's Welsh popu-lation. At the outset the argument was heard that it was unChristian to deny the English a cup of cold water, but in time many of the Welsh were enlightened. Liverpool was already taking from Lake Vyrnwy (known in Welsh as Llyn Llanwddyn) more water than it needed to slake the thirst of its inhabitants and those of populous areas of Cheshire and Lancashire. It was also reselling some of the Vyrnwy water for millions of pounds a year, in addition to meeting the needs of its own homes and industries. The demand for water was on the increase, water that could be had for nothing in Wales. They knew that water is among the most important of natural resources; in many countries, industry is located where there is a plentiful supply of water. In the United States it's quite usual for one state to pay another for the water it provides and Italy pays some of the Swiss cantons for the same resource, but there's no state or country that would dream of attacking its neighbour, destroying its society, and drowning it for the sake of acquiring its water. Because Wales was part of England (at least in English eyes), the large cities of England believed they had a right to do just that. Dr Tudur Jones, Dafydd Roberts and I went to a meeting of Liverpool Council to protest against the city's plans. Through the good offices of Councillor Murphy, an Irishman and a friend of Dr Dafydd Alun Jones, the psychiatrist, we obtained a copy of the meeting's agenda referring to a report that had been drawn up on Tryweryn. Dafydd Als, as he is known, put in some heroic work over Cwm Tryweryn. Within less than a week of his final exams at the Liverpool College of Medicine, he spent three days and nights going through the minutes of the Council's Water Committee as far back as 1865, turning up some very useful material. At the Council meeting, when the Water Committee's report came up for discussion, Tudur and Dafydd and I leapt to our feet and I tried to address the Council – through the chair, of course. The Chairman then bawled at me to shut up and sit down, but with the aid of my two companions I kept at it. Immediately in front of me, so near in fact that I was almost touching her broad shoulders, sat Councillor Bessie Braddock M.P., twenty stone of a woman with a voice to match her size. She made full use of her voice that day, and not only of her voice. She banged the lid of her desk up and down with a noise like thunder, and the other councillors followed her example. It was evident that she had put in a lot of practice at it. The chamber of Liverpool Council was now filling with the roars of hell's pit. Four policemen then pushed their way towards us through the pandemonium and carried us out into the comparative calm of the city's streets. A few weeks later I was back in order to address the Council for a whole quarter of an hour and to answer questions.

After the inaugural meetings at Bala and Liverpool, J.E. Jones arranged for others to be held in various parts of Wales. The Party published a pamphlet of mine which summed up our case and another at the end of the campaign drawing conclusions from it. J.E. worked like Hercules in sending out letters on behalf of the Defence Committee to all the local councils, the chapels and churches, the trades unions, and to a variety of societies. The support we raised throughout the country, and especially in the industrial areas, obliged the Welsh Members of Parliament in the end to lend their clear support, too. All the inhabitants of the threatened part of Cwm Tryweryn paraded through the streets of Liverpool; the only one absent was a baby less than a year old. They also went to the Granada Studios in Manchester to appear on a television programme. Their case and their ability to make it in an English richly coloured with their native Welsh awakened widespread sympathy.

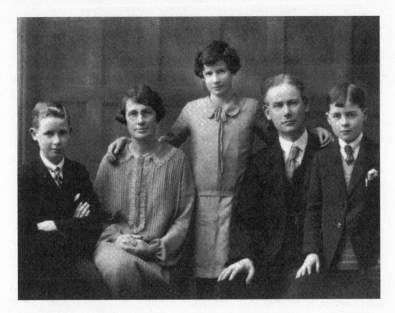

The Evans family 1925 –
Me, my Mother, Ceridwen, my Father, Alcwyn

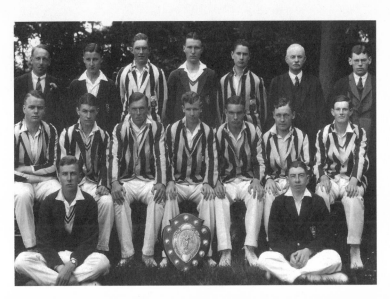

Barry County School First Cricket XI, with me at centre in
the front row.

With Rhiannon on our wedding day, 1st March 1940

*Plaid Cymru Summer School, Newport 1950. Back row –
Wynne Samuel, J.Gwyn Griffiths, D.J.Williams, Dan
Thomas. Front row – J.E.Jones, Gwynfor Evans,
O.M.Roberts.*

The official opening of Llyn Celyn, October 1965.

By-Election Victory in Carmarthen, July 1966.

With Rhiannon in discussion with Irish President Eamon de Valera.

The victory train to London after winning back Carmarthen in October 1974.

Tuning in to the first broadcast of Sianel Pedwar Cymru (S4C), November 2nd 1982.

Before the city of Liverpool could get a Bill before Parliament, it had to have the approval of a public civic meeting. Some of the Welsh people living in the city worked effectively to arrange for hundreds of their compatriots to attend that meeting. When, at half-past two, the time came for it to begin, it was obvious to the Liverpool authorities that the Welsh were in a majority, whereupon the spectre of defeat flashed before their eyes. The meeting failed to make a prompt start. The clock struck three and still it hadn't started. But over the next quarter of an hour the Corporation's employees began to troop in, some of them wearing the uniform of the Water Board. It was only when the people on the platform were certain they were in a majority that the meeting was allowed to commence.

I had an interesting meeting with Alderman Sefton, the leader of the Labour Party that ruled the city of Liverpool. The first of the two hours I spent with him was very frosty, but during the second he began to warm to me as he found that we shared many of our aims. He took great pride in the culture of Merseyside and was of the view that the north-west of England should be self-governing. By the end of our meeting he was even describing himself as 'a Scouse nationalist'. Plaid Cymru, through the good offices of J.E. Jones, of course, organized a huge rally on the banks of Tryweryn as a sign of the opposition which was now agitating the land. At this meeting I warned our people that we should have to prevent the scheme before it was passed at Westminster, for it would be too late to do anything about it afterwards. The case was opposed in the House of Lords sitting as a court of law. It had decided a little earlier to reject Manchester's more modest scheme to draw water from Ullswater in the Lake District. In spite of Merioneth Council's spending two thousand pounds on legal defence, a very large sum in those days, the Tryweryn scheme was eventually accepted in the Lords. The Liverpool Bill then came before the House of Commons, where for once there was unanimity among Welsh Members. At the second reading only one Welshman voted in its favour, and that was David Llewellyn, and yet the Bill went through with a huge majority in its favour. The English had supported their fellow-countrymen. This defeat made a lasting impression because it was a case of some importance to Wales in which the Welsh were as united as ever a nation had been. Welsh opinion was completely ignored and our interests trampled under foot by a powerful English city that acted oppressively and arrogantly, a city that had more inhabitants than the northernmost three-quarters of our counties put together. The real nature of the kind of democracy we have in Wales had been exposed.

In spite of all this we continued to take action and the Welsh Members of Parliament pretended there was still hope. The Bill had to have a third reading. In order to demonstrate their fighting spirit, Goronwy Roberts M.P. (later Lord) and T.W. Jones (later Lord), the Member for Merioneth, came to address a meeting at the chapel in Capel Celyn. It has been under water these many years. As proof of the brave fight he had put up, T.W. Jones referred to a letter he had received from none less than Jim Griffiths. The letter was in his pocket, he said. Turning to Goronwy Roberts, he asked him, 'Shall I read it?' 'Yes,' said Goronwy in that firm manner of his, 'go on, read it.' T.W. then pulled the letter out of his pocket and read two sentences which had been written in his praise by 'old Jim'; then he turned to us and said defiantly that he was going to fight to the last ditch.

The last ditch was the third reading at Westminster, a long way from Capel Celyn. It was there that the fate of a community and its rich culture was to be decided. But before one shot was fired, an understanding had been reached between Tudur Watkins M.P. (later Lord) on behalf of the Welsh Parliamentary Party and Bessie Braddock on behalf of the Liverpool M.Ps. When it came to the third reading, not a word was said by one side or the other. The unanimous view of Wales counted for nothing in the only parliament the nation had, and a great wrong had been legitimized.

The Tryweryn issue continued to agitate Wales, especially among Nationalists. In 1957, at a time when feelings were at their height, the Council of the National Eisteddfod was imprudent enough to invite the Rt. Honourable Henry Brooke (later Lord), the Minister for Welsh Affairs, to be President of the Day at the Eisteddfod held in Llangefni. This inflamed Plaid Cymru. At a stormy Executive Committee just before the Eisteddfod, a plan of action was drawn up in the event of Brooke's setting foot on the Field. It included cutting the microphone's wires on the main stage so that he would be inaudible. The Eisteddfod had to ask Brooke not to come near the place.

After losing the battle, I acted in a way that I saw later was unwise. The saving of Cwm Tryweryn's community was my only motive. I drafted another proposal, which would have given Liverpool the same amount of water without drowning any homes. David Cole, the editor of the *Western Mail* at the time, persuaded the Lord Mayor of Cardiff to host another national conference to consider my scheme. The conference, which was chaired by Huw T. Edwards, gave its unanimous approval. A strong delegation was selected to put the scheme before Liverpool Council, and there was hope that the city would at last respect the united opinion of Wales. But the journey to Liverpool was in vain. This last-minute attempt enraged certain Nationalists and it was to be an element in the unease within the Party during the early 'sixties. This was the time when some began to take direct action. The first to do so were two young men from the Rhymney Valley, 'the boys from Gwent', both industrial workers and English-speaking, by name David Pritchard and David Walters. They were caught trying to spill oil from an electricity transformer. It was nearly midnight when Elystan Morgan (later Lord), Plaid Cymru's candidate in Merioneth, 'phoned me to say two young men had summoned him to the police-cells in Bala to ask him to defend them in court. He asked whether it would be all right if he did so; I urged him to agree. During the course of his masterly defence Elystan managed to sum up the villainy of Tryweryn in a powerful way and the two patriotic miscreants were released by the Bala court. The best-known activist in the Tryweryn saga was Emyr Llewelyn, the son of the writer T. Llew Jones, who was given a year in prison for his part in direct action at the site of the reservoir, in which he had co-operated with Owain Williams and John Albert Jones.

The taking of direct action by the use of explosives increased during the 'sixties, reaching its high point in the year of the Investiture of the Prince of Wales. The feelings of Nationalists exploded at the official opening of Llyn Celyn, the reservoir built in Cwm Tryweryn. A large crowd had assembled in an attempt to stop the great ones of Liverpool, and others, from attending the ceremony, that was held in a large marquee near the enormous dam. A contingent of police had been sent to thwart us. But after the guests had assembled for refreshments in the marquee, a crowd of Nationalists led by Chris Rees rushed down the slope and brought the meeting to an abrupt end. The public address system was put out of action, so that at one point the mouth of the Lord Mayor of Liverpool could be seen moving like that of a goldfish, with no sound coming from it.

From then on, water was an issue which the Party made sure would always agitate the country. We insisted on treating it as one of Wales's most valuable natural resources for which the cities and towns and industries of the English Midlands and Chester and Merseyside would have to pay. For a quarter of a century we campaigned for a Water Board for Wales, for the whole of Wales, which would have the power to control and develop this great asset and receive fair payment for the water exported from Wales to England. The average water-rate in Wales is 30.3 pence in the pound, whereas it's 17.1 in the north-west of England and 14.22 in the

Severn-Trent area, both extensive and populous regions which receive their water from Lakes Vyrnwy, Alwen, Tryweryn, Elan, and Clywedog. Water is one of the numerous examples of how an unfree Wales continues to be exploited.

Chapter 16

A Parliament for Wales

A generation ago the people of Wales, with only a few exceptions, found it impossible to think of their country living a full national life with its own Parliament and Government. When confronted with the idea, they found it somehow odd and alien, a wholly impractical ideal. It was so obvious to them that Wales was an integral and inextricable part of Britain. Had not we Welsh only recently stood shoulder to shoulder with the English and Scots and shared their suffering in a world war as members of one great British 'nation'? Many of them lost patience with the Nationalists who were causing them discomfort by touching the raw nerve of their Welshness. Their identity was being confused – they knew that Wales was a nation but it didn't cross their minds that it should and could live as a nation; the obvious thing for them was to be British. Wales they considered a sort of sub-nation within the British 'nation'. It was to Britain that they gave their allegiance. Only Nationalists realized that Britain isn't a nation. Britain is a state which is supposed to serve a group of nations. When Scotland and Wales achieve self-government, Great Britain will disappear. If it were a nation it wouldn't disappear as a result of losing its statehood.

In those days it was ridiculous to think of living for Wales and completely unimaginable that anyone should be prepared to die for it. Welsh nationality belonged to the periphery of life. It occurred to none save a small band of Nationalists that this nation should rule itself. They didn't dream that the national entity of Wales should be the basis of economic, political, and social life and that there should be a Welsh state. It was in order to establish the fact of Welsh nationality in people's minds and connect it with self-determination that the slogans '*Rhyddid i Gymru*' ('Freedom for Wales') and 'Free Wales' were painted on many a wall and boulder throughout the land. It always seems to me that the English version has a semantic advantage over the Welsh because the word 'free' can be either a verb or an adjective.

In 1949 we launched a series of annual rallies that were to go on for more than twenty-five years. A procession, with flags flying and a brass band at its head, became an important part of our activities. They were always arranged by J.E. Jones with his usual flair. The first slogan, used at Machynlleth, was 'A Parliament for Wales Within Five Years'; we chose it in order to encourage the idea that a Parliament needed to be created as a matter of urgency. There had been no serious move in favour of self-government since the early days of Lloyd George and the *Cymru Fydd* movement at the end of the nineteenth century. The largest of the rallies was the one held at Sophia Gardens in Cardiff in 1953 when S.O. Davies, the Labour M.P. for Merthyr Tydfil, shared a platform with us, the only member of his party ever to do so. For three days a team of young men carrying a flame which had been lit at a ceremony near Glyndwr's Parliament House in Machynlleth, ran all the way to Cardiff, reaching the Sophia Gardens Pavilion when the rally was in mid-course. It was an exciting moment as the flame was borne through the huge crowd and up on to the platform. The runner was Emrys Roberts, at the time President of the Students' Union at the University College in Cardiff, who was later to make such a great contribution to the life of Wales and the work of Plaid Cymru, not least through his leadership of the Nationalists when the Party ran Merthyr Tydfil, the town of S.O. Davies, Keir Hardie, and Henry Richard.

Weak though the means of communication available to a small party may be in comparison with those at the disposal of the Government and the English mass-media, we left our mark on the Welsh consciousness. These effects were reinforced by the Campaign for a Welsh Parliament, which did some very valuable educative work. It was Plaid Cymru which planned the Campaign in the first instance, and did most of the work on its behalf. The Campaign was in fact an imitation of the Covenant Movement which, under the leadership of John McCormick, had collected some two million signatures in favour of a Parliament for Scotland. Since we shouldn't have had much support if the Party had launched the campaign, we worked through *Undeb Cymru Fydd*, the cultural movement. With the help of Dr Gwenan Jones and others, I managed to get its Council to take action without much difficulty. The secretary, T.I. Ellis, and most of the Council members, were in favour of the principle of a Parliament. A representative conference was called for Llandrindod, the one which Huw T. Edwards attacked in his pamphlet, *They Went to Llandrindod*; later on he experienced something of a conversion and joined Plaid Cymru. I went there as a speaker the day after coming out of Morriston Hospital, where I had been convalescing for several weeks after undergoing an operation. It was decided to launch a Campaign and a Committee was elected that included William George, Lloyd George's brother, who was held in great esteem throughout Wales. His son, the poet and solicitor W.R.P. George, was Vice-President of Plaid Cymru for three years. Another member of the Committee was Dafydd Jenkins, also a lawyer, who was to prove a tower of strength to the movement. He it was who, just before the outbreak of war, had organized the Welsh Language Petition. This Committee decided what kind of parliament we wanted and Megan Lloyd George was chosen as its President and Dafydd Miles its Secretary. Dafydd and his wife Charlotte, the sister of the actor Hugh Griffith, were to be in the thick of the national movement in the years that followed. The Party's Executive Committee used to meet at their home, Plas Hendre, in Aberystwyth.

One of the great difficulties Dafydd Miles faced was to get the Liberal M.Ps. to appear on the movement's platform. Although the Liberals pretended they were in favour of a Parliament for Wales, not one of their M.Ps. spoke even once. Isn't this so typical of the Welsh Liberals who haven't been seen to fight for anything this century? The great causes of Liberalism, if we are to go by reports in *The Carmarthen Journal* of Liberal speeches at Parliamentary Elections, were 'The Liberal Atmosphere', 'The Liberal Environment', 'Unity', and of course, 'Freedom' – they are as keen as the Tories on that score. The typical Liberal has been the 'I'm as good a Welshman as anybody' type, his Welshness a matter of mere sentiment, and he is content to pursue a pleasant career in local government or Parliament. They are men or women whose Welsh patriotism 'sits innocently in an armchair praising Wales as a locality and betraying it as a nation', as Pennar Davies has so memorably put it. They will never fight for Wales. They will fight for Britain but not for their own nation. I am speaking severely of the Welsh Liberals because many of them claim to be keen Welsh people. The Tories do not claim any such thing. The Tories have never pretended that Wales should live as a nation. They have objected to every progressive move. At least with them we know where we stand.

Five Labour M.Ps. spoke on behalf of the Parliament for Wales Campaign. S.O. Davies stood firm from the start and I believe it was due to his influence that the support of Tudor Watkins was enlisted. It was after a debate at the University College in Bangor between Cledwyn Hughes, the Labour M.P. for Anglesey, and me, that the other two were convinced. Cledwyn argued against a Parliament that night but it was obvious that his heart wasn't in what he had to say. After all, he had once been a member of Plaid Cymru and had believed that Anglesey would be the first constituency to fall to the Nationalists. Another former Secretary of State for Wales who used to be a member of Plaid Cymru was Peter Thomas, the Conservative. After the debate at Bangor I had a word with Cledwyn and persuaded him to lend his support to the campaign and to get Goronwy Roberts, the Labour M.P. for Caernarfon, who had also been a sort of Nationalist, to come in with him. That is what happened, and through them T.W. Jones, the third Labour M.P. from Gwynedd, also joined. When the Campaign came to an end, the five Labour M.Ps. were criticized by their own party and not a peep in favour of the cause was ever heard from four of them again. S.O. Davies was the only one to stand his ground. He put a Bill for a Welsh Parliament – drafted by Dewi Watkin Powell – before the Westminster Parliament in March 1955.

The means employed by the Parliament for Wales Campaign was to collect names on a petition. The work was quite feeble for about two years and the names came in very slowly. Dafydd Miles had to return to his post as a music teacher, but the situation was saved by Elwyn Roberts, Plaid Cymru's organizer in Gwynedd and its Financial Director, who was lent by the Party, as it were, for two years. As an organizer Elwyn was herculean in his efforts on behalf of the national movement. He proved his genius with Plaid Cymru and before that with *Undeb Cymru Fydd* and as Secretary of the National Eisteddfod in the years it was held at Llanrwst and Colwyn Bay. But his greatest triumph was in organizing the Parliament for Wales Campaign. He put new energy into every sector of the movement.

The Campaign's chief asset was doubtless its President, Megan Lloyd George. Wherever she went she drew a crowd. I spoke with her at a score of meetings – including those at Merthyr and Dowlais, Aberdare and Ystradgynlais, Rhondda and Caerphilly – and in every one the hall was full. But she was very difficult to nail down to any particular date, and this caused Elwyn headaches throughout the two years of the Campaign. It was nevertheless worth all the effort. It was on the Welsh Committee of the British Council that I first came to know Megan Lloyd George. She was its Chairman. I had become a member in order to try to help make Wales better-known abroad by ensuring that Welsh books and films were sent to the Council's libraries overseas and that Welsh lecturers and choirs visited other countries. A specific connection was established with the Welsh settlement in Patagonia. Megan had all her father's charm and quite a bit of his ability too, though little of his commitment and taste for hard work. Perhaps she was too fond of ballet and the theatre. At the outset of the Campaign she was the Liberal M.P. for Anglesey and Vice-President of her party. Once, when I was having dinner with her at Bro Awelon, her home in Cricieth, a young man called. He was shown in by the old maidservant who was responsible for Megan's conversational Welsh. The visitor was dressed like a dandy with a brightly coloured waistcoat and a large cravat. He came to the table, took Megan's hand and kissed it, saying, 'My Vice.' It was clear that he belonged to the faction of the Liberal Party represented by its Vice-President rather than to that of its President, Clement Davies. That was the first time for me to meet Jeremy Thorpe. Since Megan wasn't able to drive a car, a consequence of an accident in her youth, she relied on others to take her about. Her driver when she called once at Talar Wen was an Englishwoman. At the time my son Rhys was about two years old and my daughter Meinir seven. Rhys won Megan's heart immediately and it was evident that he liked her. Just as we were in the middle of a conversation in English, since her friend wasn't Welsh-speaking, Rhys waddled over to her with a sweet. Megan was delighted and was about to pop it into her mouth when Meinir rushed in and, summoning up her scant English, said breathlessly, 'Don't eat it. The dog's been lickin' it!'

I fought two Elections against Megan in Carmarthenshire but it had no effect on our relationship. She knew that I didn't have a hope of winning the seat. On another occasion when I was at table in Bro Awelon, Huw T. Edwards was among the guests. The first thing he did on sitting down was to recite two *englynion* which he had composed in her honour in the car on his way to Cricieth. Huw T. Edwards and Dai Francis were the last two trades union leaders with any Welsh culture, both of them Welshmen to the core, warm-hearted and genial men. I had many a kindness shown me by Dai Francis, and he made sure that the Miners' Union gave a lead in favour of a Parliament for Wales. It was he who was mainly respons-ible for establishing the Wales Trades Union Council, one of the most important developments of our time. As for Huw T. Edwards, he had been brought up in poverty at near Penmaenmawr. He suggests as much in an excellent *englyn* of his to Mynydd Tal-y-cafn:

> *Mynydd yr oerwynt miniog – a diddos*
> *Hen dyddyn y Fawnog,*
> *Lle'r oedd sglein ar bob ceiniog*
> *A 'nhaid o'r llaid yn dwyn llog.*

('Mountain of the keen wind, but snug the old cottage of Y Fawnog, where there was a shine on every penny and my grandfather wrested profit from the mire.')

For the latter part of his life Huw T. Edwards had a burning passion for Wales. He was for ten years Chairman of the Council for Wales, but resigned because the Government rejected all its recommendations. He became a political Nationalist and joined Plaid Cymru – an enormous step for someone who had been prominent in the Labour Party all his life. It's true that he left us a few years later, mainly I think because we didn't take much to his idea that a Parliament could be created merely by calling together representatives of the local councils, as we had done at the Lord Mayor's conferences in Cardiff. The two national conferences which he chaired made a profound impression on him. Despite the fact that he left our ranks, I am sure his heart was with us to the end of his days and the national movement continued to benefit from his wonderful generosity. Nobody knows, unless it was his friend Gwilym R. Jones, how much money he gave to maintain *Y Faner* when that national newspaper was in financial difficulties. We shall doubtless never see his like again.

It is not realized today just how many splendid men came into the Nationalist Party from the ranks of the Independent Labour Party. The following are some former members of the I.L.P. who joined Plaid Cymru: Abi Williams, at one time its President; the great poet T. Gwynn Jones and R.E. Holland, a Vice-President; Herbert Hughes, the distinguished headmaster of Dolwyddelan; Percy Ogwen Jones, editor of *Y Dinesydd* and father of Professor Bedwyr Lewis Jones; D.J. Davies, D.J. Williams, and Waldo Williams and his mother. These belonged to the Labour Party in its heroic phase. I came to know it at the time of its decay. The I.L.P had been the party of Keir Hardie and a very different one from that of Beatrice and Sidney Webb who had spawned the centralist policies with which I was familiar. Labour had become the party of the British State, the party of bureaucracy, the party of centralization, the party of the atomic bomb.

Another former member of the I.L.P. to join Plaid Cymru was Dan Thomas, who served as the Party's Treasurer for twenty-one years, and who became my father-in-law. He began his career as a fifteen-year-old clerk at George M.Ll. Davies's bank in Wrexham. When George decided to join the Territorials in 1910 he persuaded Dan Thomas to enlist with him. For two years George was a Captain in the Royal Welsh Fusiliers; it was he, of all people, who represented his regiment at the investiture of George, Prince of Wales, in Caernarfon. Within two years he had been converted to pacifism and had bought himself out of the army. He did his utmost to get Dan Thomas out too but the latter insisted on staying and the consequence was that he was among the first to be sent to France in 1914. A brother-in-law of his, by the way, was Richard Roberts, the first Secretary of the Fellowship of Reconciliation. George Davies was its first Assistant Secretary. After suffering frost-bite of the legs in the trenches, Captain Dan Thomas returned to Wales in 1916 as a recruiting-officer for North Wales with an office in Wrexham. One of his first sad duties was to arrest George Davies as a conscientious objector; the latter spent most of the remaining two years of the war in Dartmoor and other prisons. When the war ended Dan Thomas resumed his work at the bank and was appointed to the headquarters of Martins Bank in Liverpool. He threw himself into the work of the Labour Party, addressing many open-air meetings. He was a most powerful speaker, and as a native of Llannerch-y-medd, he had all the public speaking talents of an Anglesey man. I heard him more than once being called upon to take a chapel service, completely without warning, and we would always have an eloquent sermon from him that lasted half an hour. He usually spoke impromptu, relying on the inspiration of the moment, for he found it hard to put anything down on paper. The Labour Party thought enough of him to invite him to stand as a Parliamentary candidate, but he refused, choosing rather to immerse himself in the work of forming the National Union of Bank Employees, as it was then called. There are plenty of stories about that chapter of his life, such as the one about his walking back and fore outside the Martins Bank head offices carrying placards on his back and chest, while the directors met inside. He was then summoned to appear before them and threatened with the sack. He didn't give in and in the end, in 1937, they appointed him manager of their first branch in Cardiff, where he was to make the first loan to Julian Hodge, thus setting him on the road to success as a banker. For three years in succession Dan Thomas was President of the Union and he served it right into his old age. Among those who often stayed with the Thomas family in Liverpool was Ambrose Bebb, the writer. It was he who convinced Dewi Prys Thomas, Dan's son, and Rhiannon, his daughter, that their place was with Plaid Cymru. This means that my wife Rhiannon was a member of the Party before me. Soon afterwards they were followed into the Nationalist fold by Dan Thomas himself.

To return to the Parliament for Wales Campaign, it had collected by the end nearly a quarter of a million signatures to a petition that was addressed to the House of Commons. Goronwy Roberts presented it with a very few words and then it was put in a bag at the back of the Speaker's chair. Anticlimax though this was, the campaign had caused many thousands to think about Wales as a nation and awakened in many others the conviction that it should be

self-governing. Its effect was to be seen at the General Election of
1955. Plaid Cymru decided to contest twelve seats, but six weeks
before polling-day we had found only seven candidates. Finding
people who were willing to stand was a huge problem and I had to
scour the country in search of them. In the end we had eleven. I found
the eleventh, the candidate for Anglesey, at the funeral of Ambrose
Bebb. A short while after the Election this good man disappeared
and was never seen or heard from again. The Party received 45,000
votes, and it was said as usual that we had failed drastically and that
it was the end for us. Many of our own members believed this, too.
The truth is that it was an excellent result: an average of 4,000 votes
in eleven constituencies; the Communists and Independent candidates usually received three or four hundred. Despite its numerical
weakness, the Party had been proving for some time that it was
growing into an electoral force. In Merioneth we received a quarter
of the votes, by far the highest percentage we had ever won anywhere.
With the campaign for saving Cwm Tryweryn exercising the country
in the years that followed, we would be able to fight there in future
with hope of winning the seat.

The argument we often had to face was that Wales was too poor
to be self-governing. In vain we pointed to the success of small
countries that were far poorer than Wales. People just didn't listen
to our claim that human resources are more important than natural
resources; moreover, it also had to be proved that Wales, even as it
was, could pay its way. I went to see Arthur Beacham, the Professor
of Economics at the University College at Aberystwyth, with whom
I had been an undergraduate, to ask him to prepare a Welsh budget.
After labouring over it for several months, he found the task too
much for him, but he eventually came up with a few thousand
pounds to pay for a small group of research students to set to work
under the supervision of Edward Nevin. The outcome was the
document *Social Accounts of the Welsh Economy*, a pioneering work
the like of which had never been done before. It showed that Wales
would be able to pay its way if only a sensible sum were to be
allocated for expenditure on arms and the national debt – a debt
that had been created mainly by wars which we believed ought to
have been rejected by Wales as they had been in Ireland. Our
political opponents had real difficulty in arguing, as Jim Griffiths
tried to do in a radio programme in which he and I took part, that
Wales couldn't afford to govern itself. I did my best to persuade
Edward Nevin to serve as our economic adviser but he resolutely
refused, not for any economic reasons but because he just didn't
believe, he said, in Nationalism. Yet in a debate with him on the

subject of self-government that had been arranged in the Brangwyn
Hall by the Swansea Chamber of Commerce, Nevin dismissed those
who believed Wales couldn't afford self-government. In our opinion
the country couldn't afford to be without it. Without a government
we were unable to develop our economy, but because the people of
Wales were not persuaded of this they had to go on suffering under
the highly centralized British system.

We went into the General Election of 1959 with quite high hopes
and contesting twenty seats. One sign of growth was that, despite
such an increase in the number of our candidates, we had the human
and financial resources to fight twenty seats. In Merioneth new
members joined the ranks of old stalwarts who had borne the burden
and heat of the day; among them were a number of splendid head-
masters – W.D. Williams of Barmouth, Ellis D. Jones of
Glyndyfrdwy, R.T. Simon of Arthog, Meirion Jones of Bala, and
D.J. Williams of Llanbedr; the last named was the author and editor
of more than sixty Welsh books for children, including the series
Chwedl a Chân. Ivor Owen of Llanuwchllyn and Gwenfron Hughes
of Dolgellau are in this tradition, as were Beryl Jones the *Urdd*
organizer, and H.R. Jones, the manager of the Meirion Creamery at
the time, David Evans the coal-merchant, and Wmffra Jones the
station-master of Llyn Penmaen. These people stood firm as a rock.
Mrs Eames, Marion Eames's mother, would feed me on chocolate
biscuits, and every time I went to Llanrafon, Mrs Jones of Braich-du
would make me a flask of hot coffee. I was also pampered by the fine
family at Glyn Dairy in Blaenau Ffestiniog. The Plaid Cymru candidate in Merioneth was always spoilt! I had some lovely experiences
there, as well as some less pleasant ones. As I was coming back late
one night from Blaenau Ffestiniog, after having supper with the two
faithful sisters Annie and Leah Roberts, I spotted in my headlights
on my approach to the Trawsfynydd military camp, one of its
vehicles which had overturned at the side of the road. The dead body
of a girl lay in front of it, her head split in two by the vehicle's
windscreen. There was no sign of the driver. She was a girl from
Blaenau who had spent the evening at a pub with one of the officers
from the camp. This man had told one of the privates, against all the
rules, to drive her home. Not a word about the incident ever appeared in *The Liverpool Daily Post*, nor anywhere else for that
matter. It was very important, at a time when the Trawsfynydd
military camp was unpopular in the eyes of many, for the authorities
to suppress all mention of the incident.

Among those who came to help us in Merioneth was Hywel
Hughes of Bogota – a buccaneer of a man, well-built but bandy-

legged, with one eye missing, a keen Nationalist who had made his fortune in Colombia, where he had built up an estate by dint of his forthright character and the strength of his arm. The two words he most often used were 'honour' and 'courtesy'. He spoke Spanish in Columbia but in Wales he insisted on speaking Welsh wherever he went. When we sat down to dinner at the Golden Lion in Dolgellau, the waiter came with the menu, which was in English and French, and asked in English what we would have to eat. Hywel immediately took against him on this score. Where was the man's courtesy in speaking to us in English in Dolgellau, of all places? When the man answered back just as forthrightly, Hywel walked out of the hotel. Unfortunately, the waiter was an active member of the Labour Party and in the days that followed the story of my anglophobia was spread throughout the county.

The Election of that year was a bitter one. One of the Labour Party's dirty tricks was to arrange for personal questions to be asked about me at all Plaid Cymru meetings – they weren't put to me directly but to other speakers when I wasn't on the platform. There was a small element of truth in every story that was put about, or at least enough to make it credible. It was done in such a systematic way that even some of my own supporters began to think the stories might be true. For example, why did I employ only Italians on my nine farms? I had never owned a single farm, although I had lived in a farmhouse where an Italian prisoner of war had for a while been employed by my father. Again, why had I had English people to build my new house? True, I had a new house, but everything that went into the making of Talar Wen had been bought in Wales – the roof-slates from Caernarfonshire, the bricks from Cynghordy, the window-frames from Newport, the glass from Swansea, the slate stairs from the hills of Berwyn, the wood from Barry, and so on; and members of Plaid Cymru from Abercwmboi in the Cynon Valley had been the builders. Talar Wen was a generous wedding-gift from my father, postponed for fifteen years. The gift was my father's but the house's beauty had been created by my brother-in-law, Dewi Prys Thomas, for it was he who designed it. It added a gracious note to our family life, but at the same time gave the impression that I was a wealthy man. Another question that was asked was why did I send my children to school in England? I did have children, seven of them in fact, but not one went to school further afield than Llandovery. So why did my wife buy all her clothes in Paris? I had a wife, and she dressed smartly, with immaculate good taste, but Rhiannon never bought so much as a handkerchief in Paris. In fact, she had never been there at that time. Wynne Samuel later discovered that these questions had been drafted and duplicated at Transport House in Cardiff, the headquarters of the Labour Party in Wales, and distributed from there to the Labourites of Merioneth. Ten were collected by Valerie Wynne Williams, who spent a week in the constituency working for the Party, and in due course she published an article about them in the magazine *Wales*.

Valerie later stood twice as a Plaid Cymru candidate in Barry, one of the select band of women who have been Party candidates – Gwenan Jones, Jennie Eirian Davies, Margaret Roberts, Phyllis Cox, Siân Edwards, and Jan Power who later changed her name to Siân Meredydd. Winnie Ewing, a leader of the Scottish National Party, often used to chivvy me about the dearth of women candidates in Plaid Cymru, for did not the Scots have a dozen of them? The fact is that very few women chose to put themselves forward in Plaid Cymru's political work. Nans Jones gave a lifetime's service to Plaid Cymru in the head office where Gwerfyl Arthur is today a most effective assistant to the Party's Secretary, Dafydd Williams. It is surprising how few women have been in the vanguard of the Party nationally, though many have worked valiantly at a local level. Nevertheless, women have always made up a large part of the Party's strength. As it happens, the workers of the Llangadog branch are all women. There is a new mood among the younger generation and the Party has recently decided that half the membership of its Executive Committee and Council must be women.

We had no warmer welcome anywhere in Merioneth than at Abergeirw, which was a veritable nest of Nationalists. It was they who had the privilege of arranging the last meeting of the evening in a series held every night in the run-up to polling-day. It might be ten o'clock before I arrived, but we always sat down to a meal before making our way home. For that reason it would be midnight before I left the school at Abergeirw. On one particular night I was intending to go as far as Ganllwyd, where I was staying, only about five or six miles away as the crow flies, but twenty if you go by road through Dolgellau. I decided to try the most direct route, hoping to find the bridge over the river Mawddach. So I followed the telephone wires in the hope that they led in that direction. After about two miles the road went through a dark forest. The metalled road and the forest and the telephone wires came to a stop at a gate across the road. Daft as I was, I went on along a narrow mountain track in search of a place to turn, but there was no such place to be found. The off-side wheels of the car slipped six inches over the edge into the heather of the mountainside, and there I had to leave it since I had no hope of being able to haul it back on my own. I walked back through the pitch-dark forest. On coming out, I saw to my surprise a light on the other side of the valley. I made straight for it and came to a smallholding. It was by now two o'clock in the morning. I knocked at the door. Presently, but only after I'd convinced her as to who I was, it was slowly opened by a tidy little woman dressed in sacking from head to toe. One sack made a high peak on her head. I explained what had happened and asked whether I might spend the night in an armchair under her roof. The woman went back into the kitchen and again she was a while before she reappeared. She then asked me to come in. The kitchen was in a terrible state and there was a lot of mess on the floor. In a chair by the fire sat another woman, older than the first, and she too was dressed in sackcloth. During a conversation with these two ladies I learned that, in their younger days, they had worked at Blaen-cwm in Cynllwyd, the home of Mrs Dan Thomas. They wouldn't hear of my spending the night in a chair: a bed had to be prepared. The younger of the two then disappeared upstairs. She was there a long time. Presently she came down to show me to my room, each of us carrying a candle. There, hard against the wall, stood a feather-bed; I had never seen one before outside the National Museum. After undressing, I climbed into it and sank luxuriously into its feathery depths. I slept soundly for hours, and breakfasted on two fresh eggs and bread-and-butter made by my two guardian-angels. It was ten o'clock before I was up and seeking the help of the men from the Forestry. They were very willing to transport me to the car in a tractor and haul it back on to the road and set me on my way in the direction of the bridge over the Mawddach. But alas, by midday the rumour had run all over the county that I had spent the previous night in the company of two old maids!

My mention of the river Mawddach brings to mind a nasty turn I once had in the river Twrch near Llanuwchllyn. It was a night of great storm and I was due to give a lecture on Michael D. Jones, the patriot and founder of the Welsh settlement in Patagonia, at the Old Chapel. Having gone through Llanuwchllyn from the Dolgellau side, I took the first turning to the left instead of the second. After about a mile I could see the Old Chapel on the other side of Twrch with no bridge to cross over to it. Again I tried to turn the car on the narrow road and again it went over the edge, this time into a ditch. The meeting was due to start and if I had had to walk the two miles to the Old Chapel by road, I should have been half an hour late. Having no raincoat, and with the rain now bucketing down, I decided to make a dash for the chapel across two fields and through the Twrch. Several of the brethren were standing in the porch when a dripping spectre was washed in by the storm. Although it was past the hour for the meeting to begin and a packed chapel was awaiting me, a very kind man insisted on driving me to his home in the village to dry my hair and put me into a set of dry clothes. The lecturer stood before his audience at the Old Chapel that evening in a beautiful suit that hung on him as on a scarecrow, and with a collar that was two inches too wide.

I added very little to the sum of Plaid Cymru's vote in Merioneth in 1959, during an election campaign that was the most bitterly disappointing of all. This result contributed, together with the battle for Tryweryn, to the ructions within Plaid Cymru in the years that immediately followed. There was also a good deal of committee work, and several conferences, which weighed upon me sorely. Up to the mid-'sixties I chaired every Executive Committe and every Annual Conference without missing a single one. In due course I removed my candidature to Carmarthenshire and was followed in Merioneth by Elystan Morgan.

Chapter 17

A Nationalist Abroad

It wasn't only in Wales and the other countries of Britain that I took trips at this time. In 1958 Hywel Hughes paid for me to spread Plaid Cymru's message among the American Welsh. It was a seven-week trip, from the beginning of November to three days before Christmas. I was also taken to Toronto and Windsor in Canada as well as to towns in twenty-seven of the United States. Every day was largely taken up with travelling (almost entirely by aeroplane), with meetings of various kinds, and with interviews for the mass media. Owing to the kindness of some of Leopold Kohr's friends, I had an appointment at the International Press Club in New York, where I also took part in my first American television show. I was driven there by a dignified black man in a stretch-limousine that seemed to be twenty feet long. The programme was broadcast 'coast to coast' and was seen by twenty million people. I did a total of forty radio and television programmes during this trip, and had the experience of seeing colour television for the first time. The trip had been organized with his usual flair by Elwyn Roberts; his chief assistants in America were Colin Edwards in San Francisco, who put in some tremendous work, Glyn Lloyd Roberts in Washington, a former member of the British Diplomatic Corps and the brother of Hywel Heulyn Roberts, and in Detroit, J.R. Owen, a Nonconformist minister.

I went to America by boat. When it drew alongside the quay a gang of pressmen came on board to take pictures and do interviews with a good-looking actress. I thought she might have been Marilyn Monroe but when I asked one of the photographers, he replied, 'Oh no, just a bit of cheesecake'. I was welcomed on the quay by some friends of Wales – two of the children in Welsh costume singing Welsh songs to harp accompaniment, although their parents were from Yorkshire. There was already an interest in folk-singing in America by this time. There too were Colin Edwards and his wife, a Chinese woman of Manchu family. Her great-grandmother, Colin told me, had been

Empress of China. The photographers took a picture of me pinning a Plaid Cymru badge on her coat – the only member of a Manchu family, as far as I know, ever to join Plaid Cymru! She remained a Party member and Colin went on working for Wales on the other side of the Atlantic. His book about Yehudi Menuhin's father is to be publshed this year.

One of my three days in New York was spent in the United Nations building and part of it in the radio section where Colin Edwards, a professional broadcaster, was working for a year. Colin had been for a while in Vietnam, and other eastern countries, as a reporter for the Australian Broadcasting Corporation. We arranged with the head of radio to broadcast some programmes in Welsh on international affairs directly from the UN to Wales. But when I returned at the end of the trip we were given to understand that this was impossible since Wales had no government of its own. They were broadcasting to Iceland but they couldn't broadcast to Wales. I happened to be at a meeting of the UN when fourteen countries became new members. The delegates sat in alphabetical order, with India next to Iceland; Krishna Menon spoke on behalf of India that day. Wales, if it had been represented, would have been placed between Venezuela and the Yemen.

One of the people from whom I received great kindness during my trip to America was Thomas Llyfnwy Thomas, who was among the best-known singers in the States at that time. He came from a cultured family of Nationalists in Maesteg and it was therefore no surprise that his Welsh was as melodious as his singing voice. He looked after me for a whole day and in the evening took me to see a production of *My Fair Lady* in which his brother was singing. After the show we had supper with the cast.

I visited, of course, some of the towns of Pennsylvania where names like Bala, Cynwyd, and Corwen remind us of the Welsh Tract that Marion Eames writes about in *Rhandir Mwyn*, a fine novel that has been translated as *Fair Wilderness*. At Bangor, a coalmining town in that state, I presented the mayor with greetings, on parchment, from the Mayor of Bangor in Gwynedd.

By this time I could see how true was the description of the American Welsh given me by friends back home in Wales who had warned me that the trip would be a waste of time. With just a dozen or so exceptions, their Welshness was wholly a matter of sentiment. For them Wales didn't exist as a nation struggling for its life. Nor, moreover, do these people lift a finger, despite the great wealth that many possess, to help the national cause. One of the exceptions is Dr A.L. Roberts – Arturo de Robert when I first knew him; he used to come to see me regularly when visiting Europe. Arturo is a Welsh-speaker from the Welsh settlement in Patagonia, the great-grandson of the great patriot Michael D. Jones who was the colony's founder. He had bought the house known as Bod Iwan in Bala, his grandfather's old home, and hoped to make it into an American Welsh museum that would reflect the history of the settlement and that of the Welsh in North America. He was the founder and editor of *Ninnau*, an excellent monthly newspaper which competes among the American Welsh with the ancient journal, *Y Drych*. Arturo is warmly disposed towards Wales and Plaid Cymru.

Despite the fact that the majority of the American Welsh have an image of Wales that belongs to the nineteenth century, in one respect at least the friends who urged me not to go to America were wrong: they believed that no one would give me a hearing and that, if I went, my audiences would be small and unfriendly. But I had large meetings throughout the trip and whenever I was given time to put my case, the response was often enthusiastic. I felt at the time that if only I could have the chance to go again, in order to water the seeds I had sown, we would reap a good and perhaps an abundant harvest. But Glyn Roberts insisted that I wasn't to go around like a beggar asking for money and therefore no financial appeal was made at any stage. Nevertheless, some three thousand dollars were collected without anyone's asking for it. At a dinner of the New York St. David's Society, some of the wealthy members came together afterwards to discuss ways of helping Plaid Cymru, but though I took my leave of them with some hope, nothing came of it.

It was in New York that I had my first experience of Welsh women's societies, of which I was to see a lot later. Wasn't it the Daughters of the American Revolution who had placed a plaque on the beach in Florida to mark the spot where Madog is supposed to have landed in the twelfth century? The yarn about Madog came in very handy, particularly the true story of John Evans, the Welsh Methodist, about whom Gwyn A. Williams has written so memorably in his book, *Madoc, the Making of a Myth*: John Evans of Waun-fawr, in the eighteenth century, went as far as the Canadian border in his search for the Welsh-speaking Indians. At one of the meetings I addressed in New York a woman got up, after I had spoken, to say how proud she was of her Welsh ancestry. She had been born in the Welsh Tract of Pennsylvania where her forefathers had settled three centuries before. Her maiden name was Williams but she was now Mrs Rockefeller. She arranged for me to meet her husband in the hope of getting some financial help for Plaid Cymru, but when I went to see him at his office on the top floor of the Empire

State Building, I had no response. The top floor, I remember, was reached by an express lift to the fiftieth floor and then a local lift up the remaining thirty.

That wasn't the only disappointment I had from an American millionaire. A friend of mine had been to see Captain Potato Jones on my behalf. He was an interesting character, a Welshman who had taken cargoes of potatoes through Franco's blockade in an attempt to feed the population of northern Spain, which was still under the control of the Republican Government, during the Civil War of 1936-39. According to reports I had received, Potato Jones – a millionaire several times over – was sympathetic to Welsh National-ism and anxious to help. He had agreed to see me when I was in his part of the country. But three days before I was due to arrive, he died. There was no shortage of American millionaires who were of Welsh descent. Some were still running the steel industry and others were at the head of the largest corporations such as Westinghouse and Kodak. I visited several of the steel towns, including Bethlehem, which has its counterpart in the village of the same name in Dyffryn Ceidrych, not far from Llangadog. I attended a dinner given by a Welsh Women's Society, one of two meetings I had in Bethlehem. Fair play to these good ladies, they had prepared a Welsh meal in my honour – faggots and peas. The Society's President, who was sitting next to me, a woman of entirely English background except that she had a Welsh husband, told me they had prepared the meal the night before: they had mixed apples with the meat because, she explained, 'They don't come back on you so.'

In Toronto there was a foot of snow on the ground. A pair of rubber shoes were bought for me by David Davies who hailed from Tregaron. I flew from there to Windsor, which is on the border between Canada and Detroit, where I had a large and enthusiastic meeting, as I had in Toronto. I was taken by car from Windsor to Detroit, through the toll-gates on the bridge. When the car stopped, the officer didn't want to look at my travel visa or my luggage. After the driver had explained who I was, he said, 'What? Another bloody Welshman! Go on!' We went on to Fort Wayne, a place named after General Wayne, another Welshman from Tregaron, according to Bob Owen, and one of the fourteen Welsh generals who fought on the American side in the War of Independence. I stayed in Detroit with J.R. Owen, with whom I had once been at a St. David's Day dinner given by the Coventry Welsh Society when he was a minister in that city. The man who made the deepest impression on me in Detroit was a relative of Dr Tudur Jones who worked for the Ford motor-company. He drove a huge car with buttons to open the windows, switch the radio on, and so forth – wonders that I had never seen before. He spoke robust Welsh. He took me to see a friend in Lansing, the Governor of Michigan, who had just been elected for the sixth time. There I glimpsed an aspect of American democracy that appealed to me greatly. On reaching the Governor's house, my friend knocked on the door and walked in with a shout of 'Williams!'. The Governor came down from upstairs in his shirt-sleeves and bade us a warm welcome. I was ceremoniously made a member of the Soapy Williams Club – for that's how he was known, not because he was in the habit of using soft soap on anyone but on account of his father's having made a fortune by selling the stuff. He gave me the Club's membership badge, namely a bow-tie with white spots that I have never been bold enough to wear. Soapy swanked a lot about his Welsh ancestry. Towards the end of the 'sixties there was talk of his standing for the Presidency but nothing came of it. Another politician of Welsh descent was the Senator from Arizona who put me up at Phoenix in that state.

I hadn't imagined how big the United States was before going there. Although I knew about the three thousand miles from one coast to the other, it was the change in climate between one zone and the next that brought it home to me. We went from the heat of Arizona to the freezing cold of Utica, where the snow lay thick all about us, and from there to Washington, where the temperature was in the seventies. It was cold in Salt Lake City and hot in Los Angeles. I stayed with Welsh Mormon families in both places. In summery San Francisco I was put up with an old cultivated carpenter from Caernarfonshire, his Welsh still as fluent as it was when, half a century before, he had lived in poverty on the banks of Menai. His wife was a fine-looking woman of mixed race, and everything in their home was beautiful – the furniture, the curtains, and the pictures, the colourful bushes in the garden, and the red and yellow fruit on the heavily laden branches in the sunshine of early December. And yet in the midst of this paradise I could see that my visit was making the old boy nostalgic for Wales. As I left, he put a generous donation to Plaid Cymru in my hand.

Washington proved to be one of the most fascinating of all the places I visited. There the arrangements were in the hands of Glyn Lloyd Roberts. A large crowd, some of them from Baltimore, came to the public meeting and they contributed three hundred dollars to the collection without my saying a word about money. At one point a man wearing American Army uniform got to his feet in the front row to offer me his keen support; he was one of Leopold Kohr's friends. Next morning, Hubert Humphrey arranged for me to call on President Eisenhower at eleven o'clock, but when I arrived at the White House I wasn't allowed to see him because the British Ambassador, De Caccia, had witheld his permission at the last moment. Part of the protocol for foreign visitors calling on the President is that their country's Ambassador has to approve the visit. This was refused by De Caccia because I was a Welsh Nationalist. I was shown around the White House, but that was all. The Welsh of Washington were very angry when they heard about this let-down: they felt it to be a snub on Wales and on them. A protest meeting was held that evening and about two hundred of them gathered at the fine mansion that was the home of St. John Lewis, the Attorney General in the American Government. Back home in Wales next day, the story was given a prominent place on the front page of the *Western Mail*. I don't know how many people have been given the freedom of Washington, but I was, at a small ceremony in the Mayor's parlour where I was presented with a scroll and a large brass key in a leather case, with my name inscribed on it. Other cities followed suit – Chicago and Scranton – so I am a freeman of three American cities! Scranton was the last city to be run by the Welsh: a Welshman used to hold every post of any importance in the town, including that of fire brigade boss. The situation had been much the same in Wilkes Barre, a few miles away, but at the time of my visit the place was being run by Italians. Nevertheless, some of the top jobs had remained in Welsh hands. I enjoyed the company of the editor of Wilkes Barre's daily newspaper, a man who rejoiced in the name of Brychan Brycheiniog Powell.

In Indianapolis I met the editor of *Y Drych*, an old friend who was working hard to preserve that paper as a link between the Welsh of America. I must say it was an extremely poor publication at that time, a piece of Victoriana in both appearance and content, reflecting the Welsh attitudes of a century ago that are so typical of the American Welsh. This newspaper, which has been modernized since, was the sole survivor of the sixty Welsh journals which, according to Bob Owen, had been published in the United States in the nineteenth century; by that time the only Welsh-language thing about it was its name, meaning 'The Mirror'.

The most prominent Welshman in the United States in those days was undoubtedly John L. Lewis, the greatest miners' leader that America has ever seen. Despite the ferocity of his bushy eyebrows and his grimace, he was a wonderfully gentle man. He was terribly kind to me: besides finding time to talk at his office in Philadelphia, he went out of his way to organize a television programme for just the two of us. He said something on this programme that I can't imagine the current trades union leaders of Wales ever saying, now that Huw T. Edwards and Dai Francis are no longer with us. 'If I were your age and in Wales,' he said, 'I would be with you in this job.' At the time of my visit, the Welsh Society of Philadelphia was about to celebrate its two hundred and fiftieth anniversary; it had the distinction of being the first Welsh Society in the United States to hold a St. David's Day dinner, as long ago as 1729.

The ambience in the universities was quite different from that at the headquarters of the Miners' Union. I spoke at several of them, including Michigan and Berkeley, and at Harvard I addressed an audience hundreds strong at the famous Law School. There I enjoyed the hospitality of Meredydd Evans, who had a Chair of Philosophy at Boston at the time. He arranged an interview with *The Christian Science Monitor* for me, and I wasn't to have a more favourable write-up anywhere in America than the half-page devoted to my visit in that worthy paper. I stayed in Boston with Merêd and his wife Phyllis, who is American by birth. On the Saturday the annual football game was taking place between Harvard and Yale. Although Merêd had managed to acquire tickets, I couldn't go to the game, unfortunately, because I had to appear on television. So my host also decided to give the game a miss, in order to keep me company. During one of the broadcasts, while I was going on with some eloquence about the Eisteddfod, there was a sudden break for an advertisement about Aspirin! Although I missed the game, I did make it to a concert given by the male voice choirs of Harvard and Yale, who sang as one chorale that sounded as superb as it looked. To my great surprise, the programme included three Welsh items – 'The Men of Harlech', '*Ymdaith y Mynach*', and '*Y Ferch o'r Scer*'. Alas, I am unable to claim that these songs were sung in my honour. The explanation was that Merêd had encouraged Elliot Forbes, the conductor of the Harvard choir, to take an interest in Welsh folk-songs. He had been coming to Bangor for several years as Visiting Professor of Music, staying with William Mathias. Forbes, by the way, was a great-grandson of Ralph Waldo Emerson. After the concert we went to a party at his home and Emerson's old piano was there. It was a very lively party and Merêd was its life and soul. One of the guests was George Bundy, who was a leading member of the Kennedy administration. Despite not taking to our beds until the small hours, Merêd and Phyllis got up at five o'clock because I had to catch a 'plane to the other side of the continent. My visit to the United States didn't have much lasting effect on anybody, as far as I could tell. But it did result in the formation of three short-lived branches of a little movement formed by Colin Edwards – the Committe to Aid in the Defence of Wales (CADW Cymru).

My next visit to the United States was only of a fortnight's duration and much lighter; I travelled in April, accompanied by my wife Rhiannon. We took a direct flight to San Francisco, and since the 'plane was prevented by a snow-storm from landing at Chicago, the journey was a very long one. But there were about forty people, some of them women in Welsh costume, waiting to welcome us at the airport in San Francisco. It was Colin Edwards who once again had arranged all this, plus two hours on the radio, one of them on the station for which he worked, which relies on financial contributions from its listeners. I delivered a lecture at a large hotel that had been built from wood on a rock facing the Pacific, some two hundred miles to the north of San Francisco, a marvellous place that had been designed by a friend of Leopold Kohr's as a kind of academic tavern – one of Leopold's many ideas.

In Los Angeles we were put up in the city's most luxurious hotel through the generosity of Terry James, the hirsute musician from Cydweli who was working in Hollywood. It must have cost him a small fortune. He had lived in this place for years before moving into his own home in Beverley Hills. From there we flew to Washington to stay with Edgar Berman, another great friend of Leopold Kohr's. Berman, who had been Professor of Medicine at John Hopkin University, was a most distinguished man. He had been mainly responsible for the first heart-transplant operations and for many years he'd been consultant and personal physician to Hubert Humphrey, a leader of the Democratic Party. I was to have had dinner with Humphrey but on the very day of our appointment there occurred a great crisis in his career. He had to decide whether or not to stand for the Presidency of the United States. He decided that he would not, and not long afterwards he died. Humphrey was of Welsh descent: his great grandfather had been a ship's captain sailing out of Aberystwyth. I also spoke at John Hopkin and at four other Universities, including Loyola. I addressed the Welsh Societies of Los Angeles, Washington, Bethlehem, and Philadelphia, but the Societies of New York and San Francisco refused to extend me an official welcome, although they had done so in 1958. A good number of their members entertained me at informal dinners, among them several wealthy people who promised to help Plaid Cymru but never did.

A number of Welsh politicians have visited the United States since I was there in 1958, warning the people against Plaid Cymru and hardening their attitudes towards the Party. One of these was Ivor Richard, the British Ambassador to the United Nations at that time;

he later became Britain's Commissioner in Brussels, where he followed another great Welshman, Roy Jenkins. Like Merlin Rees, Ivor Richard, who hails from Ammanford, was one of those who called me a Fascist when I first went to Westminster. Nevertheless, he came to the party given by Frank Riccardi, another of Leopold Kohr's millionaire friends, and took me aback when he told me that he was now in favour of a federal government for Wales. The Irish had no prejudice against Welsh Nationalism; on the contrary, Paul O'Dwyer, the Mayor of New York, gave me an official reception. I also spoke at a pan-Celtic conference organized by Liam Murphy. But the most extraordinary honour that came my way in America was an invitation to speak as one of two guests at an Irish dinner in the Armoury of New York where three thousand were seated at table, including Members of the Senate and Congress, Judges and Governors. The other guest speaker was Sean McBride, who had just received the Nobel Peace Prize. In New York I also did a jolly chat show in which three of us talked from midnight until two in the morning. The programme was brought to a conclusion with a lovely Welsh folk-song sung by Maldwyn Pate, a member of the first Welsh rock-group known as *Y Blew*, who was then a professional dancer in the city; he later returned to Wales as an arts administrator.

But by far the most interesting trip I ever took wasn't to America, but to Cambodia, although it had originally been planned as a visit to North Vietnam. This was in 1967, when the bombing of Hanoi was at its worst pitch in the United States' imperialistic war against North Vietnam. One of the wonders of our century is the way in which a small agricultural nation eventually triumphed over the most powerful and richest country the world has ever known, and did so after earlier beating France and Britain in protracted wars. The victory of the Vietnamese people was in the first instance a spiritual one. They faced atrocious bombing from the air by a power that had also dropped nuclear bombs on Hiroshima and Nagasaki. The country's forests and crops were destroyed over many thousands of square miles. Tens of thousands of children and other innocent people were killed by napalm bombs that were dropped by the huge aeroplanes that ruled the skies. The epicentre of the bombing was Hanoi, the capital of North Vietnam. People throughout the world protested against the terrorism of America and its allies, but all in vain. What could we do to draw attention to this great infamy and to shame America into desisting? In their helplessness, a small group of English people, for the most part, decided on a quixotic scheme: they would go to Hanoi and stand under the bombs. The group included two Welshmen – Ifan Wyn Evans, a minister with the

Independents in Cwm-gors, who had walked on a peace-pilgrimage all the way to Moscow, and the Nonconformist rural bourgeois who wrote this book. My significance lay in my status as a Member of the Westminster Parliament. The group's leader was Michael Scott, who had proved his heroism in South Africa in his fight against apartheid, and in other countries too. I had first come across him after our sit-downs at Trawsfynydd. He later came to lecture at Plaid Cymru's Summer School in Merthyr Tydfil, staying with us at Talar Wen. He arrived in Merthyr an anti-Nationalist, but left a convinced supporter of Plaid Cymru.

The group had a long wait for a visa to Hanoi. After about three months news came, through the North Vietnamese Consul in London, that only three would be given visas, namely Michael Scott, a Catholic woman named Hastings, and myself, and that they would be handed to us in Pnom Penh in Cambodia. If the rest of the group wished to go to Cambodia in the hope of being granted visas there, they were free to do so. They decided that they would come with us. We caught a flight from Gatwick, touching down for a few hours at Istanbul and Karachi, the only time I have been on Turkish and Pakistani soil. In Karachi there were a lot of soldiers and military vehicles about the place. Between the two cities, we crossed Iran which looked from the air like one endless, mountainous desert, so different from the city that was to be our destination. Pnom Penh is the most beautiful city I have ever seen; it was built by the French, with wide leafy boulevards running down to the banks of the river Mekong. The centre was very busy with crowds of noisy people selling their vegetables and fruit and all kinds of goods in the open air. It was a happy city, with the yellow robes of thousands of Buddhist monks weaving through the crowds on every hand. The reason why the country's birth rate is so low is that many of the men become monks and are therefore celibate. Back home in Wales, my family smiled at the photographs I had taken during my trip because there were only yellow-robed monks to be seen, or so they said. Almost all were later killed by the Khmer Rouge. There are only about a thousand left in Campuchea, as the country is known today. The Khmer drove the inhabitants of Pnom Penh, a couple of million of them, out of the city into the open countryside. Three million of the country's seven million inhabitants were slaughtered. The disturbances which led to these massacres began during the mid-'sixties, when chaos was caused throughout Indo-China by the aggression of the United States, the Soviet Union, and China. At the time of my visit to Cambodia the Government in London was expecting the USA to attack that country any day from Thailand, where it had been mustering its forces. I was asked by

Harold Wilson, the British Prime Minister, to write a report on the situation on my return. I did so and gave it to William Rogers, a Minister at the Foreign Office who later became one of the Gang of Four, the group that defected from their own parties to form the Social Democratic Party.

It was the United States, which had been bombing neighbouring Laos and trying to subvert its Government, that did most to destabilize Cambodia too. In Laos it had the excuse that the Ho-Chi-Minh Trail ran through the country between North and South Vietnam. It claimed that the Vietcong were making regular use of Cambodia as a place of refuge; it was trying to prepare the way for an invasion and the overturn of the country's Government. The head of state was Prince Norodom Sihanouk, who had been King from 1945 to 1956, when he abdicated in order to lead a Government elected by the people. He was worshipped, almost literally, by his subjects, who believed him close to divinity. He was an able man who served his people well, winning freedom from the French colonialists and preserving it, while at the same time following the dangerous path of neutrality in the struggle between the Soviet Union and the United States. While he was away on a visit to Moscow, he was removed from office by the machinations of the C.I.A., as he later recounted in his book, *My War with the C.I.A.* Soon afterwards, in May 1970, America invaded Cambodia. A right-wing government was installed there under Lon Nol, who was in turn removed from power by Pol Pot and the Khmer Rouge. This led to one of the worst disasters that humankind has ever seen – another feather in the imperialistic cap of the United States.

Sihanouk was not a great man, nor a particularly good one, but he was an able patriot and an engaging and warm-hearted person. Michael Scott and I had a long talk with him and afterwards he entertained us to dinner; the conversation was pleasant enough, the food excellent, and the wines of the very best; or so I was told! I presented him with a copy of *A Book of Wales*, the anthology edited by D. Myrddin Lloyd and his wife, and he said with a straight face that he would keep it on his bedside table. From him I received in turn a round silver box in which to keep my cigarettes, although I don't smoke! He also showed us two films which he had both produced and acted in. The leading role in one of them was played by his wife, a beautiful French woman; it was set among the splendid architecture and sculpture of the temples of Angkor Wat, one of the wonders of the world. The temples were built during the period of Cambodia's grandeur, which extended (to put it in terms of Welsh history) from the age of Rhodri Mawr to that of Owain Glyndwr.

They were much appreciated by the French who had ruled the country after 1860, and had been restored to their former glory. French was Sihanouk's first language and that of his Government. It was also the language of the only daily paper in Pnom Penh. The paper attacked us bitterly and called for our expulsion until Sihanouk put a stop to whatever they had to say. Was he, I wonder, right to suppress it?

Since the American excuse for their military threats against Cambodia was that it was being used as a refuge by the Vietcong, we examined this allegation in some detail. Michael Scott and I paid visits to the missions of Canada, India, and Poland – the three countries that formed the International Commission that had been set up by the Geneva Convention of 1954 – in order to review the situation in Cambodia. In their unanimous opinion there was absolutely no evidence to suggest that the Vietcong were using any part of Cambodia on any appreciable scale. The Commission had published several reports to prove this and we were given copies of them. On my return to London I enquired about them in the library at Westminster, but no one knew of their existence. Everyone accepted the American story. It was also believed by the British Ambassador in Pnom Penh, for when I asked him for proof, he raised his eyebrows in astonishment and said, 'Everybody knows it, old boy'. There was no need for evidence when the facts were so well-known. During our stay in Pnom Penh we received a good deal of help from Wilfred Burchett, the jovial Australian journalist who was out of favour with the Government of his own country. He had settled in the city and married a Cambodian woman. Since he was the leading expert on Vietnam, I later arranged for him to address a group of Parliamentarians at Westminster.

All this time we had been waiting for visas, but they didn't come through. It was the North Vietnamese Ambassador who was supposed to provide us with them. This man was terribly polite towards us, saying the reason for the delay was that Hanoi was unwilling to accept responsibility for us while the situation remained so dangerous. Furthermore, there was only one flight to Hanoi; the small plane held only seven passengers and had just been shot down. One day the Embassy gave a reception for the whole group. Michael Scott and I hurried there from the Canadian Embassy on the other side of the city. The heat and the Vietnamese delicacies on an empty stomach proved too much for me, and I fainted – the only time in my life I have ever done so. I remember the lovely sensation to this day. Since we were unable to remain for much longer waiting for visas, Michael Scott and I left after about a fortnight, having failed in our mission but not having altogether wasted our time. The rest of the group stayed on for another fortnight. On the way home we had to spend a night and a day in Bangkok, a beautiful city but nothing to compare with Pnom Penh. There I saw how the material wealth and cultural tastes of America contrasted with the way of life of old Siam, now called Thailand – the literal meaning of which is Land of the Free.

On the day of my return to Westminster a three-day debate began on foreign policy. I was intending to speak on the second day, after having an opportunity of putting my impressions in some order, but Horace King, the Speaker, sent me a note asking me to see him. He asked me whether I would speak that very evening because the House wanted to hear me – an exaggeration if ever there was one! I went into the library for half an hour and was called upon just after coming back into the chamber. I was able then to bear witness to the destructive effects which the struggle between the Soviet Union and the United States of America was having on one of the most beautiful countries in the world.

Chapter 18

Victory

The Welsh awakening has depended on the building of a strong national movement which fights for Wales on all fronts. The most crucial battle has to be fought within the nation itself. If external factors should overwhelm it, the reason will be attributable to internal turpitude. The nation's life can be maintained and restored only by the moral forces within it. What is done to it by Whitehall reflects the internal condition of Wales itself. The chief importance of sending Nationalists to Westminster has been that they demonstrate the vigour of Welsh nationality. The British parties have made no contribution to the national awakening. Their most positive activities in Wales have been in reaction to the vitality of political Nationalism. The most essential task for anyone who is serious about Wales is to help build a national movement that is determined to work in the political, economic, cultural, and social fields. Sympathy for the cause of Wales which is not organized in a political party always proves ineffective. Our task as Nationalists has been, and will continue to be, the gathering together of the country's life-giving forces. This process has been the major creative development in the life of the nation during the present century.

On the language front a great deal has happened. A brave stand was taken by Trefor and Eileen Beasley of Llangennech when they refused to pay the Llanelli Council's rates demands because they were in English only. We arranged with Dr Harry Davies of Ammanford to buy back the furniture that had been removed from their home by the local authority. Another blow for the language was struck in a most unexpected way. I had been trying to persuade Gwynfor S. Evans of Y Betws to contest the County Election in April 1958. Although he was for long unwilling, on the day the nominations were to be handed in he decided that he would stand, but he had no official English forms, only some Welsh ones which had been manufactured by Plaid Cymru. He rang to tell me this and I urged

him to hurry up and fill them in with the requisite ten names and
hand them in by mid-day. He did so, but because they were in Welsh
the forms were rejected by the returning officer, W.S. Thomas, the
Clerk of Carmarthenshire Council. So we decided to take our case
to the High Court in London, for which the Party had to find some
three hundred pounds in expenses. Our barrister was Dewi Watkin
Powell, who acted free of charge, and not for the last time either. I
can put it on record here that a good number of Nationalist lawyers
have given their services free in the defence of fellow-Nationalists or
by representing them in other ways in the courts. Dewi argued with
uncommon skill and the case was won. The court refused permission
for the County Council to appeal and it had to pay costs. Thereafter
all the electoral forms and posters in Carmarthenshire were bilingual
in both local and Parliamentary Elections. But the most important
consequence of this case was the setting up of the Hughes Parry
Committee in 1963, which looked into the legal status of the Welsh
language and led to the Language Act of 1967.

I had been trying for some while to bring the weight of the chapels
and churches behind the cause of the language. I wrote to the
Nonconformist denominations, and to the Church in Wales and the
Roman Catholic Church, asking them to appoint delegates to a
national committee in the hope that they would also contribute from
their coffers towards the cost of employing an organizer. The outcome was the setting up of the Interdenominational Committee for
the Welsh Language (to give its Welsh title in English), with Dr
Lewis Evans as its Chairman, the Reverend Gwilym R. Tilsley its
Vice-chairman, and the Reverend Dafydd Edwards its Secretary.
This Committee did some effective work for Welsh-medium education for both children and adults, in the use of the language in local
and central government, and in public life generally. But it didn't
manage to find money to appoint an organizer, and because this
work was onerous for an unpaid Secretary, who couldn't afford to
travel on the Committee's business, the work began to languish after
a few years. It must be admitted that the churches themselves were
rather sluggish in this respect. The Independents published a pamphlet entitled *Gwerth dy Grys* by Pennar Davies, Alwyn D. Rees and
myself, calling on them to take action. This pamphlet demonstrated
the interdependence of the chapels and the Welsh language. It was
the chapel which more than anything else has upheld the Welsh
language during the greater part of the last two hundred years. But
if the language depended on the chapels, then the Welsh chapels also
relied on the survival and restoration of the language. They were
badly affected by the decline of the language. There was, however,

still a close relationship between the language and the churches even in the early 'sixties, when some eighty per cent of Welsh-speakers belonged to a chapel or church, according to statistics published by the denominations; only about fifteen per cent of the English-speaking Welsh were members.

In November 1963 the Council for Wales and Monmouthshire (to give it its full title), under the chairmanship of Richard I. Aaron, Professor of Philosophy at the University College of Wales, Aberystwyth, published an exceptionally useful report on the Welsh language. Its main proposal was the granting of official status to the language, and it defined what it meant by this.

The most important step forward in the interests of the language took place at Plaid Cymru's Summer School in Pontarddulais in the summer of 1962. We had been discussing for some while the need for a language movement that would concentrate its efforts on campaigning for the wider use of Welsh in public life. This was necessary from the Party's point of view as well as for the sake of the language, for we had always suffered from the allegation made in some quarters that we were mainly concerned with language and culture. We weren't able, in our view, to combine fighting effectively for the language and working as a political party. That was why Plaid Cymru had to reject the appeal made by Saunders Lewis in his powerful radio lecture, *Tynged yr Iaith* ('The Fate of the Language'), in February 1962. It was at the Plaid Cymru Summer School in Pontarddulais that *Cymdeithas yr Iaith Gymraeg* was formed, with Tedi Millward as its Chairman and John Davies its Secretary; its aim was to take direct action on behalf of the language. Over the next twenty years the Society enlisted some of the nation's best young people, encouraging them to stand up and be counted, and in many hundreds of cases to be gaoled as a consequence. There is nothing grander in the history of Wales than the struggle they have waged.

But the greatest victories were won in the field of Welsh education. At the beginning of the war, Sir Ifan ab Owen Edwards, the founder of *Urdd Gobaith Cymru* and a great benefactor of the youth of Wales, had made one of his substantial contributions by establishing a Welsh-medium school at Lluest in Aberystwyth. There were many Welsh-language rural schools in existence by this time, with head-masters of conviction and vision, but only one that was designated a Welsh School. In order to ensure and safeguard the Welsh character of a school it is still necessary to designate it as a Welsh School. It is only in a Welsh School that Welsh is the official language and used as the medium of instruction. The historic achievement of Ifan ab Owen Edwards was to do this and, moreover, to do it in an

anglicized town like Aberystwyth. There were only seven pupils at
Lluest at the outset, but the school had a brilliant teacher. It was
Lluest that launched Norah Isaac on a career in which she was to
accomplish so much for the enrichment of our national life. The
school grew steadily and proved that it's possible to provide a
first-class education and at the same time ensure academic success
through the medium of Welsh. That is now the common experience
of the Welsh Schools. I once heard the dramatist Matthew Williams,
a Schools Inspector in Llanelli at the time, saying that he would have
had to pay hundreds of pounds a year to provide an education
similar to the one his daughter was receiving at Ysgol Dewi Sant in
the town, the first Welsh School to be set up by a local authority,
thanks mainly to County Councillor Lottie Rees. Its splendid headmistress was Olwen Williams. We have good cause to be grateful for
the magnificent headteachers who have taught in the Welsh Schools.
We have recently lost one of them in the person of Enid Jones Davies,
the wife of the old Republican, Ithel Davies. In Barry the first
headmistress of a small Welsh School of fifteen pupils was Elinor
Davies. That school, like most outside Flintshire, was established as
the result of a lot of hard work over quite a long period. The
committee met throughout its campaign at my parents' home, and
my father's vans used to transport the children to the voluntary
nursery school. This was the school that prepared English-speaking
pupils for primary school. Among the most prominent members of
the committee were the writer and broadcaster Aneirin Talfan
Davies and Raymond Edwards, the Schools Inspector who laboured
with such zest on the language's behalf.

Today more than six hundred Barry children receive their education through the medium of Welsh, at nursery, primary, and
secondary level – and some ninety-seven per cent of them come
from English-speaking homes. My brother Alcwyn and his wife
Llywela were able to ensure a better and more Welsh education for
their three daughters and three sons in a large anglicized town like
Barry than my three daughters and four sons ever received in the
rural, Welsh-speaking area of Llangadog. Five of them were educated at the University College at Aberystwyth, a family record!
Although Welsh is a second language for Alcwyn and Llywela –
neither of her parents had any Welsh – it is the language of their
home and their children have been thoroughly immersed in the
values of Wales. The eldest went to the Welsh Comprehensive
School at Rhydyfelin near Pontypridd, where ninety-eight per cent
of the pupils, as in Caerphilly, come from homes which have no
Welsh. Others attended the Welsh Schools at Llanharri and the

youngest was a pupil at Ysgol Glan Tâf in Cardiff. In Barry there are also Welsh classes for adults, as is to be expected in the town where Chris Rees lived. Chris, who has been a Nationalist since his early youth, has done so much in this field. It was he who brought Ulpan classes into our lives, a method of teaching a language to adults which was pioneered in Israel. The number of pupils at Welsh-medium nursery, primary and secondary schools in the counties of Glamorgan is now getting on for twenty thousand, and that's in an area where there wasn't a single Welsh school a generation ago and where those who were able to speak the language could be numbered only in hundreds. Why do so many of the English-speaking parents of Glamorgan send their children to Welsh Schools? Because their national consciousness has been awakened by Plaid Cymru and they have been given enough pride in their Welsh identity to insist on their children having the language.

In the Welsh-speaking parts of Wales the story is different. The influx of English people has changed the language of many rural schools that were completely Welsh twenty years ago. Schools in areas where sixty per cent of the population are Welsh-speakers should be officially designated as Welsh Schools. In these the language of instruction should be Welsh, no matter how many English-speaking children attend them. I know of successful schools in country areas which are wholly Welsh in language, despite the fact that only between fifteen and twenty per cent of the pupils come from homes where Welsh is spoken. Success often depends more on the headteacher's conviction than on the policy of the local authority, however important that may be. It is always an advantage, of course, to have a Welsh-medium nursery school, to prepare the children for their education in Welsh at primary level.

With the honourable exception of the late Lord Heycock, it's strange how consistent the opposition of the Labour Party has been to Welsh-medium Schools. After going over to Labour, even a Welshman as keen as Lord Elystan Morgan felt obliged to oppose the opening of Ysgol Penweddig at Aberystwyth, and like other Labourites in that town he sent his children to the English Secondary School. Much the same goes for Gwynoro Jones, formerly the Labour M.P. Carmarthen. I also remember Dr Roger Thomas, when he was Labour M.P. for the county, making an ass of himself in a radio programme in which he and I took part: he chose to argue that bilingual Comprehensive Schools actually did harm to the Welsh language! As proof of this he cited four boys he had heard speaking English outside the bilingual Comprehensive at Ystalyfera. The implication was that if it had been an English school, they would have been speaking Welsh! He also had two other serious complaints about Welsh Schools. They were unfair to the English schools because they deprived them of parents who took an interest in the education of their children, and they were schools for the children of posh people – the crachach – he said. Three days before he was to make these sweeping statements on the radio I had heard that a hundred fathers of children at Ysgol Maes Garmon, a Welsh-medium Comprehensive School in Flintshire, had lost their jobs in the steel-industry at Shotton. In the opinion of Dr Thomas, the only place to fight for the language was on the hearth: if parents insisted on speaking it to their children it would be safe. This is the attitude of people who saw the number of Welsh-speaking children in the schools of the old county of Carmarthenshire fall from eighty-four per cent in 1936 to forty-five per cent in 1960 and to fewer than thirty per cent in 1980.

Few people realize how serious the crisis faced by the language is in what used to be Welsh-speaking Wales, not only as a consequence of the erosion that's been taking place for many years now as a result of the English education provided in the schools, English television, the English press, and many another anglicizing factor, but also in particular as a result of the influx of huge numbers of English people who have poured in during the last decade or so, and who continue to do so. Take for instance the upper part of the Tywi Valley and its environs from Nantgaredig to Rhandirmwyn. Today, and I am writing in 1982, it is only a minority of children in the primary schools who come from Welsh-speaking homes. This has been the situation in Llandeilo and Llandovery for two generations or more, but it is now happening in the rural areas as well. This is the picture in the schools:

	from Welsh-speaking homes	from English-speaking homes
Cynghordy	6	14
Cilycwm	3	26
Myddfai	20	6
Llanwrda	15	18
Llansadwrn	9	27
Llangadog	38	36
Llanddeusant	18	2
Gwynfe	5	8
Tal-y-llychau	3	10
Salem	1	19
Maes-y-bont	0	23
Trap	13	10

Llanarthne	27	32
Brechfa	14	26
Abergorlech	7	4
Nantgaredig	50	62

Almost without exception, there are more English-speaking immigrant children to be found among the classes of younger pupils. The situation is much the same in Carmarthenshire, Cardiganshire, and northern Pembrokeshire, all three of which used to be bastions of the Welsh language. While passing through Tal-sarn in the Aeron valley recently, I called at the post office. The postmaster informed me that there were English people in two out of every three houses in that neighbourhood, including the farms, from Tal-sarn as far as Llangeitho. I could tell of a similar situation in many a district in Dyfed where Welsh culture was strong up until recently. It is true that the chapels are emptying as a consequence of the ebb of Christianity, but the English incomers weaken them so much more quickly, and with them go the various cultural societies, the Sunday Schools, the evening-classes, and the local eisteddfodau. And of course it worsens the situation in the English secondary schools such as Pantycelyn in Llandovery, Tregib in Llandeilo, and the one at Ammanford. Although these schools have always had an anglicizing effect on their pupils, their English character didn't do much harm for as long as a core of the pupils were Welsh-speakers. But when the majority have no Welsh, as is the case today, it can place the language in mortal danger. The great majority of primary schools do sterling work in turning out Welsh-speaking children who come from English-speaking homes, but after two or three years at secondary school their Welsh is lost. For how much longer are these large English-language schools going to undo the splendid work of the teachers in the primary schools? And it must be asked what will the fate of the language be in ten years' time while these fortresses of English are maintained by the influx of English people who threaten to overwhelm us?

The main hope for reversing the decline of Welsh culture in these areas is to be found in a combination of television and education provided in the Welsh language, together with a growth in national consciousness and the people's pride in their Welsh identity. In the primary schools we must have heads and teachers of conviction and forthright personality who can teach children all day, except in English lessons, through the medium of the Welsh language, and follow that course never mind how many English-speakers there are in the class; and we must also have bilingual comprehensives to carry on their work. A host of schools throughout Wales have shown that this does a great deal of good to a child's academic career, as well as making him or her a more rounded person.

But at the critical time I have been writing about the Labourites of the Carmarthenshire constituency, under the leadership of Dr Roger Thomas M.P., chose to join with the Tories in renewing their attacks on the Welsh primary schools and the bilingual Comprehensives. These schools, declared Dr Thomas and the Labour Party's constituency committee, were dividing the community, and they would in time create a situation like the one in Northern Ireland! The responsibility for maintaining the language belonged in the home, they said. 'The language,' said Dr Thomas, 'has to be spoken vigorously and naturally in the everyday lives of the children for it to prosper.' He did not say how this was to be accomplished in the homes of the thousands of English people who had recently moved into Welsh-speaking Wales, buying up house after house, farm after farm, as well as pubs, post offices, garages, and small businesses, and there was no mention of those who had come in without any prospect of work whatsoever. Both the Labour and the Tory Party were offering a recipe for the demise of the Welsh language and the civilization of Wales.

The English flood still sweeps through Wales, but it would have been even greater if some had had their way, with the overflow from cities such as Liverpool and Birmingham. These people, who approved of the inundation in the early 'sixties, were anxious, with the co-operation of certain Welsh authorities, to transfer scores of thousands of English people to Welsh-speaking areas in Anglesey and in Merioneth, where the Labour M.P. was very much in favour of the scheme. T.W. Jones, the M.P. for Merioneth, claimed that there was no likelihood whatsoever that ten thousand English people would harm the fortunes of the Welsh language in the vicinity of Bala, which has a population of about two thousand. When Jim Griffiths was appointed as the first Secretary of State for Wales in 1964, his sole idea was to resettle sixty thousand of the inhabitants of Birmingham in a new town in Montgomeryshire, a county which has about as many people. The same kind of thinking was behind a scheme to develop a huge town on the banks of the Severn, to be known as Severnside, to the east of Newport. These schemes were fiercely resisted by Plaid Cymru and eventually we met with success. Although many English people have flooded into Wales, deliberate attempts to drown the country have been confounded. Despite stout resistance on our part, the Severn Bridge was built. We wanted the money spent on building the Bridge to be used instead on making a dual carriageway from Cardiff to Merthyr and then on to Holyhead via Wrexham. This road would have led to economic initiatives in the valleys of Glamorgan, in mid-Wales, and in Clwyd and Gwynedd. So far there is a good new road from Cardiff to Cilfynydd, a little to the north of Pontypridd; I'm told that it's known locally as Welsh Nash Way. But the road that would be the backbone of Wales remains a dream that has not yet been fulfilled. The authorities argued that the hills were too high, that the winter snow is too heavy, and anyway, they said, there was no industry in mid-Wales to speak of. So different was the attitude of the Italian Government towards the *Autostrada del Soli* which runs down the spine of that country. There it was argued there was no industry and so they had to have a motorway. A Welsh Government would have given priority to a highway that would have served as the country's backbone, drawing its various parts into a single economic whole.

It's an enormous task to win a nation's freedom without creating an independent Welsh way of thinking. A strong Party must be built in order to concentrate on the objective. It's nonsense to claim that self-government will come on the skirts of the British parties' policies, without any effort at all on our part. This is the greatest political objective for which we as Welsh people can work. To achieve it, the moral resources of the nation must be harnessed within a National Party. This alone will bring the necessary pressure to bear. Even when Plaid Cymru was a very small party, without ever coming anywhere near serious electoral success, it proved that an independent Nationalist Party had power and influence. In his book *The Party System in Great Britain*, Bulmer Thomas wrote as long ago as 1950 that 'the determined work of the Nationalists of Wales has forced the old parties to acknowledge Wales as a nation.' In 1961 it was said in *Local Self-Government*, a book published by Political and Economic Planning: 'The government of the United Kingdom will meet the demands of the Nationalists by granting under pressure a greater measure of self-government'. Although Plaid Cymru was small, the Establishment had to take action in order to minimize its potential for threatening the British order of things. It was this that spurred us into building the national movement.

The Party's growth in Carmarthenshire had been very slow. It is the fighting of Parliamentary Elections that signals a party's effectiveness, and in 1955, with Jennie Eirian Davies as its candidate, Plaid Cymru had contested Carmarthenshire for the first time. Four years later Hywel Heulyn Roberts was our excellent candidate. He served the Party most effectively as Chairman of its Finance Committee and was for years among the most steadfast men in local government in

Wales. He too was the first Chairman of the new Dyfed County Council. Yet, despite the strength of our candidate, the Party won only about five per cent of the votes, much fewer than we had in Llanelli, which had been contested three times by the staunch Eirwyn Morgan when he was a minister at Bancffosfelen. There was a call within the Party for more efficient organization at this time. Members of staff from Trinity College, Carmarthen – men like the educationalist Jac L. Williams and the poet Bobi Jones – had lent us their strength over more than a quarter of a century. It was Bobi Jones who proposed dividing the Carmarthenshire committee into two constituency committees. But we didn't succeed in setting up an effective committee in Carmarthen until we had acquired the services of a man who in the fullness of time would also be on the staff of Trinity College. This man was Cyril Jones, a native of Old Colwyn, a History teacher at Ysgol Pantycelyn at the time and later headmaster of Ysgol Dyffryn Ardudwy. Cyril married a lovely girl from Caeo and they had made their home in the village of Pumsaint in that parish. Under his leadership the village became the cultural centre of northern Carmarthenshire. The appointment of Cyril Jones as Secretary proved to be a turning-point in the fortunes of the constituency committee and from that moment on it developed in strength and efficiency; the fruits of its work were to be seen in the three Parliamentary elections that were fought within the four years after my becoming the Party's candidate. Cyril was my agent in all three. He gathered about him a cheerful and effective group of workers who included two of the Parc Nest brothers – Aled Gwyn, who was later to leave a deep impression as a District and County Councillor, and Jim Jones, yet another member of Trinity College's staff. Among Jim's accomplishments is *Dan y Wenallt*, his marvellous translation of Dylan Thomas's *Under Milk Wood*. I might as well mention here a very pleasant evening I once spent at Laugharne watching the original version of the play in the company of Saunders Lewis and Kenneth Davies, a great benefactor of the arts in Wales whose flat in Tiger Bay was one of the wonders of the city of Cardiff. We travelled down to Laugharne in his large and comfortable Daimler. I had gone as far as Carmarthen from Llangadog in an old van that had seen better days, and when I got back to it after midnight, I couldn't start the engine. That was another night I spent at the roadside!

I fought Carmarthen for the first time in 1964. I had a number of advantages. By dint of my work on the County Council I had become fairly well-known. Over the years I had been addressing cultural societies and all kinds of other organizations up and down the

county, and in Carmarthen town itself. The most notable of the
town's societies was the English Fellowship at the Welsh chapel
known as Tabernacl. About a hundred men came together every
Sunday afternoon under the leadership of T.J. Evans, the Treasurer
of the county's Education Committee. For a quarter of a century,
beginning in the middle of the war, I had been addressing this society
once a year. The Party's vote in 1964 was doubled, having been
increased from 2,500 to 5,500 – the largest vote ever received by a
Nationalist candidate up to then, though it wasn't enough to save
our deposit. At the General Election of March 1966 we received
7,500 votes, again the largest number ever given to the Party.

In Merioneth, Elystan Morgan was the Plaid Cymru candidate in
1964; before that he had been an effective candidate in Wrexham on
three occasions. But the Party's Merioneth vote fell from 5,500 to
3,500. In the year following Elystan stood against Chris Rees for the
Vice-Presidency of the Party, and Chris was elected. In October 1965
the news reached my ears that Elystan was talking about joining the
Labour Party. I went to Wrexham to see him. It was true, he said,
that he was thinking of going over to Labour but he hadn't yet
decided. Two things that came out of our chat were that he believed
Plaid Cymru's vote had reached what he called a plateau, and
wouldn't go any higher, and that it was essential to reinforce the
movement within the Labour Party in favour of an Elected Council
for Wales. After a long discussion, I left Wrexham with the feeling
that Elystan wasn't likely to turn his back on us. However, after a
short while I heard from a reliable source that he was still seriously
considering going over to Labour, and that his friend John Morris
M.P., who had been at Ardwyn School in Aberystwyth with him,
and was now a Minister in the Labour Government, was urging him
to do just that. I asked Elystan to meet me at the Metropole Hotel
in Llandrindod. At the end of our conversation I asked him to
discuss the matter with Lewis Valentine, the veteran Nationalist who
lived in Rhosllannerchrugog. A few days later Elystan 'phoned to
say that the shilly-shallying was at an end and that he had finally
decided to stay in Plaid Cymru. I should hear no more, he said, about
his joining the Labour Party, because that chapter was now closed.
Yet within two months I was told that he had defected to Labour,
and after a few weeks he was selected as that party's candidate in
Cardiganshire. Six months later he was a Member of Parliament and
within the year he was in the Government. His defection was a heavy
loss to Plaid Cymru, for Elystan was a clever and warm-hearted man.
If he had stood as a Nationalist in Cardiganshire, it's possible that
he would have been elected as a Plaid Cymru M.P. and the land

between Holyhead and Cardigan today would have been Free Wales.

It was an episode of particular significance, Elystan's turning his coat against Welsh Nationalism. Although many had done so in the past in order to join one or other of the British parties, there was no one of Elystan's calibre among them. He was one of Plaid Cymru's main leaders and considered by many to have the makings of a President. His defection threw a spotlight on the gap that exists between what it means to be a Welsh Nationalist and being British in political terms, and on the pressure that can be brought to bear on a Welshman who wants to be a British politician to renounce the struggle for Wales and militant Welshness. A militant Welsh stance is the only effective means of tackling the needs of Wales today. Those Nationalists who in the past have given their loyalty to Wales, not Britain, were militant Welsh people. For the sake of Wales they faced a long period in the political wilderness. Should they have met with political success, they had made a commitment to refuse all jobs and honours in London. To join them was an act of self-denial. The spirit of the true Nationalist was summed up in the well-known poem by Prosser Rhys, an extract from which I shall give here in an English version by D. Myrddin Lloyd:

'Ah no! I can no other
Than stand here, come what may,
True to the land that bore me
Though sad her plight today;
With all her faults, my Wales has grown
Into the marrow of my bone.

And with the few who love her
Through every strain and shock,
Dreading no boorish insult,
Scorning the knaves who mock,
I call upon our nation's youth
To come to terms with her ancient truth.

And when the supercilious
Uprooted, upstart crew
Maintain it is but folly
That moves our loyal few –
Then come what may, I'll stand or fall
With the little band that gives its all.'

In turning his back on Plaid Cymru, Elystan ceased to be a fighter for Wales. He became what is sometimes called 'a good Welshman', which means a Welshman who has a sentimental

regard for Wales but gives his first allegiance to Britain, swimming
on a British tide that has carried so many in recent generations to
brilliant careers, fame and honours in London. Elystan even went
so far as to oppose the opening of a bilingual comprehensive school
in Aberystwyth, the town where he had been educated, and he sent
his children to the English Secondary School. In the tradition of
Welshmen who make their careers with the British parties, he now
used his Welshness instead of fighting passionately for it. He had
become a Britisher and took the British view on the great questions
of the day. On a television programme soon after he had become a
Minister in the Government, we faced each other over the question
of sending British troops to Northern Ireland. Elystan was in
favour of doing so.

Since my public activities were eating up so much of my time, my
wife Rhiannon had to give me quite a bit of help in raising our family!
In August 1955 Branwen was christened, the youngest of our three
daughters, at Islaw'r Dref near Dolgellau, in a small chapel that
stands in a deep valley on the bank of the Gwyrddail brook, where
the splendour of Cader Idris can be glimpsed through the branches
of the trees. Rhiannon's cousin, Griffith Griffiths, was still farming
Gallestra in that wondrous district which has always been an inspiration to me. There were once seven farms on Gallestra's land. There,
on the slopes of Pared y Cefn Hir in the mid-'forties, Dan Thomas
had scattered the ashes of Richard Roberts, his brother-in-law and
first Secretary of the Fellowship of Reconciliation, in a small service
conducted by George M.Ll. Davies. At the side of the Pared, about
a mile and a half up into the mountain from Gallestra, stands Ty'n
Llidiart, the house where Rhiannon and I spent our honeymoon. She
and her brother Dewi Prys Thomas and their mother used to spend
every summer and Easter holiday there from the end of the war
onwards, when the family was living in Liverpool, and Dan Thomas
would spend every weekend there. When our children were small, it
was there too that we would take our summer holidays, and I would
go up and stay with them at weekends. That is why Branwen was
christened there. She is the only one of our seven children who has
chosen as a profession the care of children with serious physical
handicaps – a calling which appealed to her even when she was very
young. On 1st August Rhys was born, the seventh of our children,
and the Benjamin of the family. Rhiannon wouldn't have any more
children after him because she had heard that every eighth child born
into the world is Chinese! Having been much taken with that
American book, *Cheaper by the Dozen*, I wanted twelve. I have no
difficulty in remembering Rhys's birthday for a good reason: the

Party's Summer School was held at Porthmadog that year and I had just gone up on to the rostrum when a telegram was handed to me. I opened it in full view of the audience and as the news was happy, I read it out loud. It said that a boy had been born to us. Some of the people present asked what his name was to be, and Eirian Davies shouted, 'Madog!'. But the name by which he was christened was Rhys. Sixteen years had gone by since I had heard on the telephone that Alcwyn, our eldest son, had been born. In one respect, at least, Rhys follows in the family tradition: he belongs to a musical group. In fact, he has been a member of several groups; the name of the one he belongs to at present is *Bando*. I have been well-educated in pop and rock music because another son, Dafydd Prys, joined the first Welsh rock-band, *Y Blew*, whose sole record is now a collector's item. They used to rehearse at Talar Wen until the people of Llangadog about a mile away began to complain about the din. It's a good thing that *Y Diliau*, the group to which Meleri belongs, was not so noisy. But their style is very different from rock. My own taste is catholic enough to enjoy both, and yet one of my regrets is that not one of my family plays jazz. The Welsh music scene is now well-developed, so much so that the impression is sometimes given that young people don't much care about anything else, except perhaps rugby. But it's a good thing that so much of the world of pop in Wales is in Welsh when so much else is carried on in English. The singing of Welsh hymns by the crowds at rugby-matches has almost completely died out, replaced by Max Boyce's 'Hymns and Arias', although Welsh rock seems to be enjoying a tremendous vogue.

In May 1966 the calm of family life was interrupted, if that's how I should put it, by the news that Megan Lloyd George had died. She had been seriously ill for some while, too ill to take part in the Election held in March of that year. And so the fateful by-election was called. Despite the fact that Plaid Cymru was ten thousand votes behind Labour and eight thousand behind the Liberals, we knew that we could do well in a by-election, and even climb into second place. I'm afraid it was this that was uppermost in my thoughts as I stood at Megan's grave in Cricieth on the day of her funeral, with the mountains of Snowdonia a majestic circle around us against a cloudless blue sky. On my way home from the funeral, I called at Islaw'r Dref. The spray on the rocky Gwynant had never been whiter, nor the dress of the valley's trees greener, than on that May afternoon. The sunshine poured warmly over the blue of the Crogenan lakes as I lay on a slope of the hill above them, with the great towers of Cader Idris rising to my right and the lovely peaks of Pared y Cefn Hir to the left. On the horizon the Arennig and Aran Benllyn stood silent in the sunshine. I am quite aware how silly this may sound to the reader, but at that moment I felt Wales breathing quietly all around me.

There was excitement among Nationalists right from the start. In such fine weather we were able to canvass happily all day and into the evenings. It was a pleasure, rather than a duty, to stand and address small clusters of people in the villages and larger gatherings in every market-place. A splendid group of workers gathered around Cyril Jones, some of them sixth-formers from the Grammar Schools at Carmarthen. Among their number were Geraint Thomas (known as the Prof), Siân and Catrin Edwards, Tony Jenkins, Yvonne Davies, Dai Lewis, John Lewis, and Sharon Morgan. They were joined by Phil Henry and Eifion Thomas and many another of their generation. The canvassing was led in the hilly parishes of our area by members of my own family – Alcwyn, Dafydd, Meleri, Guto, Meinir, and Branwen – and the pleasant manner of these young workers left a deep impression wherever they went. No election was ever better organized than this one. Cyril Jones had the help of J.E. Jones and Elwyn Roberts, both full-time officers of the Party. The brilliant leaflets and handouts that we published contributed to our success. One of these consisted of eight lively pages written by the novelist Islwyn Ffowc Elis. He had had experience in contesting Montgomeryshire twice for Plaid Cymru, and there's no doubt that his literary prowess was a great factor in our success.

The day before polling day I stood in the crowd around the ring of Carmarthen Mart listening to the witty auctioneer selling cattle. Since he was a friend of the cause, he took the opportunity of drawing attention to my presence. He was accepting bids for a cow in the middle of the enclosure. 'Eighty pounds I am bid . . . eighty pounds I am bid. Are you in, Mr Evans?' 'No,' I replied, 'but I shall be tomorrow night.' At the huge meeting held in the Celtic Cinema that evening, when the building was full and overflowing into the foyer and street outside, I told them this story. Suddenly a man jumped up in the middle of the gallery shouting, 'I was that man! I was that man!' Many of those who were present at that inspirational meeting, which was perhaps not unlike a revival meeting, said they were certain that I was going to win, but I didn't believe it. I had fought eight elections before and lost my deposit in six of them.

Some time after midnight I went to the count, crossing Nott Square (the general, by the way, was the great-great-grandfather of the Minister for Defence in the present Government). Outside the Guild Hall in Carmarthen Elwyn Roberts was waiting for me. He had just come out of the count with the news that I was in. Though he swore this was the Gospel truth, I just couldn't believe it. But as soon as I went into the Guild Hall I could see that it was true. After declaring the result inside, the returning officer went out on to the balcony to announce it to the crowd filling the town's square. When they saw me standing behind him, they went wild with joy. They knew that a Nationalist had carried the day at long last. The headline in *The Daily Mail* next day was 'Welsh Win Carmarthen'. The Election had been held on 14th July and many saw significance in the fact that on 14th July 1789 the Bastille had fallen. On 14th July 1886, eighty years to the day, the great Liberal Tom Ellis had been elected to Westminster as the Member for Merioneth. On 14th July 1404 a Treaty had been signed in Paris between Owain Glyndwr and the King of France! The result was greeted by Cliff Protheroe, the Labour Party's chief officer in Wales, with some unhappy words. 'This,' he said, 'is the beginning of the end for Welsh Nationalism.' David Williams, the historian, took a different view: in his classic work *Modern Wales* he described Plaid Cymru's victory as 'a watershed in Welsh political history'. Harri Webb wrote a ballad about the victory, which also inspired his famous poem, '*Colli Iaith*' – '*A Chymru'n dechrau ar ei hymdaith*' ('And Wales now sets out on its journey'). Within eighteen months the victory for the cause of Wales was to have clear reverberations in Scotland. At two in the morning I was carried on the shoulders of my supporters to a car that would take me home to Talar Wen. There was great rejoicing. It seemed to me that everyone was happy except the victor himself, though he too had to put on a broad grin. His happiness was clouded with the thought of the burden of new responsibility which would now weigh upon him, and the fear that he might disappoint his people. Talar Wen was like a beehive. At ten the following morning I was back at our office in Carmarthen to lead the triumphant motorcade around the constituency.

For most of the next three days I was travelling around the county that had elected a Nationalist – the Great Cantref and the Small Cantref as it was known in days gone by, the land of Gruffydd ap Rhys and his son, the great Prince of the ancient kingdom of Deheubarth in the twelfth century, Rhys ap Gruffydd – although I also had to give a good deal of my time to the media, and some to make a record that was later released by Gwasg y Dryw. There are numerous accounts of how the news of our victory was received. I liked in particular the story told by Eic Davies about his calling at a newsagent's in Gwauncaegurwen at seven in the morning on his way home from Carmarthen. 'Have you heard that Gwynfor Evans has gone in at Carmarthen?', he asked the woman who kept the shop. 'Poor dab,' she replied, thinking no doubt of St. David's mental hospital, 'I hope they won't have to keep him in too long.' The news was broadcast in many of the countries of the world. It made the front page of *Pravda*. The Chief Constable of Carmarthenshire later told me that he had read it at Madrid airport and had danced with joy, to the great embarrassment of his wife. The news received a warm welcome in some pretty unlikely places. Everywhere people felt well-disposed towards Wales and the Welsh felt more pride in their nationality. The telegrams and congratulations flowed in; I don't know how many there were by the end – anything up to a thousand, perhaps. Islwyn Ffowc Elis would know, for he took responsibility for acknowledging them all. The wording on the telegram from Harry Secombe read, 'Harold Wilson will have to learn to play the harp now.' Many papers carried pictures of the triumphant scenes after the count and in the days that followed. The one I liked best was of the nine members of the family on their way to chapel on Sunday morning. Television crews came from far and wide. I ran into a spot of bother with one from the Netherlands. They wanted to shoot the family coming out of the house and getting into the car, as if we were already on our way to London. We all trooped out of the front door of Talar Wen one by one and packed into the car exactly as directed, only to find that the car refused to budge and so we had to go through the whole charade again.

The Nationalists had demonstrated their organizational abilities. It was because the Welsh have these talents in large measure that Ernest Renan, himself of Breton stock, once wrote that they are the Teutons among the Celts. It's a shame that they haven't had a chance to show their talents in organizing the life of their own country. The arrangements made by the Party were immaculate within the constituency and smooth outside it. A special carriage was reserved for the family and friends in the train that took us from Carmarthen to London on the following Wednesday, with room for about fifty of our supporters. At every stop in Wales we were waved on our way by a crowd of jubilant Nationalists. At Cardiff and Paddington stations they sang '*Hen Wlad fy Nhadau*', and the national anthem was also sung by the hundreds who turned up at the Lyons Café near Leicester Square. It was sung again, and more than once, by the crowd of Welsh people who had gathered outside the entrance to the Palace of Westminster when I arrived there on the Thursday. It seems that the square had never seen such scenes. As a rule, crowds are not allowed to assemble there, but at the windows there appeared the faces of civil servants who were enjoying the singing, the like of which had never before been heard there. Several of them later told me how much they had enjoyed the occasion. For a few hours that day the police and authorities were filled with goodwill towards Wales and the Welsh. In an attempt to disperse the throng in a friendly fashion, a Welsh-speaking policeman handed me a loudspeaker so that I could make a speech from the steps of Westminster – again something without precedent. I felt a bit like Chesterton's donkey, for I also had my hour. Then in we went to the great Gothic hall where each of the four patron saints of the countries of Britain looks down from his arch – Andrew the Jew for Scotland, Patrick the Welsh-speaker for Ireland, George who probably never existed for England, and David the Welshman for Wales.

At a half past three that afternoon I stood at the bar of the chamber in the House of Commons with S.O. Davies and Jim Griffiths, my two sponsors, on either side of me. I had asked S.O. for obvious reasons and Jim Griffiths because he was the other M.P. from Carmarthenshire. It was Prime Minister's question-time and all parts of the chamber were full – the press gallery, the public gallery, and the Members' green benches, with scores standing tightly against the chair of the Sergeant at Arms and near the doors. When the Speaker called my name we all three took five steps forward and then bowed, three more steps and bowed again. We had rehearsed it all earlier in the day. My two sponsors then left my side and I walked forward to the table in order to take the oath and write my name in the Members' Book. At this point, to my great chagrin, there was a hitch. I had expected to take the oath in Welsh. I had even been to see George Thomas, the Secretary of State for Wales, about the matter that morning, and then Horace King, the Speaker. I had been given to understand by both of them that there would be no difficulty. But this was refused there and then. I moved forward to shake hands with the Speaker and then I did something that caused great laughter around the chamber: I sat down amidst the Government Ministers on the front bench. In the minds of the Honourable Members the fellow from rural Wales had dropped a clanger. But I wanted to address the House and nobody can do that unless he rises from his seat when called by the Speaker. I had to sit before I could rise! So I got to my feet and asked on a point of order whether I might take the oath in Welsh. The Speaker wouldn't allow it and read out a long statement explaining why no one could speak in Parliament in any language save English. He quoted from authorities and from precedents that proved that the House could be addressed only in English, without going as far back as the fifteenth century, it's true, when the language of the place was French. I rose to my feet twice again, 'further to the point of order', to say that it was an intolerable insult that I, in the only parliament that the Welsh people had, was not allowed to utter one word of Welsh, the language spoken in Wales for nearly two thousand years. The Speaker then resumed his explanation of why I couldn't and other members got to their feet to make points of order. Seven of them made contributions to the debate. Sir Harmond Nicholls tried to maintain that in speaking I had already made my maiden speech, but the Speaker rejected that idea. Emrys Hughes made the point that in swearing the oath I was addressing God rather than Parliament and that He had no prejudice against the use of Welsh. Eventually they promised to set up a working-party to look into the matter and, after the next Election, Members were allowed to take the oath in Welsh without anyone's objecting to it. I don't think any took the opportunity of doing so at that time, but in 1974, of course, the two Nationalists and one or two others did.

My first question to the Prime Minister was whether he would present a Bill for the setting up of a Parliament in Wales. His answer was 'No'. When I said that the three candidates supporting the principle of a Parliament at the Carmarthen by-election had received ninety-five per cent of the votes between them, Harold Wilson replied that only one member of the Westminster Parliament had been given a mandate to call for a Parliament for Wales. He was right, of course. A vote for the Liberal or the Labour candidate was not considered to be a vote for a Welsh Parliament. Then Jim Griffiths thanked Harold Wilson for all he had done for Wales and I was urged to co-operate in the reorganization of local government rather than chase after what he called 'will o' the wisps'. In the Election of 1945 Welsh self-government had been a part of Jim's electoral address. On being reminded of this, he responded by saying that the circumstances had changed. But what had changed were Jim Griffiths's circumstances.

Chapter 19

Punishment at Westminster

My great friend at Westminster was Emrys Hughes, the Labour
Member for South Ayrshire, who looked after me like a father from
my very first day. Emrys had been born in the Rhondda, a great-
grandson of John Hughes of Pontrobert, the mentor of the hymn-
writer Ann Griffiths. During the First World War he had spent
eighteen months as a conscientious objector in a cell at Caernarfon
castle. He married the daughter of Keir Hardie and wrote a biography of his father-in-law, among other books. His home in Cannock
had been Keir Hardie's and I visited it when I went to lend my
support to the Scottish Nationalists in the by-election that was
caused by his death in October 1969. I was very glad of the opportunity to see Keir Hardie's old home, for of all the Labour leaders,
it is with him and George Lansbury, his spiritual successor, that I
have the warmest sympathy. It's possible that this has something to
do with the fact that Hardie was a Scot and Lansbury half-Welsh,
since his mother was a Welsh-speaker from Breconshire. Labour was
returned at that by-election with no difficulty. Their candidate was
Jim Sillars, who, having made a futile attempt to start a Scottish
Labour Party, is now a member of the S.N.P. Jim once told me that,
during a speaking-tour of the United States in the company of Neil
Kinnock, he had come to the conclusion that it was the latter's lack
of Welsh which was behind his animosity towards the language and
the political claims of Wales. Emrys Hughes had been a school-
teacher and later a journalist. The lively Socialist weekly *Forward*
had no better editor. I subscribed to it for years before the war when
Emrys was in the editorial chair and found it much more human than
The New Left Review, the Marxist magazine that I also used to take.

On my first day at Westminster, it was Emrys, the author of a
definitive book about its rules and rituals, who showed me around
the House. He told me a story about the sober-sided procession of
the Speaker who leaves his rooms with his attendants at precisely

2.28 pm, all frills and buckles in their knickerbockers and black silk
hose, and then processes in stately step along a long corridor before
turning into the great foyer under the enormous oil-paintings depict-
ing scenes from English history. In the foyer hundreds of people are
marshalled by a squad of policemen into a neat circle. These are the
lucky ones with tickets for the public gallery which is to be opened
in about five minutes' time. As this dignified procession draws near,
the raucous voice of a policeman calls for silence, and in the religious
hush that follows the retinue proceeds as if on wheels, with the
Sergeant at Arms carrying a great sword and mace at its head, the
Speaker in his periwig in the middle, and lastly the Chaplain walking
behind two attendants in breeches. According to Emrys, some chap
who was a bit of a rough diamond once came into the foyer just as
the procession was approaching and, seeing a friend of his on the
other side of the hall, cried out, 'Neil!', whereupon the crowd all
obeyed the command, solemnly kneeling down where they had been
standing! I might as well follow the procession to its end. In the
Chamber perhaps ten members will be on their feet in readiness for
the prayer meeting when the Speaker comes in. As a rule, these are
the ones hoping to take part in question time, which is now about to
begin. The doors are then closed and an attendant outside is heard
shouting, 'Speaker at prayers!'. When the Chaplain calls for prayer
the Members all turn to face the wall. The Chaplain then prays for
the Queen, the Prince of Wales, and members of the Royal Family,
and then the Lord's Prayer is said. I broke the Westminster rules by
praying in Welsh.

As he showed me around the tea-rooms, Emrys Hughes pointed to
the Welsh table, saying, 'I wouldn't sit there if I were you. Your name
is mud there.' So I never sat there in all the four and a half years of my
first term at Westminster. Apart from Elystan Morgan I didn't have
a friend in the place among the Welsh Members. Some of them made
no attempt to conceal their animosity. Ness Edwards, the Labour
Member for Caerphilly, refused to speak to me at all and Goronwy
Roberts used to pass me in the corridor without looking at me. The
only time Iorwerth Thomas, Labour M.P. for the Rhondda, spoke to
me was when he chastised me for asking questions about constituencies other than Carmarthen. I would see Donald Coleman every
Monday morning at Neath railway-station but he never greeted me,
either there or at Westminster. They wouldn't lower themselves by
speaking to a 'Fascist'. On the other hand, Cledwyn Hughes was
always polite and kindly disposed towards me, but because he had a
job in the Cabinet I didn't see much of him. Roy Hughes, the M.P. for
Newport, was very friendly but most of my friends were members, like

Emrys Hughes, of the Tribune Group on the left wing of the Labour
Party. They knew that I was on their side in the social struggle. One of
the campaigns in which Emrys Hughes and I co-operated at Westminster was an attempt to do away with titles. From the outset
Michael Foot was friendly towards me; I always found him courteous,
sincere, and warm-hearted.

I saw quite a bit of Elystan. We had coffee together one Thursday
afternoon to discuss the forming of a group within the Labour Party
that would take action in favour of Parliaments for Wales and
Scotland, of which Elystan was willing to serve as Secretary. Nothing
came of it because that weekend Harold Wilson 'phoned him with
an invitation to become an Under-Secretary at the Home Office. By
the Monday following he was a member of the Government and
thereafter Wales never had his services at Westminster. As a minister
at the Home Office he had to answer questions from the front bench.
It was funny to see Wil Edwards, his Labour friend, sitting on the
back benches and pulling faces behind his back. In November 1967
the great victory of the S.N.P. at Hamilton swept Winnie Ewing into
Westminster and from then on I had a partner in the Parliamentary
struggle. Emrys Hughes took to her too: he was in the habit of
introducing us as 'my two illegitimate children'!

Unlike the 630 other Members of Parliament who were, appar-
ently, in their element in the Palace of Westminster, I found it hard
to put up with the place. Its smug English character weighed sorely
on my spirits and I found the atmosphere of London uncongenial
too, except for a few strolls in St. James's Park. If Megan Lloyd
George was like a fish out of water when not at Westminster, that's
how I felt within its walls. Perhaps it would have been different if I
had been younger, but I was fifty-three when I was first elected as
the Member for Carmarthenshire. What's more, Westminster is the
most powerful English symbol that exists, more potent than even the
English Crown. A picture of the Palace of Westminster is used daily
on television before political news programmes, such as the one that
is provocatively called 'Nationwide' as if the Welsh nation were part
of a larger 'British nation'. Westminster is, in fact, the very symbol
of the complete subjugation of Wales, the most mighty manifestation
of the Britishness, that's to say the Englishness, that is killing our
country. Its central place in the history of England underpins the
power of Britain. In the enormous pictures that hang from its walls
only English history is shown and English is the only language
spoken there. The Great Hall of Westminster, the oldest part of the
building, was built on the foundations of the palace of King Canute,
the Dane who first united England as part of his empire. He showed

more sympathy for the language and life of England than the English have ever shown for the languages and lives of the nations they have conquered. It was the French-speaking Edward the Confessor who built the Hall of Westminster and it was extended by William the Conqueror, who was also a French-speaker. French had supplanted Saxon as the language of government and law in England in the twelfth and thirteenth centuries, at a time when the language of law and government in independent Wales was still Welsh. Westminster Hall was first used as a meeting place for the English Parliament in 1547, some eleven years after the annexation of Wales by England. The most remarkable feature of the present fine buildings, built in the nineteenth century, is the hour-bell known as Big Ben after the husband of Lady Llanover who was once Commissioner of Works. During my first term at Westminster I had no room or desk or telephone. I used to work in the library, a pleasant enough place but quite inconvenient. When I was returned in 1974 I was given a lovely little room facing Big Ben which filled the place with its chiming when it struck the hour and its quarters. Since this was Plaid Cymru's office at Westminster, I shared it with Heulwen Huws, our cheerful and efficient secretary.

I wasn't born to be a Member of Parliament or a professional politician. I am always astonished when I hear someone talking about following a career in politics, as if politics were just one profession among many. Several Nationalists who look on politics in this way have joined the Labour Party or some other party because that was the only means of promoting their careers. I was driven into politics for the reason that it's in the political field that important decisions are made which affect the life of the Welsh nation. As a consequence of my lack of confidence, which arose in turn from my other shortcomings, I used to have nightmares in the years I was at Westminster, during which things got so disastrously out of hand that I would be woken up by my own screams. It's more than likely, moreover, that all this, together with the anxiety and stress that I felt, had a lot to do with the series of illnesses for which I had to undergo surgery. I can give a good enough account of myself on a platform when I have time to prepare what I have to say. Whenever I speak in public about such familiar matters as Welsh history, peace, Nationalism, or Plaid Cymru and its policies, I can be quite effective. As a rule I spoke without notes on these topics, except at conferences and on special occasions. I wasn't too bad either at answering questions put by someone else or by a panel or by other speakers. Among the best things I ever did were as a participant in the television programmes 'University Challenge' and 'Celtic

Challenge', and in radio debates with Iorwerth Thomas and Jim Griffiths, and once in an hour's debate on the wireless with Lord Ogmore – that kind of thing. But no one could call me a great Parliamentarian. I drew some comfort from a conversation I once had with Horace King when he was Speaker. He had organized a fund for the erection of a statue of Keir Hardie at Westminster. The only people to be commemorated in this way are great Parliamentarians. The two in this century upon whom this honour has been bestowed are Winston Churchill and David Lloyd George, and in that order. After a statue of Churchill in heroic pose was put up, some insisted that Lloyd George should be shown in a challenging pose as a partner to him in the Members' foyer, which is next to the holy of holies. In arguing for the putting up of a statue to Keir Hardie, Horace King had to admit that the Scot was not a great Parliamentarian. He had hardly played much part in the activities of the House. King's argument was that Keir Hardie had led, and to a large extent created, the Labour Party which had played such a great part in Parliament's work during the twentieth century. For this reason it was agreed that the statue should be put up. Hardie's bust stands today in a corner on a landing that leads down to the lower refectory. Of course, I don't have Keir Hardie's ability and I have done little to compare with what he accomplished, but I too have used whatever talents I may possess in the building of a party.

My experience in Parliament was similar to that on the County Council. In both places, and for most of the time, I was on my own as the only Welsh Nationalist; in both places the Labourites were particularly hostile towards me. I was given the traditional silence to deliver my maiden speech, but after that a number of Welsh Labourites, with Jim Griffiths prominent among them, came into the chamber to interrupt and heckle. Welsh question-time would always include a contest between me and George Thomas. In those days two direct questions could be put and two supplementaries, although only one was allowed in the last session I attended. The treatment that was handed out to me by Labour came as a shock to Winnie Ewing and she made a point of coming into the debate whenever I was speaking, in order to lend me her very audible support.

It may be difficult for some readers to recall how vicious George Thomas could be. Last year he spent a whole week at the National Eisteddfod happily enough, like a man in his element. He said he was never happier. This was not the same chap as the George Thomas I first knew as Secretary of State for Wales and later as leader of the Welsh group of Labour M.Ps. In these capacities he was extremely set in his anti-Welsh sentiment and savage in his readiness – always with a smile – to cudgel a Nationalist about the head and stab him in the chest or from behind. He was the very scourge of Welsh Nationalism and the Welsh language. Leo Abse was tender-hearted in comparison. His favourite targets were Plaid Cymru and *Cymdeithas yr Iaith* – the Welsh Language Society. At Westminster, with the might of the British Government at his back and his hounds about him baying for blood, he found the lone Nationalist sitting opposite him tasty prey.

At about this time the troubles began again in Northern Ireland. In the opinion of anti-Nationalists this proved how dangerous it was to have a devolved Parliament: they said it was the Parliament at Stormont that was the root of the troubles. The Assembly's very existence was alleged to be the cause of the awful violence. (After the situation deteriorated with the winding up of Stormont, the British were later to yearn for its re-establishment.) They also tried to claim that the I.R.A. demonstrated the perils of Welsh Nationalism. Time after time Wales was warned by George Thomas that campaigning for the Welsh language, though the methods used were completely non-violent, was sure to lead to a situation of terror like the one in Northern Ireland. Here is a quotation from an article in *The Guardian*: 'For anyone to say that what has happened in Ulster cannot happen in Wales,' George Thomas declared, 'is refusing to measure up to the facts that stare us in the face. What we have heard from the Eisteddfod in the last week could well have been the voices of General Amin and Enoch Powell. I am considering the formation of a league of English-speaking Welsh people to redress the balance of interest in the Principality. I am prepared to call a meeting of responsible people to form such a league. The BBC is already at the mercy of the Welsh Language Society.'

There was a lot of seething anger among workers for the language when the Gorsedd of Bards decided to admit George Thomas to its ranks at the National Eisteddfod held in Barry in 1968. They felt that this diplomatic flattery of the language's chief enemy was a betrayal of their cause. The officials of the Gorsedd were astonished by the reaction against its decision. They were afraid that a great commotion might harm the peace of the Eisteddfod and arranged for a large detachment of policemen to protect the Minister from the wrath of his compatriots. So many police had never before been seen on the Eisteddfod Field and they have never been since. But they weren't enough to guarantee the peace in the opinion of the Gorsedd. I received a request over the telephone from the Archdruid Gwyndaf, a friend from our student days at Aberystwyth, that I should walk with George Thomas in the Gorsedd's procession on the Eisteddfod Field. Since I didn't feel that I could do that, Gwyndaf asked whether he could come and have a word with me, and he drove from Llandudno all the way to Llangadog. A great commotion could do irreparable harm to the festival, he said, but to have to cancel a visit by the Secretary of State would have even more far-reaching consequences. So I agreed to do it. We changed into our white robes at Gladstone Road School, where I had been a pupil so many years before, and were transported by bus to the Eisteddfod Field. As we stood at the entrance, George said to me, 'My knees are like jelly, Gwynfor.' Then, escorted by police, we walked on to the Field, George and I at the head of a procession of bards. Just inside the entrance I spotted a large, fierce and resentful crowd of young people who had a menacing look about them. But when they saw that I was walking at George's side, the pressure on the police was suddenly lifted and we reached the Pavilion without anything being thrown at him or the striking of any blow. The doors were opened and the procession moved down the aisle towards the stage. Three rows from the front George came to an abrupt halt and stood still, and the long procession also stopped. His mother was sitting in the seat next to the aisle. As we all know, George adored his mother and it's to his credit that Mam became quite a well-known character after his elevation to the Speaker's chair. He leaned over to her and his loud whisper broke the hush of the pavilion: 'It's all right, Mam, Gwynfor is with me.' After we had left the Field, at the end of the Chairing of the Bard ceremony, George asked what he could do for me. If only I had asked for a Parliament for Wales, I might have got it that afternoon, but all I asked him to do was carry my white robes back to Gladstone Road School, and this the Secretary of State did willingly enough.

George Thomas stopped hounding the Welsh-speaking Welsh after leaving his party political job and becoming one of the Chairmen of the House of Commons. On the retirement of Selwyn Lloyd as Speaker he was one of the candidates for the position. He asked Dafydd Wigley and Dafydd Elis Thomas and myself for our support and we three Plaid Cymru M.Ps. gave it. George Thomas was one of the best Speakers in the history of Westminster. In thanking Selwyn Lloyd for his fairness in the chair, I managed to utter two sentences in Welsh without his trying to stop me, and two hours later I was asked for a translation so that what I had said could be printed in Hansard. When George Thomas took the chair I congratulated him too and wished him well in Welsh. I noticed there was a broad grin on his face. My Welsh words were recorded in Hansard but not his grin. Wales saw the best side of George Thomas thereafter. The sad thing is that the anti-Welsh side of his personality looms larger in the recent history of Wales than the man who was one of us on the Eisteddfod Field at Machynlleth.

One of the most effective methods I developed at Westminster was to interrogate the Government with both written and oral questions. This was the first time, as far as I know, for this technique to be used so persistently. Since it wasn't possible to ask more than two oral questions every six weeks – that's the measure of the democratic answerability of the Welsh Office – the questions for the most part had to be written ones. I asked nearly a thousand a year and the Welsh Office started complaining bitterly about the cost of their replies. It claimed that the cost of answering my questions was running into thousands of pounds a year. But within a few months Elystan Morgan began competing with me on this score and I have noticed that Members' questions have greatly increased since then. In imitation of the Government's habit of publishing its policies in White Papers, I too published a selection of my questions, together with the damning answers given by the Government, under the title *Black Papers on Wales*, in which the Government stood condemned out of its own mouth. These documents had covers similar to the Government's White Papers except that they were black. I once happened to be sitting in the library at the same table as Enoch Powell with the first of the *Black Papers* in front of me on the day of its publication. On spotting it, he took hold of it and said like a flash, in Welsh, 'The Black Book of Carmarthen, is it?'. This was a reference to a famous medieval Welsh manuscript and those were the only words of modern Welsh that I ever heard him utter in private conversation, although he had once had a good academic knowledge of medieval Welsh, enough to edit a a manuscript of the Welsh Laws with Professor Stephen J. Williams. I remember asking him him how on earth he had managed to speak Welsh so fluently on a television programme without having spoken it from one year's end to the next. His reply was that he had been working hard at brushing up his Welsh the previous day.

I had the willing support of many members of Plaid Cymru during my time at Westminster. My agricultural consultant was Gareth Evans, who had fought Cardiganshire for us twice, and Dafydd Wigley, who was living at the time in Hounslow and working for Mars, the chocolate-makers, advised me on industrial matters. He came regularly to Westminster and I visited his and Elinor's home several times. Dafydd had worked for Plaid Cymru as a schoolboy and had been a staunch Nationalist ever since then. I was able to speak with authority on housing because Eurfyl ap Gwilym was feeding me with information. At the only sitting of the Welsh Grand Committee where this matter was discussed, the material at my disposal was superior to anyone else's, thanks to Eurfyl. My daughter Meleri Mair, who had done a course in shorthand and typing at a technical college, worked from home as my secretary, though Rhiannon was also kept busy answering the 'phone and standing in for me at meetings that I was unable to attend. Clem Thomas, by now editor of *The Carmarthen Times*, was appointed part-time organizer after Gareth Evans had made enquiries about him and reported that he was genuine. He had been for a while Megan Lloyd George's agent, until he found that his wages weren't being paid regularly enough by the Labour Party.

Among the probable consequences of the by-election was the Government's decision not to go ahead with the building of a huge dock at Portbury, near Bristol, which would have dealt a grievous blow to the docks on the Welsh side of Severn; the Government also decided to establish the Royal Mint in Wales instead of putting it, as was generally expected, somewhere in the north-east of England. In his great disappointment over this, poor Dan Smith, the leader of the north-east, commented, 'What we need here is a couple of Nationalists.' Furthermore, Harold Wilson paid two visits to Carmarthen, which hadn't seen a Prime Minister ever before. On his second visit he announced his intention of having a new bridge built over the river Tywi. The bridge hasn't been much help in reducing the town's traffic-congestion but it did a good deal to increase the Labour vote in the constituency.

I shall not try to give an account here of my first term at Westminster, for much of it will be found in the book *The Welsh Question* by Alan Butt Phillips, but I should refer, because of their continuing importance, to two things in particular. One is the Welsh Language Act that was passed in 1967, a little more than a year after the Carmarthen by-election. This was the fruit of the Hughes Parry Committee which had been examining the status of the Welsh language in public life. Although it conceded equal validity rather than equal status, its preamble can be interpreted as a statement in favour of the latter. There is a real and substantial difference between the two. What is certain is that we should not have had such an Act, if any at all, had it not been for the electoral success of Plaid Cymru. The Hughes Parry Report would probably have been shelved, just like the Reports of the Welsh Advisory Council, chaired by Huw T. Edwards, were in the 'fifties.

The second matter to which I shall refer was a four-day debate on the Common Market. The question was whether Britain should apply for membership. The Government had decided by an overwhelming majority in favour of applying, but Great Britain was put to shame by a veto by De Gaulle. The debate was opened with a speech lasting an hour and half by Harold Wilson, who was keenly in favour of joining. I argued against, basing my speech on two main points. One was the economic harm that British membership would cause in Wales and the other was the danger that the Community would develop into a great military power possessing nuclear weapons. I argued that such an eventuality might lead to a war that would destroy the civilization of Europe. I spoke as a keen European; no one who has been so greatly influenced by Saunders Lewis could do otherwise. But the Europe I wanted was a Europe of the small nations and the historical regions that make up its civilization. I pleaded for their unification in a loose confederation that would allow that civilization to grow, but I rejected the concept of a federal Europe. Today it's more than likely that pulling out of the European Community would do more harm than good to Wales. But with the terrifying growth of the nuclear threat, Europe's great need seemed to me then to be the coming together of its peoples in the cause of peace and against nuclear arms, not a political and military union of just a part of the continent which was armed with nuclear weapons against the Soviet Union. Our primary task in Europe on both sides of the Iron Curtain was to rid ourselves of nuclear arms.

After its victory at Carmarthen, Plaid Cymru's growth continued up to the tribulations of 1969, albeit at a slower pace than that of the S.N.P. after Hamilton. In 1967 and 1968 we were fortunate enough to have by-elections in the Rhondda and at Caerphilly after the death of Iorwerth Thomas and Ness Edwards, two bitter enemies of the national movement. Iorwerth Thomas was a Welsh-speaker from Cwmparc in the Rhondda, although I never heard him utter a word in the language. He was brutish in his hatred of things Welsh. From the end of the 'forties he kept on attacking 'the Welsh nationalist fanatics who by their conduct and propaganda will put Wales back to the low levels of peasant economy.' He and Ness Edwards had two of the largest majorities anywhere in the countries of Britain and they had no need to lift an electoral finger to keep their seats. The only thing Iori Thomas used to do was call in at some of the drinking-clubs of the Rhondda Fach on the eve of poll. In fact, his nickname was the King of Clubs. Our candidate at the by-election was Vic Davies, a man of sound judgement, who still works for the Party in the Rhondda. On seeing Plaid Cymru's progress, the Government hurriedly passed a Leasehold Reform Act in order to curry favour with the people of the Rhondda, many of whose homes were leasehold rather than freehold. They and people like them in other parts of Wales have Plaid Cymru to thank for the slight easing of their situation that wouldn't have happened had it not been for the Party. Plaid Cymru still fights, under the leadership of Owen John Thomas, against the iniquities of the leasehold system by which people can be deprived by their landlords of the homes in which they have lived all their lives. The high point of the by-election in the Rhondda was the unforgettable meeting at the Parc and Dare Hall at a moment when we were beginning to think we might win. With another week in which to campaign we might well have done so, and what a breakthrough that would have been. Alec Jones, a former teacher and Iori Thomas's agent, was elected but the Labour majority was slashed from 16,888 to 2,306. It was a close-run thing.

Our experience at Caerphilly was even more wonderful. There the Party's candidate was Dr Phil Williams, whom I once heard described as a genius. He is an example of the great ability among Welsh Nationalists which has convinced me that Plaid Cymru could easily form a Welsh Government as capable as any of the British parties'. It was interesting to hear Sir Goronwy Daniel, who had a distinguished career in England before becoming head of the Welsh Office, saying recently that it wasn't among those who had got on in London and overseas the most able Welsh people are to be found, but among those who have stayed at home in Wales. Phil Williams had been Chairman of the Cambridge University branch of the Labour Party. He had fought Caerphilly twice before on behalf of Plaid Cymru and this time he led a terrific campaign. The most notable event was a motorcade a mile long that wound its way from Bargoed all the way to Caerphilly. The momentum with which our message was put across gathered pace from day to day. Fred Evans, another ex-teacher and agent to Ness Edwards, was elected, but the Labour majority went down from 21,148 to 1,874. The day after the poll poor old Fred Evans was showing the bruises on his arm which he claimed Fascist Nationalist hooligans had inflicted on him after the count. But the worst damage done to Fred was the bruising of his pride. At about this time, too, Jim Griffiths became anxious to retire from Parliament and go to the House of Lords, but when an opinion-poll of the people of Llanelli revealed that Plaid Cymru was likely to win the seat at a by-election, he decided to stay on in the House of Commons.

With the growth of Nationalism in Scotland running hand-in-hand with the Welsh awakening, Harold Wilson and his Government – as always happens when Nationalism is gaining ground – felt obliged to move in an attempt to prevent its progress by making a concession. What it did this time was set up a Commission and give it substantial powers, a Royal Commission in fact, to study the constitutional status of Wales and Scotland and to make recommendations. In forcing the Government for the first time to take the national future of Wales seriously, Welsh Nationalism had its greatest success to date. Lord Crowther, the economist, was the Commission's first Chairman, and after his death, he was followed by Lord Kilbrandon, and it's by the latter's name that the hefty Report became known. Two members of the Commission were stalwart Welshmen who had given a lifetime of valuable service to their country – Sir Ben Bowen Thomas and Sir Alun Talfan Davies. Both had at one time been members of Plaid Cymru. The Party gave oral evidence on two occasions, one in Cardiff and again at Aberystwyth, and it presented a mountain of written evidence. Crowther paid particularly warm tribute to the economic plan for Wales which had been prepared by Dafydd Wigley and Phil Williams. Several possible versions of a constitution for Wales were included in the Commission's majority and minority reports. Six of its members supported a Parliament for Wales. However, by the time the final Report was published, both Winnie Ewing and I had lost our seats, and although Donald Stewart was returned to Westminster for the Western Isles of Scotland, the British parties then took it for granted that the threat from Nationalism in our two countries had blown over. For that reason they gave the Report a cool reception and prepared to let it gather dust in Whitehall. But they were to receive a terrific shock at two subsequent by-elections, one in Merthyr Tydfil and the other in Glasgow. Plaid Cymru's candidate in Merthyr was Emrys Roberts, who was later to lead it on the local council when the Party came to power in the town. His contribution to Plaid Cymru's work had already been enormous as an organizer and as its General Secretary. Years before, he had been given twelve months in prison for his stand against military conscription. Although it was Labour that won the seat, Ted Rowlands's majority was only 3,700, whereas S.O. Davies had been used to getting a majority of anything between 17,000 and 22,000. The Liberal received 765 votes. At Govan in Glasgow Margo McDonald won the seat for the S.N.P. Once again the Nationalism of our two countries had demonstrated its strength and the consequence was that the Government had to reconsider the future of Wales and Scotland.

In the mean while, the life of Wales had taken a serious turn with the growing use of violence by those who had despaired of ever achieving electoral success. Whenever there was an explosion in

Wales, and it happened more frequently than in Scotland, politicians from the British parties always put the blame on Plaid Cymru, and one of the allegations brought against us at every Election, including the one at Carmarthen, was that we were encouraging the use of violence. This charge had been regularly made for twenty years or more. It was the main theme of Huw Thomas's campaign when he stood as Liberal candidate at Carmarthen in 1970. He tried to make out that I was some sort of jack-booted Nazi. They are still at it, tirelessly. We had a brilliant example in February of this year from Dr Alan Williams, who speaks from the anti-Welsh heart of the Labour Party the kind of language that used to be heard on the County Council a generation ago. In one of the long-winded letters he sends to local newspapers throughout Wales, Dr Williams went on about a little speech I had made as Day President at the National Eisteddfod in Machynlleth. The observations, mainly historical, which I had made in the same capacity at the Ammanford Eisteddfod, were also targeted by the Labour Party. As he came at last to the point of his letter, Dr Williams gave the awesome background to what he had to say: 'Over the last fifteen years we have witnessed in Wales an escalating catalogue of violence . . . Throughout this period Gwynfor Evans has been conspicuous by his silence in condemning such violence . . . On the contrary, he visits the trials and the prisons for (*sic*) those prosecuted, thus giving moral support and encouragement. During the Fourth Television Channel campaign Gwynfor himself threatened a hunger-strike, unless the Government reversed its U-turn. Hunger-strikes are no part of the Welsh heritage. Indeed, they belong to the Maze Prison in Northern Ireland – and it was largely because of fears that a Northern Ireland-like situation could develop in Wales if Gwynfor carried out his fast unto death, that the Government capitulated. From his "victory" on the issue, the duty of a genuine patriot was then to defuse the strong passions he had aroused. Quite to the contrary, Gwynfor has tried to raise passions still higher. As President of the Day at the National Eisteddfod in Machynlleth, addressing 5,000 of our people in the pavilion, and tens of thousands more through the media, his speech sounded like a war-cry. He said, "Patriots have fought and died for their country. In Wales's past there have been sufficient patriots prepared to lay down their lives for their country." It was left to the listener to interpret. What did he mean? Fought and died? Lay down their lives? Was he asking for more hunger-strikers? Volunteers to be killed in action? A bloody uprising? ', and so on, and so forth. My transgression had been to quote from our national anthem – '*Ei gwrol ryfelwyr, gwladgarwyr tra mad, dros ryddid collasant eu gwaed*'

('Her brave warriors, most excellent patriots, spilled their blood for freedom').

In his next letter Dr Williams, the Labour Party's leading intellectual in Carmarthen, said that he too sometimes sang '*Hen Wlad fy Nhadau*': 'I enjoy singing our National Anthem, along with 50,000 fellow-Welshmen at Cardiff Arms Park, and such places, but to passionately support Wales on the sports field is as far as my nationalism goes.' Although he wasn't a Nationalist like me, he said, he was the better Welshman, because his blood was purer. He said of it, 'It is pure, undiluted, Welsh-speaking, Welsh blood. Indeed, my pedigree is a good deal better than yours.' Thus we learned that not only has Dr Williams a body full of red Welsh blood but that it also speaks Welsh, which is more than I can claim for myself. Even the Nazis, who based their race and nationhood on their Aryan blood, didn't assert that it was German-speaking! Nor has Plaid Cymru ever declared that Welsh nationality depends on blood or anything of that kind. For us, in the words of the poet Glyn Jones, anyone can choose to be Welsh as long as they are prepared to take the consequences.

The Labour Party has reared some great thinkers to lead it in Wales, but the Tory Party has been just as fortunate. On a radio programme in which he and I once took part, Delwyn Williams – then Tory M.P. for Montgomeryshire – claimed that he was the better Welshman because he had many centuries of Welsh blood flowing in his veins. He too was alarmed at my violent methods. Indeed, he managed to accuse me on the one hand of being a bloody terrorist and, on the other, of being too much of a coward to defend my country by using the nuclear bomb. As I write these words he is calling for Britain's military invasion of the Argentinian mainland. Delwyn is quite fearless. He is no more afraid of invading Argentina than he is of attacking Wayne Williams for his stand on behalf of the Welsh language.

After several explosions had occurred, I began to have frequent visits from the police. In the case of the large explosion at Clywedog they had more reason than usual for calling on me. On the night of the blast I had been within a few miles of the place, addressing a meeting at Caersws. Two days after the incident, police-officers called at Talar Wen with a cap and scarf they had found near the dam, to see whether they fitted me. The Birmingham police also had an excuse for paying me a visit after an explosion at the offices of the Severn-Trent Water Board in that city, for a little while earlier I had led a Plaid Cymru deputation to the Municipal Offices, calling for payment for the water of Wales. But the explosions were exploited by the politicians quite cynically, in order to do the Party harm. One repugnant example of this was the behaviour of George Thomas after an officer was hurt in an explosion at the RAF station between Penbre and Cydweli in 1968. George Thomas alleged that a Nationalist was responsible, although he knew only too well that this wasn't true. A few days later he went still further. He came down from London to Carmarthen specifically to visit the wounded officer at Glangwili Hospital. He had never visited a miner who had been injured underground, because he wasn't able to lay the blame on Plaid Cymru for that. I heard shortly afterwards who in fact had been responsible. The person's vicar wrote to me saying that he couldn't remain silent while Nationalists were being blamed. The man under suspicion was an RAF cadet from a small town near Coventry, who had been at Penbre for the four days prior to the explosion. The vicar told me all about him in a long letter and confirmed the main facts in a second letter. It included an account of the young man's obses- sive interest in explosions and fires. Shortly after the incident he was taken into the psychiatric wing of an RAF hospital in England. At the time a Scotsman by the name of Jock Wilson was in charge of the squad of English plain-clothes police who had been sent to Wales, much to the annoyance of their Welsh counterparts, to look for the perpetrators of the explosions. I asked him to come to see me to discuss the explosion at Penbre, and he came in the company of another police-inspector. I showed them the vicar's letters, but there was nothing in them that these two hadn't seen before. They knew everything about the case, they said, but they didn't have enough evidence to take action against the young Englishman. Of course, if they had done that, they would have made fools of the politicians who were lambasting Plaid Cymru. In public they went on saying that they were looking for a Welsh Nationalist, and George Thomas persisted with his claim that the bomb had been placed by a Nationalist. When I drew his attention at Westminster to the evi- dence against the RAF cadet from the English Midlands, without naming him or giving his place of birth, George Thomas responded by saying that I was slandering an innocent Englishman. The culprit was never apprehended.

The police made use of a number of *agents provocateurs*. These men would pretend to be keen Nationalists, but their real purpose was to encourage Welsh people in the use of explosives so that the police could catch them in the act. This ruse had three objectives: to enable the police to prove they could be successful in apprehending miscreants; to give Nationalists a bad name; and to discourage potential Nationalists, as when Inspector Pat Molloy arrested fifty innocents and had them locked up in cells about three years ago. One agent managed to cajole three young Nationalists into laying dynamite at the base of a monument near Holyhead harbour. It was he who supplied them with the explosives and manufactured the bomb. He too informed the police about the lads. This man's address was a farmhouse in Radnorshire, but we were told that he had come from Hamilton, Winnie Ewing's constituency, where again he had pretended to be a keen member of the S.N.P. Winnie went to see his mother, who signed an affidavit that her son's room was full of police equipment. I tried to get *The Times* to give the case some publicity in order that the matter might be taken to a court of law – in those days the newspaper used to do quite a bit of that kind of reporting. Two journalists went up to Hamilton but the man's mother refused to speak to them. The three Welsh youths were defended by Dewi Watkin Powell, who managed on appeal to get the prison sentence reduced from eighteen months to nine.

There were regular press reports about the antics of the Free Wales Army. We considered them a comic opera that only added to the tension of the times. Doubtless Plaid Cymru suffered by being tarred with the same brush as the FWA. We hoped that its members would in due course be prosecuted for parading illegally in military uniforms, for that would have rid us of the nuisance. But the authorities had a cunning plan to use the group in order to do us further harm. I never thought for a moment that the FWA were likely to shoot anyone. Their function was to mask much more serious activities. This became evident at the trial and subsequent imprisonment of John Jenkins, the leader of a group calling itself *Mudiad Amddiffyn Cymru* ('Movement for the Defence of Wales'), who was given ten years. I had a lot of respect for John Jenkins. A sergeant in the British Army, he in fact considered himself to be a soldier fighting for Wales and he scorned my way of working. Saunders Lewis, too, was of the opinion that the FWA were soldiers fighting for Wales and he was magnaminous enough to attend their trial. I believe my refusal to accompany him contributed to the coolness between us for some years thereafter. But we were later reconciled. When our estrangement was at its frostiest, Rhiannon and I received an invitation from Nesta Howe to have dinner with Saunders and dear Mrs Lewis at her hotel in Barry. Nesta was my favourite cousin, a gracious and lively woman, and the only one among my cousins to show warm sympathy for Wales. Her death at an early age was a great loss. It was a first-class dinner and the high-point of the evening was a bottle of Bordeaux '46. Saunders leapt like a stag when the bottle was brought to the table and spoke earnestly in appreciation of the qualities of Bordeaux wine from that year. My heart warmed to him as I watched him enjoying it and I sipped my Jaffa Juice '69.

The year 1969 saw the launch of the noble but quite unpopular campaign of *Cymdeithas yr Iaith* against monolingual English roadsigns. This was to cause more bad feeling than anything else up to then because it was evidence of what was called 'vandalism' in most parts of Wales. A wave of righteous anger swept through the country. The crescendo of the Society's tumultuous activities was reached at the time of the investiture of Charles Windsor as Prince of Wales in July 1969. The main reason behind the timing of this occasion, I'm convinced, was to do the maximum harm possible to Plaid Cymru in the dilemma with which it was faced. On the one hand, our instinct prompted us to oppose the investiture because the crown and title of the heir to the throne was a potent symbol of our subjection as a nation and our incorporation into England. On the other, since the Welsh are so unhealthily monarchist, to have opposed the event would have been sure to damage Plaid Cymru. We had had bitter experience of that in 1936 when the Party had boycotted the coronation, under the leadership of Professor W.J. Gruffydd, who at the time was its Vice-President, Saunders Lewis being in prison for his part in causing the Fire at Penyberth. This had contributed to the stemming of the great progress the Party had made after the burning of the bombing school and the imprisonment of Saunders Lewis and his two companions. To have opposed the investiture vigorously, in our opinion, would have done more harm to the Party than a boycott of the coronation, for the reason that it was being held in Wales. This was the biggest act of propaganda ever seen in our country and there was world-wide interest in it. It was shown on television in the four corners of the world, including the United States where many millions watched it. It was evident that the Government, which had had such a shock in Carmarthen, the Rhondda, and Caerphilly, believed that it had hit upon an ideal way of harming Plaid Cymru. But the Party's Conference displayed its political maturity in deciding, with only two votes against, to leave on the table the motion that we take action against the investiture. The Party's policy was to ignore the whole spectacle. But the response of the Welsh Language Society was quite different. With an abundance of self-respect, it attacked the show in vigorous fashion, with the prophetic passion of the philosopher J.R. Jones spurring it on. It was a triumph of meticulous organization on the part of the authorities that the trial of the FWA was timed to last for a fortnight prior to the investiture and to end neatly on the very day it took place. On the great day there were many flags flying in Wales, both large and small, and the most prominent among them was the Union Jack.

The day of the investiture happened to be Welsh Questions Day at Westminster. I had put two questions down on the day's order papers but I was the only Welshman in the House that day. The Welsh Members were at Caernarfon castle – Elystan Morgan and Wil Edwards, Cledwyn Hughes and T.W. Jones, and all the Socialist Labourites in their silk hats and coat-tails, and George Thomas in his splendour presenting 'the golden rod' to Charles. The night before, at Abergele, two young Welshmen were killed by the explosion of their own bomb as they carried it to the railway-line along which the royal train was due to arrive. They were not members of Plaid Cymru. As I got to my feet to ask my first question, a roar of angry baying arose from the Labour and Conservative benches, and for a little while it was impossible for me to hear my own voice. Of course, there was no one there from the Welsh Office to reply. After I had managed to put my question so that it could be heard, it was answered quite brusquely by Judith Hart without any reference to its content; rather, she went on about an attempt by Welsh Nationalists the previous night to blow up the line on which the royal train was to arrive. The same thing happened with my second question.

When Charles came to Carmarthen on his triumphal tour of Wales after the investiture, as the M.P. for the constituency I had to shake hands with him, but I wasn't bidden to the feast at Golden Grove later that morning. Instead, I drove home past the mansion, stopping for petrol at Wynford Morgan's garage at Ffair-fach. The village square was filled on all sides by a crowd of people waiting to see Charles as he made his way from his lunch to Ammanford. The village was one of my strongest bastions, where I could usually rely on a warm welcome. On this occasion, however, I got out of the car and stepped into a deafening silence like that of the grave. Through the chilly atmosphere I went into the shop to look for Wynford, and it persisted as he put petrol into my tank, and then in the unsmiling silence I drove away.

During the second half of 1969 I saw my support slipping away. I don't doubt that the painting of slogans and the bombs and the witty attacks on the monarchy did some people's spirits a power of good, and that it has lasted to some extent ever since. But many people were estranged from Plaid Cymru which, for three years previously, had been growing apace. When Elfyn Talfan, the brother of Aneirin and Alun, who had for years been a mainstay of the cultural life of Brynaman, went selling the Party's newspaper, *Y Ddraig Goch*, on the road to the Black Mountain, where he had been used to selling a dozen copies, he couldn't sell one. Although we had won back quite a bit of ground by the time of the Election, the harvest was a bitter one in terms of votes. On the whole I am pretty sure the effect was a beneficial one for Wales, however.

On 4th February 1970 I came out of the chamber in the House of Commons to face a crowd of reporters. Did I know, they asked, that my daughter Meinir was in a cell under the law courts near the Strand? This was the first I had heard about a raid by members of the Welsh Language Society led by Ffred Ffransis on the court where the famous case of Convoy Q17 was being heard. In order to draw attention to the status of the Welsh language, they had gone into the court, where the international press was assembled, and sat down on the floor in front of the judge, singing Welsh hymns and folk-songs. The judge, who had never before suffered such an insult to his dignity, was extremely annoyed. He demanded an apology from the transgressors and, when they refused, they were sent to prison for six months for contempt of court. Having had the news from the journalists, I immediately went over to try to see Meinir. On the steps at the magnificent building's entrance, I was spotted by a BBC reporter. During an interview that was broadcast throughout the countries of Britain, and which shocked many a staid voter in the constituency of Carmarthenshire, I admitted that I was full of admiration for Meinir's courage. I found her, together with four other girls from the University College at Aberystwyth, to be in high spirits, though locked in an underground cell. Despite the fact that they and the lads who were with them had decided not to appeal against any sentence, I persuaded them to let me try to arrange for an appeal, and I went to see Dewi Watkin Powell who had helped me on so many previous occasions. He explained that it wasn't usual to allow an appeal against a judge's decision when a court had been held in contempt.

A week later, the girls having been in Holloway Prison, Rhiannon and the other parents attended the hearing. It was Lord Denning, attended by two judges, who presided on the bench. Dewi excelled himself, and there is good reason to believe that his own subsequent elevation to the judiciary had something to do with the brilliance of his defence that day. The five were released, but because the lads had refused to plead, they had to spend months in Pentonville Prison, where I visited them every week. The following year, Sir Goronwy Daniel and his wife Lady Valerie were kind enough to invite Rhiannon and me to dine with them in Aberystwyth, when Lord Denning and his wife were among the guests. During the meal Denning said to me, 'When I saw those lovely innocent girls in front of me, I knew I couldn't send them back to prison.' So there had been something else, besides Dewi's brilliance, to explain their release! I should like to pause at this point to mention the many good turns Goronwy Daniel has done for the Welsh language, but I must press on with the main story. Not long after this, Meinir was in prison again – at Pucklechurch in Gloucestershire, since there is no women's prison in Wales. When I went to see her, we weren't allowed to say a word in our own language, and the same was true when Rhiannon visited her. Having to speak English to each other made our relationship seem most strained, as if we were strangers. That was the only time we had ever spoken to each other in what we Welsh call 'the thin language'. She had been imprisoned this time because she had stood up in the public gallery of Swansea Courthouse to make a statement in favour of the Welsh language during a case brought against members of the Society. A little earlier she had been jostled by the police and pushed down some stone stairs leading from the Court. The behaviour of the police towards language-protestors could be ferocious, but there's nothing to suggest that any of them ever struck back. The self-discipline they have shown over all the years of the Society's existence is one of the wonders of our national life. The charge brought against the leaders of the *Cymdeithas* at Swansea was conspiracy; they included Ffred Ffransis, Gronw ap Islwyn, Robat Gruffudd, and Dafydd Iwan. This charge is usually brought when there's no proof that the defendant has committeed any offence, as in the case of Wayne Williams. Dafydd Iwan, doubly famous for his political work and for his folk-singing, demonstrated debating skills of the first water. On hearing him presenting his case so powerfully and cross-examining and answering questions with such clarity, I was convinced that a new leader had arisen in Wales. Later, of course, in addition to making a unique contribution with his voice and guitar, he grew into one of Plaid Cymru's most formidable leaders. Not long afterwards, Meinir was back in Holloway for several months in the company of Enfys Llwyd, after a number of *Cymdeithas* activists had broken into the headquarters of the BBC in London; she had been found guilty of scattering documents to do with Winston Churchill and the coronation of 1953. Holloway is among the worst of prisons, completely degrading in its regime and conditions. Meinir believed that everyone who had been locked up there came out a worse person than when he or she had gone in. The only privilege she enjoyed was that she was allowed to receive and write letters in Welsh and that was because Mrs Wing, to whom I have already referred, was the Governor, and a Cornishman, the father of Tim Saunders, the Chaplain; he very kindly pretended that he was able to understand Welsh. After Kathleen Smith, the Vice-Governess of Holloway, became the Tory Parliamentary candidate for Caernarfonshire, of all places, Meinir took part in a quite difficult programme with her on television.

When Meinir and Ffred married, he too was expecting to return to prison. Altogether he has spent a total of five years in prison as part of his long fight for the language. He was given a year for climbing a television mast with intent to damage it and two years at the Mold court for conspiracy. Ffred was sent to prison in Walton Gaol for a year for the offence of having in his pocket a small map of a transmission area in the north of England that other members of the Welsh Language Society had raided. By then he was a married man and Meinir the Society's Secretary. After losing a baby, she came to live in Llangadog to keep the shop known as *Y Cwch Gwenyn*, that sold just about everything, but without much in the way of capital. It was she who ran the shop while Ffred was in prison and she was living there when Lleucu and Carys were born. In prison Ffred used to dream of starting a business selling Welsh crafts that would employ half a dozen members of the *Cymdeithas*, who would spend the other half of the year working for the Society. This exceptionally gifted young man worked hard to keep the business going without any capital behind him, and despite an incredible series of mishaps, while at the same time his strength was taxed by his prodigious labours on behalf of the Welsh language.

The 1970 Election was announced while I was in Middlesex Hospital, having recently undergone a serious surgical operation. For days before I had been observed at Westminster like some oriental spectre, my skin yellow and a faraway look in my eyes. Winnie Ewing had the same kind of shock as had my friend Reggie Walters when, in 1959, he put his head around the door of the ward at Glangwili Hospital and saw me looking poorly and with tubes stuck into me after treatment to my throat performed by the surgeon popularly known as Slasher Morgan. Reggie broke the bad news to my friends that he feared the worst. But Gwynoro Jones didn't fear the worst; he was the energetic Labour candidate in the Carmarthenshire constituency in October 1970 when the campaign started, within a month of my operation. Gwynoro confidently forecast that I had only six months to live, but he was exaggerating as always. It was no surprise to me that I lost that Election by some three and a half thousand votes. The surprise was that I hung on to nearly fifteen of the seventeen thousand I had received in July 1966. The candidate who undoubtedly had the biggest disappointment was the Liberal, Huw Thomas. Like so many Welsh Liberal candidates, he had been successful in his career, as a television presenter. I had noticed it was a successful career, and not any conviction about the cause, that was generally regarded as the main qualification for Liberal candidates, and this one had succeeded, like so many of them, in London. Although he had never been known to do the slightest thing for Wales, he came to Carmarthen as the country's saviour. He was ready to do battle on behalf of Wales unto his last breath, and for the other vague Liberal causes such as Freedom and Unity – or so he said. He would stand firm against all disunity. As a television personality he had charmed the ladies and appealed to farmers in particular. With so many qualifications for a Welsh leader, he was expecting to regain the seat for the Liberals. Indeed, he thought he had won it up to about midnight on the night of the count. I happened to be near the door when he arrived, all smiles, looking every bit the victor. I saw the Liberal agent quickly moving across to him and heard him say, 'You're a bad third.' Huw Thomas's face then fell and the smile was wiped from his face, just as it was from the faces of the rest of the Liberals present. They huddled together in a sullen little cluster. Their candidate said nothing to raise their spirits. After the result had been announced inside the hall, we moved out on to the balcony where the returning officer was to read out the voting figures to the large crowd that had gathered in the square below. The crowd's roar came up to meet us as we appeared at the window, the returning officer first, next Gwynoro Jones, myself third, and then Huw Thomas trailing behind me. But he didn't come out on to the balcony. Before reaching the window, he suddenly turned on his heel and said, 'If this is your bloody Wales, I'm never coming back here.' And as far as I am aware, he never did come back. Wales had lost another of its saviours. But no matter, it had gained Gwynoro Jones.

Chapter 20

The Nation of Dewi and Glyndwr

Although not able to lay claim to being a literary man, I have written quite a lot – because as a propagandist I believe in the power of the written word as well as the spoken. The element of propaganda was to be seen in my most ambitious work, an outline of the Welsh historical tradition which I called *Aros Mae*. It was the first attempt to present a history of Wales in one volume since O.M. Edwards published his book *Wales* in 1901. My work tried to look at our country's modern history as well as the Middle Ages, tracing the story of a nation whose life has been quite different from England's and giving it a pattern. The little Welsh history taught in schools in my day was merely an appendix to the history of England, the story of a conquered province from which all colour and light had been drained under the deep shadow of its conqueror. Most of our historians had seen Wales as a province of England. At the University Court in the 'fifties an Englishman who was Professor of History at the University College in Cardiff objected to my attempt to secure a Chair of Welsh History in the College on the grounds that the history of Wales was merely local history. I argued that the history of this nation should be the basis for the teaching of all history at both secondary and tertiary level. The subject should be extended to the history of England, Europe and the world after grounding the pupil or student in the history of his own community and nation. After all, that's what happens in every free nation.

The history of Wales must be put in the hands of every Welsh man and woman. Its history is its memory. Where there is no history there is no civilization. In the history of the nation Welsh people will find their roots and learn about that part of European civilization for which they have responsibility. When they take possession of their history they will be in no doubt but that they are Welsh – not abstract beings, and certainly not a British amalgam unsure of whether they are English, Welsh, or British, or even British Welsh or Welsh

British. They will then be sure of their national identity. It is the confusion in the Welshman's identity which is mainly responsible for the ineffectiveness of the nation and for the servility of so many Welsh people. If they had possession of their country's history, they would be stronger and more dignified and confident. This confusion is reflected in their political and economic life, for the link between a lack of confidence and an unhealthy economy is a strong one. Furthermore, the psychological servility of the Welsh will not be removed by presenting their history to them as if it were part of English or British history. Although the situation has greatly improved with the emergence of a new generation of Welsh historians, the blight of much recent writing about modern Welsh history is that it has been heavily under British influences. But although too many Welsh historians, especially those on the political left, still view the history of Wales through English or British eyes, ignoring for example the central place of the Welsh language, it's been most heartening recently to see the emergence of a brilliant generation of independently minded Welsh historians.

And what a history the Welsh have! We see them beginning to form themselves into a community as early as the year 383 when Magnus Maximus, known in Welsh tradition as Macsen Wledig, departed from the Isle of Britain with his hosts under the Red Dragon flag, leaving the Welsh to defend their enchanting land. I think we should reject the pedantry that refuses to call it Wales in the centuries that followed the Roman period. A fact that made a deep impression on me is that Wales became a nation in the Age of the Saints, whereas Great Britain didn't come into existence for another twelve centuries. I am trying to establish the custom of considering 383 as the year which marks the beginning of our national history and to have it celebrated in 1983. I wrote a pamphlet about Magnus Maximus with this purpose in mind and asked Dafydd Iwan to compose a song for the occasion; the result was the thrilling '*Rŷm ni yma o hyd*' ('We are still here'), one of his greatest songs. After Macsen Wledig, over the next two centuries, the Welsh were possibly the only people in the Roman Empire to defend their country against attack from the Teutons, if we except the kingdom of Strathclyde on the northern side of Hadrian's Wall, which disappeared as an independent Welsh kingdom in the eleventh century. The story of the Welsh defence during the thousand years that followed is an inspiring one. It abounds with rich characters, and the heritage that was so stoutly defended and handed down to us is just as great and rich. The survival of the Welsh tradition and its literature over so many centuries can only be regarded as magnificent and astonishing, from the Golden Age of the Saints to the Steel Age of the People in the nineteenth century. In Welsh we use the word *gwerin* to denote the common people and it's a far better one than 'working-class' in the context of the recent history of Wales. For the Welsh haven't been serfs in England's back-yard: they have lived as a people a national life of great dignity that has been safeguarded over the last two centuries in the cruel circumstances of both town and country by the great heritage handed down to them through the medium of the Welsh language. The richness of their intellectual life has been quite unique. Despite all the cannibalising of the nation over the last hundred years or so, the rich vein running through the nation's life in our own abject time has not been exhausted. Though the nation itself may be falling apart, the foundations are still firm. It is for that reason we claim the right, in the words of Robin Oakey, 'to represent humanity on this patch of land'.

In my book *Aros Mae* I tried to discover a pattern in the story and make it easy to remember. I believe a people's sustenance is to be found in its history as a people, even among those who have only a tenuous grasp on it in the form of myth. We ought not to undervalue the part played by national myth; no one has yet attempted to measure the contribution made by Geoffrey of Monmouth and Theophilus Evans's book, *Drych y Prif Oesoedd*, in upholding the Welsh historical entity. I fully expected professional historians to make little of *Aros Mae*, but it wasn't so. It was generous of Tudur Jones and E.D. Jones to read the manuscript and to think well of it. It had a favourable review from Professor Glanmor Williams in the *Western Mail* and was highly praised by David Williams, my old County School teacher. Gwyn A. Williams said the book was a good example of what he called 'useable history'. When it was translated into English, Professor Alun Davies and his wife Margaret read it through before it went to press. Margaret was the Justice of the Peace who was sacked by Lord Hailsham for supporting the Welsh Language Society. The kindness shown to me by her husband Alun, whose untimely death was such a cruel blow, and by Drs Tudur Jones and E.D. Jones, was typical of the limitless help that made it possible to publish the book so quickly, and of the friendship that exists among the scholars of Wales. I wrote the first two pages of notes on Christmas Day 1970 and within seven months it was in the shops and on sale at the National Eisteddfod. This would have been impossible without the co-operation of Elfryn Thomas and the John Penry Press, of which I had been Chairman for six years. I myself did as much as possible to help, of course. Several times I took photographs to Bath and collected the blocks that were made of them there. Tegwyn Jones and my son Alcwyn Deiniol, the photographer in the family, were of great assistance with the illustrations and the jacket; I went up the Rhondda to arrange for the binding; O.M. Lloyd corrected the proofs; Professor Stephen J. Williams and Dr Lewis Evans read the work through to check the quality of the Welsh; the poetry was expertly translated by Professor Gwyn Williams of Trefenter; Elwyn Roberts made the arrangements for launching the book and, of course, Trebor Lloyd Evans, Secretary of the Union of Independents, showed his customary care and attention to detail from first to last. The five thousand copies of the first impression sold out fairly quickly, since Plaid Cymru took most of them; it also took the profit, and in due course there was a second impression. But of all those who helped, my wife Rhiannon was the heroine. It was she who typed the entire work from my poor handwriting, just as she had been the amanuensis for so many of my books, pamphlets, and articles. No one received any payment for the onerous work that had been undertaken on this occasion.

In May 1973 I addressed the Cardiff Business Club, one of the capital's posher societies, on Wales and its history. The chairman was Kenneth Davies, who had been a pioneer in the aviation industry and was at one time Chairman of Cambrian Airways. After the lecture he gave a dinner for thirty of the city's leading business people. Kenneth made sure that Wales was kept at the centre of the table-talk that evening. One of those present was Geoff Rich, the editor of *The South Wales Echo*, a paper which was then and still is tiresomely anti-Welsh in its editorial attitudes. It is an influential newspaper with twice the circulation of the *Western Mail*. That night, perhaps as a result of my lecture and the good food, the editor warmed towards Wales. He pushed a note across the table asking for something that seemed incredible at the time. It was a request for me to write ten articles on the history of Wales for his newspaper. I jumped at the chance, of course. We had a brief chat about it after the dinner and next morning he kept to his word. The articles were published as a centre-spread, with a line drawing to accompany each one. More than that, they were later collected and soon published as an attractive booklet on good-quality paper with a striking cover and colour illustrations. The edition of twenty thousand copies sold out in no time at all, at fifty pence a copy. Unfortunately, it was felt to be too expensive to print more, but I translated the booklet into Welsh and five thousand copies of that edition were also printed.

I have often made use of material relating to the history of Wales, as I did at the Cardiff Business Club, while addressing a variety of cultural societies or St. David's Day dinners. A run of these speaking engagements had the effect of making me put on weight from year to year. Among them were the dinners of Welsh Societies at Colleges and Universities such as the Dafydd ap Gwilym Society at Oxford and the Mabinogi Society at Cambridge. It was at a dinner of the Mabinogi that I first met Dr Gareth Evans, who was working at the Cavendish Laboratories at the time. I was later to work closely with him. But I don't think he was present at the Mabinogi dinner the evening a gentle woman of great dignity came over to thank me for my address. I was given to understand that she had never heard anything so wonderful. I later learned that she was Norah Chadwick, the great historian. She had done the most exciting work on the early centuries of Welsh history, much of which is to be found in her three substantial volumes published by the Cambridge University Press. From these I had taken a good deal of the material I had used in my lecture to the Mabinogi Society that evening! Later on, the University of Wales Press published her book on the Druids, which deserves much more attention than it has so far received. In her will (she died in 1972), Norah Chadwick left a small fortune for the creation of a Chair of Celtic History at Cambridge, but it seems the sum was insufficient for the purpose. I remember asking Professor Glyn Daniel, my old schoolfriend, whether St. John's College, his own College, with its Welsh connections, could find the rest of the money, but I never heard that anything was done about it.

Having heard that there was call for an English translation of *Aros Mae*, Elin Garlick approached me on the Eisteddfod Field offering, with great generosity, to undertake the work as a labour of love. The result was *Land of my Fathers*. I took advantage of this opportunity to add a few passages here and there, some thirty pages in all, perhaps. I believe about two thousand copies were made of the book's English version and it was reprinted three times thereafter. In a letter I received during the summer of 1981 from W. Rhys Nicholas, who kept an eye on the books printed at the John Penry Press, he said my book was the best-selling title of all the many they had ever published. I also heard from readers overseas, and from the other countries of Britain, some of them claiming that my book had made Nationalists of them. I have no idea how it had come to their attention, for the John Penry Press can't really afford to advertize any of its books.

I had been so impudent as to write a book about the history of Wales, despite my obvious lack of qualifications, because I couldn't get anyone else to write it, and not for want of trying. I am no scholar and even if I did have the talents of a historian, I had been too long growing tomatoes to have given them much exercise. In our family the historian's instinct belongs to my sons, Dafydd Prys and Guto

Prys, although I must also acknowledge that some of it was found on Rhiannon's side in her brother Dewi Prys Thomas, the great-grandson of Gweirydd ap Rhys. Despite having had no more than four days' schooling, in 1872 this weaver published one of his substantial books, *Hanes y Brytaniaid a'r Cymry*, a history of the Britons and the Welsh, in two large volumes, containing five hundred double-columned pages, 750 words per page and detailed notes on sources at the foot of each. The heroism of the Welsh Victorians was indeed remarkable. I had called on Prosser Rhys at the offices of Gwasg Aberystwyth as early as 1938, to ask him to find a writer who was enough of a historian to write the story of the Welsh nation. The only outcome had been to get the historian R.T. Jenkins to translate the booklet that J.E. Lloyd had written for the sixpenny series published by Benn, under the title *Golwg ar Hanes Cymru*. A more significant success was in persuading the Broadcasting Council to ensure the publication of a series of radio lectures that later appeared in print. It was Aneirin Talfan Davies who took this in hand, like so much else. There were two excellent series by our leading scholars and they were published in two volumes under the title *Wales Through the Ages*, under the editorship of A.J. Roderick.

In 1968 I became a member of the History Section of the Board of Celtic Studies with the sole purpose of persuading it to publish, under the imprint of the University of Wales Press, a series of books on Welsh History that would make one standard history, like those published at Oxford and Cambridge on England's history and by Edinburgh University Press on Scotland's. In discussion, the older historians maintained that the idea was completely impractical because, they said, another generation's articles and books on local history, histories of specific periods, histories of personalities and institutions, and so forth, were needed before they could think of putting together one comprehensive history of Wales. The younger generation, on the other hand, thought the idea practical, and the work was put into the hands of four among them. Glanmor Williams, who has made an outstanding contribution to the writing of our history, was appointed editor of the series. Last year, thirteen years on, the first volume in a projected series of six was published jointly by the University Presses of Wales and Oxford, namely *Rebirth of a Nation* by Kenneth O. Morgan, a history of Wales from 1880 to 1980. Some years will go by, I fear, before we see the rest, but it's encouraging to know that the increasing number of scholars working in this field have now made such an ambitious scheme a practical possibility.

In an attempt to nurture a greater interest in the history of Wales,

Plaid Cymru has brought out a variety of books and pamphlets. In 1936 it published a book of lectures on the history of the Act of Union of 1536. In 1946, at the Summer School held in Abergavenny, I planned a programme of lectures on the history of Welsh Nationalism, with a view to publishing a volume of them in due course. The result was the volumes *Seiliau Hanesyddol Cenedlaetholdeb Cymreig* and *The Historical Basis of Welsh Nationalism*. These books consist of some excellent lectures by A.W. Wade-Evans, T. Jones Pierce, Ceinwen Thomas, A.O.H. Jarman, and D. Gwenallt Jones; there is also one by me that's not in the same league as the others. Ceinwen Thomas published a long series of articles on the history of Wales in the *Welsh Nation*; she also contributed one of the essays in the little book on the Princes of independent Wales which was entitled *Ein Tywysogion*. The poet Gwenallt Jones wrote an essay on Michael D. Jones for *Triwyr Penllyn*, which also dealt with two other great sons of Penllyn, namely O.M. Edwards and T.E. Ellis. Four years prior to delivering his lecture at Abergavenny, Professor A.O.H. Jarman – our chief authority on the earliest period of Welsh history and literature – had been in prison for refusing military conscription.

At about this time we erected a number of stones in commemoration of some of the nation's great men, such as the one on the wall of Bodiwan, the home of the patriot Michael D. Jones, in Bala. At the beginning of the 'fifties we commissioned R.L. Gapper to carve in granite from the Trefor quarries the defiant words spoken to King Henry II by the Old Man of Pencader in the twelfth century – words that should be learned by heart by every schoolchild in Wales. Dafydd Orwig was Plaid Cymru's Organizer in those days and under his supervision the great stone was transported to Pencader in Dyfed. Meetings were held at every stop along the way and there was a great rally at journey's end. The memorial stone was unveiled by Dr William George, who also spoke at the rally. At Hendy-gwyn (Whitland) the Cymmrodorion were persuaded by Dewi Watkin Powell, the Chairman of their Council, to place a stone in commemoration of Hywel Dda, the king of that part of Dyfed in the tenth century and a great law-giver; a commemorative garden, designed by Peter Lord, was later built at Hendy-gwyn. This year I am attempting to awaken interest in Rhys ap Gruffudd, the king of southern Wales, who was born in 1132, and trying to induce the Government to restore his castle at Dinefwr, perhaps the most important castle in the history of Wales, and one which to our great shame is fast falling down. Would it, I wonder, be an idea for the women of Wales to do something to honour Gwenllian, his mother, who was killed in battle against the Normans near

Cydweli? The field is still known as Maes Gwenllian. But the most striking monument in which I had a hand was the one to Llywelyn ap Gruffudd, the last Prince of independent Wales, at Cilmeri on the road out of Builth, that was put up under the aegis of Breconshire County Council in association with Caernarfonshire County Council. By now the group known as *Cofiwn* is busy doing the necessary work of reminding our people of its great men and women in visible ways. There are scores of others in our history who deserve to be commemorated.

One thing in which I take pride is that I helped to arrange a meeting at Llandybie where tribute was paid to Gomer Roberts, the historian who was the very embodiment of the strength of the Welsh-speaking Nonconformist people, the richness of whose life was commented upon by Professor Zimmern, the renowned Professor of International Politics at Aberystwyth in the 'twenties. Gomer Roberts was held in high respect throughout Wales as an outstanding historian who combined his work as a scholar with his heavy duties as a minister of the Gospel without ever being afraid of showing his stout support for Welsh Nationalism. As a young man he had worked as a collier. When he felt the urge to go to college, six of his comrades in the anthracite coalfield published a selection of their poems in a volume entitled *O Lwch y Lofa*, which they sold in order to raise money to help Gomer on his way. That was the splendid thing about the robust old tradition of the Welsh people. In what country other than Wales could such a thing happen? It would be a mistake to think that the genius of our people has been extinguished. The radio programme *Talwrn y Beirdd*, presided over so wittily by the poet Gerallt Lloyd Owen, reminds us weekly in the most wonderful way that our people's talents and culture continue as before.

I entertain some hope that the sixteenth day of September will eventually be established as the Festival of Owain Glyndwr. He was proclaimed Prince of Wales on 16th September 1400. I have been trying to promote the idea for some years and I believe it is gradually catching on among our people. The reasons for celebrating the Festival of Glyndwr are obvious. He is the great national hero nearest to us in time, a man who created an independent Welsh state out of next to nothing and, according to J.E. Lloyd, he was the father of Welsh Nationalism. Providence gave us a patron saint in Dewi, who is known in English as St. David, and he unites the whole of Wales; it is good to know that the Festival of Dewi has been celebrated for centuries. He was commemorated in Philadelphia as early as the beginning of the eighteenth century and the soldiers of Henry VII celebrated him at a feast for which the king himself paid.

Dewi was a saint and preacher, a religious leader, and it is at St. David's Cathedral in Dyfed that we remember him. Glyndwr, on the other hand, was a patriot and warrior, a political leader, and his memorial is the Parliament House at Machynlleth. Dewi lived in the sixth century, whereas Glyndwr achieved his heroic feats in the fifteenth. We celebrate Dewi on the first day of March. Nearly six months later, on the sixteenth day of September, we celebrate Owain Glyndwr, at the beginning of autumn when Nationalists' thoughts turn to the busiest time in politics. The two men counterbalance each other, as do the two dates. Wales has need of the spirit and vision of them both, Dewi and Glyndwr.

Chapter 21

Success and Failure

One of the problems facing Members of Parliament who have lost their seats is that they have to look for another job in order to maintain their families and homes. That was now my problem too. After the Carmarthenshire by-election of July 1966 my brother Alcwyn, who has always been wonderfully generous towards me, was kind enough to take responsibility for looking after the greenhouses at Llangadog. It wasn't a terribly successful business and after Britain joined the Common Market it quickly went down hill. Even in the summer of 1970 it was obvious that I wasn't going to be able to make a living from it, and I hadn't taken a penny out of it since I was elected. Alcwyn kept it going because some of the men working there had been with me for many years. Two attempts to find Welsh people to take over the business proved unsuccessful and there was no sign of any other Welshman who would buy it. Very few Welsh people seem to be in this kind of business, anyway, although it would have been easy enough to find an English buyer. Alcwyn went on shouldering the increasing financial burden up to the winter of 1982, when two of the greenhouses were blown down by a hurricane the like of which had never before been seen in these parts; everything growing in the other greenhouses was frozen over because the high winds had brought down the electricity lines. Without power it was impossible to keep the coal-fires going. For weeks on end the temperature remained far below zero. It was time to call it a day.

While I was looking for a way of earning a living, Elwyn Roberts came to my rescue – not for the last time either. He found an English-speaking Nationalist, whom I'm not allowed to name, who paid me, until I was re-elected in 1974, the three thousand pounds that I'd been receiving at the end of my first term as an M.P. It was marvellous that a business man who loved his country should have agreed to help someone who was still prepared to work for Wales. His generosity gave me the freedom to continue with my proper task.

I was still able to work for Plaid Cymru in the Carmarthen constituency, where I remained as candidate, and in other parts of Wales. I could travel throughout the country as the Party's President, and to some extent help the national cause in other countries such as Euzkadi, Catalonia, Corsica, Britanny, Ireland, and Scotland; Brussels, too, became an important centre that I had to visit from time to time. I was able to go on working on the County Council and to give some of my time to the Union of Independents, of which I remained Treasurer. I was also able to give more time to my writing, publishing two more books – *Wales Can Win* and *A National Future for Wales*. The first book I had ever written was *Plaid Cymru and Wales* in 1950. The Silurian Press, the English-language imprint of Llyfrau'r Dryw (later Christopher Davies), had asked the leaders of the four political parties in Wales to write a short book on their respective parties, but the one on Plaid Cymru was the only one to appear. In it, as I said in the preface, I 'tried to convey some sense of the urgent and imperative need for a Welsh Parliament'. In 1964 my book *Rhagom i Ryddid* appeared and in 1967 the very substantial volume entitled *Celtic Nationalism*, published by Routledge & Kegan Paul. The section on Scotland in this book was written by Hugh MacDiarmid; Owen Dudley Edwards wrote the Irish part, and Ioan Bowen Rees and I were jointly responsible for the section dealing with Wales; it was Ioan who did most of the work. A fine historian was lost when Ioan, who stood as Plaid Cymru's candidate in Conwy and Merthyr Tydfil, went into local government, although Wales was to benefit greatly from his appointment as Chief Executive of Gwynedd County Council in 1980. His is the best mind in the field of local government in Wales and his book, *Government by Community*, which presents the attitudes of Plaid Cymru, is a classic work which has had a good deal of influence. His lecture in Salzburg in April 1982, at the international symposium organized by the Government of that region in honour of Leopold Kohr, left a deep impression on all who heard it. On the same occasion I took as the subject of my lecture 'The Fight for a Free Wales'.

Peter Hughes Griffiths brought his infectious enthusiasm to the task of developing the Party's organization in the Carmarthen constituency and his influence blew through the town and its environs like a fresh breeze. A large number of meetings of one sort or another were held up and down the county, including well-organized social evenings that brought many people together in a pleasant atmosphere. I must put on record the jolliest night of the year at Carmarthen – the Plaid Cymru eisteddfod in which the Party's branches competed against one another in quizzes in which the questions all had a political slant. The star on this occasion was Gwyneth Evans who became a valuable member of staff after the Party's success in 1974. She was our expert on social questions. A powerful political machine was built up with thirty-two branches operating where there had been none a quarter of a century before. By the time the General Election was upon us in February 1974 we were spoiling for a fight. That Election now belongs to political legend in Carmarthen. When I arrived at the count it was very late and the tension was filling the place. There were really only two horses in the race and nobody could say for sure who was going to win, Labour or Plaid Cymru, Gwynoro Jones or I; sometimes he had seemed to be ahead, and sometimes I had been in the lead. Poor old Gwynoro was on tenterhooks at the count, moving restlessly from one pile of voting papers to the next, often stopping at the table where the totals were displayed, and every now and then going over to the returning officer to inspect the slips that had been spoiled. He would hold one up against the light and examine it closely and anxiously, making doubly sure that it wasn't a vote for him. I left this work to my agent, the redoubtable Cyril Jones. By the time the count was over I was two votes ahead and, of course, there had to be a recount. I withdrew to a small room at the side of the main hall to enjoy the drama from afar. Cyril or someone else kept on coming in to report on what was happening. At the end of the second count it was Gwynoro who was in the lead. By now it was two o'clock in the morning and everyone was very tired, so it was agreed to postpone the count until the following midday, by which time the tension had if anything increased. The voting slips were once more spread out on tables in front of the tellers, who put them in tidy piles for each of the candidates. When the pile reached a hundred it was taken to a table on the stage. There it was obvious that Labour and Plaid Cymru were neck-and-neck with each other. The spoilt voting-slips were scrutinized time after time. The result of this huge exercise involving some fifty thousand slips was that Gwynoro Jones was three votes ahead of me, but only by three. Cyril now urged me to demand yet another recount, for hadn't I been ahead at the first count? But I didn't want to. For one thing, I could have been five votes behind in a fourth count, and besides, my position would be much stronger by the next Election if I had lost by only three votes than if I had won by three. And so it turned out. Despite the fact that the result announced on 1st March showed that Plaid Cymru had lost by three votes – by far the smallest majority in the countries of Britain – on the following 10th October we won a majority of 3,640. These are the figures announced on 1st March:

Labour	17,165
Plaid Cymru	17,162
Liberal	9,698
Conservatives	6,037

And here are the votes on 10th October:

Plaid Cymru	23, 325
Labour	19,685
Liberal	5,693
Conservative	2,962
British Party	342

We had received more than twice as many votes polled by Plaid Cymru throughout the country at the General Election of 1951.

It was Brisbane Jones, a likeable old Cardi well over eighty years old, who received the 342 votes as a Briton. Since he was standing in the first place against Welsh Nationalism, he'd been claiming that he was certain to win the seat. Moreover, he had announced that Plaid Cymru was sure to lose its deposit, and to show his good will, he said, he would be prepared to pay the deposit of any of the candidates who lost theirs. The Liberal and the Tory accepted their hundred and fifty pounds with gratitude.

The Election of 28th February 1974 was given a lot of coverage on television and in the press because it was expected to be a close-run thing. But on the evening of 10th October the media throughout the countries of Britain gave more time to Carmarthen because the singing of the large crowd, led by Inspector Fisher of the Dyfed Powys police, was so terrific. He had begun to conduct them because women were fainting as they were crushed against the barriers. They were being carried into St. Peter's Hall where the count was taking place. After the Inspector had been leading the singing for quite a while, he would return to the hall, but soon one of the television people would come hurrying after him to persuade him to go back out on to the balcony. London couldn't have enough of the magnificent singing on their screens.

The next time I came across Gwynoro Jones was on the panel of a brains trust arranged by the Liberals of Carmarthenshire in the Spring of 1981, on the very day that he announced his membership of the Social Democratic Party. Three months previously he had been on the short-list of Labour candidates for the constituency of Gower, when Gareth Wardell was selected. The news of his switching party caused a good deal of excitement among Liberals on the night of the brains trust. Some of them urged him in my hearing to promise there and then to stand for them and the S.D.P. at the next General

Election. They weren't to blame for the fact that nothing was decided that evening. At the 1979 Election, just two years previously, some Liberals had roundly cursed the Labour Party, and yet, although Gwynoro insisted that he believed in exactly the same policies, and that it was his former party and not he who had changed, he was embraced by the Liberals that night as if he had been a Liberal from the womb.

The experience of losing by a mere three votes at the beginning of the year turned out to be a source of great strength for Plaid Cymru and it reinforced the positions of Dafydd Wigley and Dafydd Elis Thomas who went on to win resounding victories in Caernarfonshire and Merioneth. They added to the heavy pressure that came from Scotland, where seven Nationalists had been elected. It was the strength of the Nationalist movements in our two countries which, of course, forced the Government at Westminster to start drafting a Bill that would give Scotland its own Parliament and Wales an elected Assembly. In the October of the same year the number of Welsh Nationalists was increased from two to three and the seven from Scotland to eleven, one more than the number of Liberals in the House of Commons. The Government now had a majority of only three over all the other parties and later on this shrank to just one. That was the most promising position we had ever been in. We now saw our Party growing in its political clout sufficiently to oblige the Government to yield a measure of self-government to Wales. It was true that the proposed Assembly would have been weak and it wouldn't have had the power to legislate except on insignificant matters, but what I believed to be crucial was not that it should have legislative powers, but that the people of Wales should have an elected Assembly which would draw the nation together and give it direction. A nation must start somewhere in walking the path to complete self-government. We shall never win full national status in a single leap. The setting up of an Assembly elected by the people and reflecting the opinion of the electorate and giving the nation a voice in its own affairs for the first time in its history would have been a revolutionary step in the right direction. That is not too strong a description of it. For the first time ever Wales would have had a national body politic that thought in Welsh terms. More interest in its deliberations could have been expected than has ever been shown in Welsh affairs at the Westminster Parliament. Its business would have been followed from day to day by the media and that would have nurtured among the people a Welsh way of thinking, thus weakening the hold of British habits on their minds. Despite the fact that its powers would have been few, I decided that I should henceforth seek election to the Assembly in Cardiff rather than stand again for Westminster, because I thought more could have been achieved in our own capital than in London. There we could make policies and plans for Wales and press them upon the Government. If the Assembly's voice were to be ignored, its members and the whole of Wales would be greatly put out, thus helping public opinion to mature politically. I was sure that once the Welsh people had been given the smallest taste of responsibility, they would ask for more. It was reasonable to expect that the call for financial and legislative powers would increase and that it would be difficult for the Government to resist it. The setting up of an elected Assembly would bring Wales a long way down the road to full self-government.

I wasn't on my own by a long chalk in believing that an Assembly would transform the national life of Wales and grow in due course into a Parliament. That was the fear of the Tories and Labour, too. The basic argument they brought against the proposed Assembly was that it would put Wales on 'the slippery slope' towards complete self-government. All the other arguments were secondary to this one. True, they argued that the Assembly would add another tier of government in Wales, but that already existed in the shape of the Welsh Office and the civil service. The Assembly would have made it answerable to the people and rendered it democratic. As much as possible was made of the likely cost and the impression given that the Welsh would sink under the weight of the taxes raised to maintain the Assembly. The truth is that it would have cost the people of the countries of Britain a little more than a halfpenny per head per week – a good deal less than a Welsh television channel. It was also argued that an Assembly would have had an inimical effect on the status of the Westminster M.Ps. because it would be to the Assembly members that electors would have taken their problems. This was doubtless true and in the opinion of Nationalists it was yet another argument in favour of an Assembly. This in fact was only a variation on the theme of 'the slippery slope' – that really was the basic argument against.

At the outset, a single Bill was drafted for both Scotland and Wales. Things started to look as if they were going wrong when opponents succeeded in making two Bills out of it, one for Scotland and the other for Wales. The discussion of the combined Bill and then the two separately took up a good deal of the House's time over about three years. When the moment came for the debate on the Welsh dimension, its opponents immediately went into the lead, taking up most of the time available. They included three-quarters of the Welsh Members, for the only ones who lent the Bill their clear support were the three Nationalists, the two Liberals, and the

Labour M.Ps. John Morris, Cledwyn Hughes, Roy Hughes, Caerwyn Roderick, Elystan Morgan, Denzil Davies, and Tom Ellis. Our opponents were enthusiastically led by a number of hostile English and Scottish Members, but no Englishman or Scotsman rose from the back benches to support the Bill. The Welsh Labourites who were against the proposed Assembly were led by a committee of four – Neil Kinnock, Leo Abse, Fred Evans, and Ioan Evans – and Donald Coleman and Ifor Davies served as whips. The Bill's opponents were by far the most voluble on the Labour benches, while every one of the Welsh Tories contributed his piece with the help of several English Members on the benches opposite. The three Nationalists were less active than they would have wished to be because our opponents had claimed that the Assembly was National- ist policy. Our frequent intervention would have weakened rather than strengthened the case in favour. The impression given in debate was that those who supported the Bill were a small, lacklustre coalition whereas its opponents were abounding in self-confidence. Yet if only the Government had stood firm in its resolution, it would undoubtedly have succeeded in its aim. Our opponents' most suc- cessful stratagem was to insist on a referendum before the Bill could be passed. Our rejection of that clause had to be masked because it would have been an admission of weakness. Up to that point the opposition, although strong, hadn't been all that significant, for it was only to be expected that the discipline of the Labour Party would ensure the support of its Members in the lobbies. But when another clause was inserted to the effect that forty per cent of the electorate would have to vote for the Assembly in a referendum, we knew we had lost the battle.

For about a year during the second half of that Parliament the Government was kept in office by a pact that had been struck with the thirteen Liberal M.Ps. Even then it tried to enlist our support, and I had two meetings with Jim Callaghan, the Prime Minister, but after the Liberals withdrew their support, it was on the three Welsh Nationalists and one Irishman, who was seldom at Westminster, that the Government had to rely for the last nine months of its life. It certainly couldn't rely on the support of the Scottish Nationalists. Since Michael Foot was the Leader of the House and Deputy Prime Minister, we saw a lot of him. I had a good dozen meetings with him in his room, sometimes in the company of the two Dafydds and at others on my own. During the summer of 1978 we met twice at the home of the friendly Caerwyn Roderick, Foot's Parliamentary Sec- retary, in Rhiwbina, a suburb of Cardiff. Michael Foot's aim was to retain our support and ours was to squeeze out of the Government as much as we could get for Wales. Several times I tried to persuade him to ensure that the Labour Party in Wales held public meetings and seminars to explain the content of the Wales Bill, about which the public was woefully ignorant. But I pleaded in vain and nothing was done. I was just as unsuccessful in trying to get Jim Callaghan to give a public lead in favour of the Assembly. Our Labourite and Tory opponents had their way just as easily in the country as they did at Westminster. Nevertheless, it was the Welsh people and not the Government who must take the heaviest responsibility for the fiasco that followed.

During these three years, the three Welsh Nationalists won more for Wales than the other thirty-three Welsh M.Ps. had done in a generation. The most important thing we achieved was the setting up of the Welsh Economic Development Agency and the hundred million pounds which was its capital. It was this which finally established Wales as an economic unit. Plaid Cymru had been pressing for it for about forty years. Of great benefit to the quarrymen of Gwynedd was a Bill to provide compensation for those suffering from silicosis, and their widows. This Bill was a great embarrassment to the Labour Party, for it should have passed such a Bill a generation earlier. Thirdly, the sons of farmers were given the right of inheriting their tenancies. Fourthly, we won a small measure of justice over the question of the supply of water. Some three million pounds was paid to the Welsh Water Board, which brought the cost of water in Wales somewhat nearer to that in England. One of the first acts of the Tories when they were returned to power was to do away with this payment. Lastly, the Government was pushed in the direction of starting work on the Welsh television channel, for which we had been pressing. A sum of eighteen million pounds was made available so that the engineering work could be put in hand in Wales several months before it began in England. However, the Government was to fall before a start could be made on the work. The Scottish Nationalists could have saved the Government but they were too incensed by its attitude with regard to self-government to lend it their support. They paid a horrifically heavy price for this.

Plaid Cymru's status was reflected at Westminster during my second term in my personal life. Instead of being a pelican in the wilderness, I was now one of fourteen Nationalists, instead of a pariah I was now a respectable and important personage, acknowledged as a party leader. I had a pleasant room and was often invited to meet various VIPs, sometimes in the magnificent setting of the Speaker's House where dwelt George Thomas, who filled the post with wisdom and a sense of humour. George was wonderfully generous towards us throughout the life of this Parliament. Rhiannon and I received invitations to dine with other party leaders and the wives of those who were married. Harold Wilson was among them, as were Edward Heath, the Liberal Jeremy Thorpe, Donald Stewart of the S.N.P., and James Molyneaux the Ulster Unionist. On yet another occasion I attended a dinner in the presence of Harold Macmillan, James Callaghan, Douglas Home, Edward Heath, Harold Wilson, and the Duke of Edinburgh. The only woman present that evening was the Queen.

By the middle of that Parliament I wasn't in the best of health. In February 1977 my wife had to fetch me home from London and I was in quite a bit of pain as I lay on the back-seat of the car. That evening Rhiannon was woken up by a sound rather like that of a rifle going off – it was my hiccups rattling the bed and the furniture in the bedroom. They continued for a whole week. When Rhiannon came into my room I was unusually talkative, chatting away quite cogently but completely irrelevantly. Although it was two in the morning, she rang for the doctor and Dr Ieuan Davies, poor chap, turned out in his usual gracious manner. He gave me a number of sleeping-pills and, since I was still as lively as a lark, pumped enough morphine into me to send an elephant to sleep. But I was still chatting away nineteen to the dozen, without any sign of falling asleep. It was my natural courtesy that kept me awake. Since a gentleman had been kind enough to call on me, I felt that it was my place to entertain him, and there I was, with poor Dr Ieuan himself almost dying for sleep, chattering on about heating-systems and the like, without an inkling as to why Rhiannon was splitting her sides by my bed. At about three in the morning she suggested that I might pay the good doctor a compliment if I showed that his medicine was beginning to work. So I lay back in my bed and fell immediately asleep, only to find myself a little later being woken up by two burly men and being bundled into an ambulance. By the time we reached Glangwili Hospital it appears that my chattering was wonderful to hear, extremely lively but complete gibberish. Later that evening the nurse was terrified on hearing a very loud noise coming from the ward where I was supposed to be lying in bed. She rushed in and found that I was trying to make for the toilet, dragging in my wake all the paraphernalia – the tubes in my nose and arm, the bottles, and so forth. After about a week a doctor friend, another National-ist, called to see me. His advice was that I should accept the fact that I could never work again as I had been doing up to then, but he comforted me by saying that there would still be a place for me in the life of Wales – as a symbol. Within six weeks I was once again

being cared for by the solicitous nurses of Glangwili, having undergone surgery there. It was the month of May before I was able to
return to my Parliamentary duties and travel the length and breadth
of the country again.

Eighteen months later the countries of Britain were beginning to
experience 'the winter of discontent' that preceded the referendum
on Devolution which was to take place on St. David's Day 1979.
Almost everything went wrong that winter, including the weather.
When I went to hold meetings in favour of the Assembly in the
uplands of Glamorgan and Gwent there were hardly any vehicles on
the road, so deep was the snow. I went canvassing through snow and
ice. As a rule it was only Nationalists who canvassed for the Assembly. That was about all they could do. Although the inter-party
committee chaired by Elystan Morgan was supposed to be organizing matters, in practice there was no effective campaign in favour of
the Assembly. In the ranks of the Labourites and Tories who opposed the idea there were high spirits. Despite the fact that the Wales
Bill had been proposed by the Labour Government, the Party did
not so much as put out a leaflet explaining its contents, and not a
single branch in South Wales, with the possible exception of Llanelli,
was known to work seriously on the Bill's behalf. The meeting held
in support of an Assembly at the University College in Bangor under
the chairmanship of the Archbishop of Wales was an exception in
the success it encountered, despite Michael Foot's speaking rather
disappointingly and showing reluctance to admit, significantly
enough, that Wales was a nation. More typical was the meeting
which launched the campaign in Carmarthen, at which John Morris,
the Labour M.P. for Aberafan, was the chief speaker. He had agreed
to be present on condition that I shouldn't be on the platform. So I
stood in the background as a symbol of Plaid Cymru's role in the
proceedings.

The result was a rout from the point of view of Wales but a
resounding success for the Labour and Conservative Parties. Wales
was degraded in the sight of the world and humiliated in the eyes of
its own people by the hugely negative result. Four times as many
voted against an Assembly as voted in favour. Even in Gwynedd,
where two of the M.Ps. were Nationalists, there were twice as many
against as in favour. That day, 1st March 1979, went down as the
blackest in the history of Wales.

A month later the Government fell, because the Irish Nationalist
had failed to turn up for the vote. The General Election that
followed was held on the same day as elections for the District and
Community councils. Although it held Caernarfonshire and

Merioneth with increased majorities, there was a substantial drop in Plaid Cymru's vote in the rest of the country, and in the local elections it lost scores of seats. In Carmarthen the BBC took part in the Election by publishing the result of an opinion poll on the Tuesday evening before the Thursday on which voting was due to take place. The poll had been taken the week before and it showed that the Tories were second to Labour with Plaid Cymru a poor third. I heard about a Young Farmers' meeting at Glan-y-fferi (Ferryside) on the Wednesday evening at which it had been decided, in the light of the poll published by the BBC the previous evening, to switch their support to the Tories in an attempt to stop Labour from winning. Doubtless many others came to the same conclusion. Here are the results of that Election:

Labour (Dr Roger Thomas)	18,667
Plaid Cymru	16,689
Conservative	12, 272
Liberal	4,186
National Front	146
Keep Britain United	126

Once again I was out of a job.

Chapter 22

A Television Channel for Wales

After the dashing of its hopes by the referendum of St. David's Day 1979 and the disappointing result of the General Election that followed, the morale of Plaid Cymru was at its lowest ebb. Ten years previously it would have been more than pleased to have had two Nationalists at Westminster of the calibre of Dafydd Wigley and Dafydd Elis Thomas. But this manifestation of the Party's strength did little to soothe the anguish among its rank and file. Their confidence had been completely undermined by the disgrace of the referendum's result and their spirits had taken a knock by the falling away of support at the Election. In this dark hour the Tory Government decided to take advantage of Welsh Nationalism's weakness by striking a sudden and pitiless blow against our language. On 12th September 1979, in Cambridge, the Home Secretary, William Whitelaw, announced in a surprise statement that the Government did not after all intend to set up a Welsh television channel, as it and the Labour Party had earlier promised.

Our despair plummeted to new depths. The winning of the TV Channel had been the greatest victory of the national movement in recent years, and the cost had been heavy terms of imprisonment for some patriots. English television was destroying the Welsh language before our very eyes. Without a Welsh television service at peak hours, the language wouldn't have much longer to live. Now the Government was killing off that hope. The blow fell upon people who had lost the will to fight back, creating a crisis more serious than anything Wales had seen during my lifetime. The Thatcher Government was attacking Wales on every front. For ten years and more English people had been streaming into the Welsh-speaking parts of our country and overrunning the bastions of our language. Even the best of our people seemed paralysed and helpless, lacking spirit and hope. Once again it was demonstrated how completely Wales relied on the national movement and Plaid Cymru in particular. If it lost its spirit the people would perish. But in the words of T. Gwynn Jones,

> '*Ysbryd gwlad! Os bradog lu*
> *Cas lwyth fu'n ceisio'i lethu,*
> *Iddo trwy hyn ni ddaw tranc,*
> *Heb ddiwedd y bydd ieuanc!*'

('A country's spirit! If a treacherous and vicious throng have tried to quench it, it will never be overcome by this, but will remain endlessly young!')

Neither a Government's neglect nor exterior forces can kill a nation unless the moral demise of its Nationalists goes hand in hand with them. They are the nation's soldiers. If the soldiers of Wales should lose their will to fight, they are sure to be defeated. The worst thing about October 1979 was that the Party's spirit was faltering. The most dangerous foe was depression, and it was in the minds of our own people. In this situation to have gone on working only in the conventional political way, given that the will to work could have been restored, wouldn't have been enough. Even the kind of non-violent direct action that had taken place magnificently in the recent past appeared to be inadequate for the situation now facing us. The circumstances called for the taking of some short sharp action that would be sure to prove costly, and might even mean the loss of life. I was self-important enough to believe that it was only action on my part which would be sufficient to touch the heart of Wales and turn the situation around. The goal at which I thought I could aim was the renewal of Welsh Nationalists' spirits, though the political goal would be to restore the Government's commitment to a Welsh TV Channel. I had already decided that I had to take action when Meredydd Evans called to see me to get my response to the self-sacrificing act which was in his mind and that of Ned Thomas and Pennar Davies – an act in the tradition of the young people of *Cymdeithas yr Iaith* and the three men who burned the bombing-school at Penyberth in 1936, an act which would perhaps send them to prison for a long time and which demonstrated the conscience of the nation's best people in the profundity of its crisis. It was so wonderful that three men of their stature – among the foremost writers and thinkers in Wales – should be prepared to commit a misdemeanour for the sake of Wales in a way that would be so costly to them. In approving of their intention and expressing my admiration for them, I told Merêd that I too was thinking of taking action, but I said no more than that for the time being. The three carried out their plan at Pencarreg and another four of the nation's best took action at Carmel, namely Millie Gregory, Maldwyn Jones, Cynog Dafis, and Iwan Meical. All these militants took action against television transmitters.

Up to this point I didn't know exactly what the nature of my action would be. I had considered several courses that were quite serious in their different ways, but had rejected them one by one. In the mean while Plaid Cymru's Council had called upon Welsh people to refuse to pay their television licences. The same afternoon I went from its meeting at Neuadd Pantycelyn, the Welsh students' hostel in Aberystwyth, to announce that decision at a television rally in the Old College, where Meredydd Evans, Ned Thomas, and Ffred Ffransis were to speak. The arrangements for this campaign were put in the capable hands of Peter Hughes Griffiths and by the following September he was able to announce that two thousand people had refused to pay – all of them quite respectable people who had never before thought of deliberately breaking the law. The response of the authorities to this ever-growing movement was slow and cautious, for nothing like it had ever been seen in Wales before; the campaign was a notable example of the non-violent action which had been such an important element in the victory which had been won in the first place. When in due course the summonses started arriving, the majority refused to pay the fines that were handed out by the courts. As a result, about twenty people were sent to gaol; that was just the beginning. Among those who were imprisoned were two former bank-managers, Douglas Davies and D.O. Davies, and T.C. Jones of Penrhyndeudraeth, who was in his seventies, spent a fortnight inside Walton Gaol in Liverpool.

By the end of the year I had decided that my most effective course of action would be to go on hunger strike until the Government announced that it would keep its word and carry out its promise to establish a Welsh TV Channel. I didn't expect it would respond positively. When I discussed the matter with Rhiannon, she gave the idea her full backing, and a little later I shared the secret with our children, one by one. I also went to Swansea to discuss the morality of my action with Pennar Davies. The next thing was to decide the best moment for announcing my intention and then carrying it out. This wasn't something to be done hastily. I therefore decided that the announcement should be made in the spring. Before the end of January I had confided in Peter Hughes Griffiths and Dafydd Williams for, as the Party's officers, they would have a lot to do with the arrangements and publicity. Towards the end of February, having been at a St. David's Day dinner with him at Llanberis, I told

Dafydd Wigley of my intention. As far as I am aware, no one else outside the family was told. The plan so far was that I should go on hunger-strike in a room above the Plaid Cymru offices in Cathedral Road in Cardiff, since they were a convenient place from which to handle publicity. But later on, Dafydd Williams took the view that this would place too great a strain on Gwerfyl Arthur and other members of the Party's staff. So the location was changed to my study in Talar Wen, which was much better for me, of course, despite the smell of cooking which sometimes wafts into it. On 31st March a letter of mine was published in the columns of *The Times* calling on the Government to keep its word, without revealing anything of my plan, of course. In April, with the help of the writer Emyr Humphreys, I prepared the statement that I would make in announcing my intention. By then I had decided that I should go public at the beginning of May.˙My son-in-law, Ffred Ffransis, suggested that it would be appropriate if the Government were to be given a clear six months' warning. In the end, I gave it five months, making an announcement on Monday, 5th May, that I would be starting my fast on Monday, 6th October, unless the Government in the mean while had made a statement to the effect that it would honour its pledge. This ample warning was given so that the Government would have plenty of time to think again, that is to make the proverbial U-turn that Mrs Thatcher had never made up to then and hasn't made since, unless her reaction to the miners' strike can be put into that category. More importantly, in my mind, for I had no expectation that Mrs Thatcher and her Government would think again, I wanted to provide an opportunity for the arranging of a great campaign throughout Wales. I gave 5th October as the date when the fast would begin because the months of October and November would be a good time for the campaign to reach its crescendo. Furthermore, Parliament would be returning at the beginning of October and Plaid Cymru's Annual Conference was to be held at the end of the month.

As I might have expected, the announcement caused general shock and I was interviewed and cross-examined by people from the media. The response among Welsh-speakers was mixed. The Establishment, including the directors and friends of HTV, were on the whole antipathetic, of course. The weekly newspaper *Y Faner* opposed the idea and was never to admit that we had won a victory of any substance. But the national movement took heart. The Welsh Language Society returned to the fray and later on a high price was paid by Hywel Pennar, Meurig Llwyd, Euros Owen, Angharad Tomos, and Wayne Williams, for the part they had played in the renewed Welsh television campaign. Plaid Cymru sprang back to life, throwing itself once more into its fight against unemployment that was increasing on all sides. The Party's new spirit was demonstrated when Mrs Thatcher paid a visit to Swansea to address the Welsh Tories on 20th July. The anger of Wales was expressed that day by more than a thousand Nationalists who had gone there with the express intention of greeting her. Before the Prime Minister arrived, however, hundreds of Labourites led by Neil Kinnock and other M.Ps. paraded along the road that leads to the Patti Pavilion, brazenly facing the scorn of Nationalists who hadn't appreciated Labour's treachery in the referendum on a Welsh Assembly. If Kinnock's head was held low that morning as he walked the road to the Patti, Mrs Thatcher's limousine didn't venture along it at all. She took a minor road and then went into the hall by a side door, slipping in past the toilets and through the rear of the stage. She left in the same way, from backstage past the toilets and out through the side door, into her sleek limousine, escaping from the town along another minor road. When, I wondered, had the Prime Minister of Great Britain had a similar experience?

The publicity about my intention to go on hunger strike increased with every week that went by. It was given a boost by the rally organized by *Cymdeithas yr Iaith* outside HTV's pavilion on the Field of the National Eisteddfod in Dyffryn Lliw. From the start there were regular reports in the Welsh, Irish, and Scottish newspapers. By the beginning of May every British daily had carried the story; long articles, and sometimes more than one, appeared in *The Guardian*, *The Sun*, *The Mail*, *The Express*, *The Mirror*, *The Telegraph*, and *The Times*; the Thunderer published a supportive leading article as well as many letters. Some of the Sundays, such as *The Sunday Telegraph* and *The Observer*, made much of it, and *The Sunday Times* even carried a sympathetic leading article in Welsh. There was also a good deal of interest shown by television. I did quite a few interviews, some of them like the one for *Panorama* bringing pressure to bear on England, and others in Edinburgh which helped the national cause in Scotland. Television crews from Germany and Canada turned up at Talar Wen. It may be that the coverage given by the foreign press did as much as anything to shake the Government. For example, the news was given prominence on the front page of a Catalan paper in Barcelona that had a daily circulation of a million. Most of the front page of a Stockholm paper was taken up with the story and in Finland a paper accompanied it with large photographs and bold headlines. Three articles appeared in *The New York Times* and two in *The Christian Science Monitor*. The story was given a lot of coverage in other famous journals such as *Time* and *McLeans* in Toronto. The national cause of Wales was thus brought to the attention of several countries overseas, since I took good care to give all correspondents a full picture of the plight of the Welsh nation, together with a description of the work and aims of Plaid Cymru.

By mid-July it was clear that the campaign was gaining momentum. Many a public body came out in support and there were such demonstrations as the vigil arranged by a number of young Welsh Independent ministers during meetings of the Union. But while they supported my aims, many wondered at my determination to fast unto death. I don't know how many people told me to my face or in writing that my death would be futile, since I could have achieved so much more if I remained alive. I didn't agree, of course. Perhaps I was suffering from a swollen head in thinking that I was a kind of symbol and that my dying for Wales – for that's what it really entailed – would have a lot more effect than anything I could do with the rest of my life. I had a hint in July that the Government was beginning to be seriously worried. Lord Cledwyn arranged for me to receive an invitation to meet Nicholas Edwards, the Secretary of State for Wales. We had a secret meeting on 21st July at St. Fagans, near Cardiff, at the home of Sir Hywel Evans, the head of the Welsh Office at that time, with Sir Hywel himself present. In a two-hour discussion we discussed every aspect of policy, including, of course, who would make the programmes to be broadcast on a Welsh Fourth Channel, what relationship it would have with the BBC and HTV, who would run it, and so on. The Secretary of State paid particular attention to the likely cost, which he maintained made a Welsh Channel an impracticality. The impression he gave me was that he had come there not to listen nor to discuss so much as to lay down the law. I wasn't surprised by this at all. As a matter of fact, I didn't expect anything different. I knew as well as anyone about the intransigence of the Thatcher Government. One interesting question which was asked by Sir Hywel Evans towards the end of the afternoon was whether I should be content if twenty-two hours of Welsh programmes were to be screened without interruption on week-nights, but on two channels. I replied that I should not, nor did I think the idea a practical one. I left St. Fagans more certain than ever in my mind that the Government would never give in.

Meanwhile, many a friend of the cause who wasn't a member of Plaid Cymru showed concern and was anxious to help. In July the Archbishop of Wales, the Very Reverend Gwilym O. Williams, told me that he, Sir Cennydd Traherne, the Lord Lieutenant of

Glamorgan, and Sir Goronwy Daniel were hoping to see the Prime Minister and that he had been given to understand that Nicholas Edwards was arranging a meeting. With a view to preparing for this meeting, he invited me to have dinner with him at Dolserau near Dolgellau. I have no idea why they didn't see the Prime Minister. Be that as it may, at the request of the Council of the National Eisteddfod, the Archbishop, together with Sir Goronwy Daniel and Lord Cledwyn, met William Whitelaw, the Home Secretary, on 10th September, almost a year after Whitelaw's statement at Cambridge that the Government was reneging on its promise to establish a Welsh Fourth Channel. I believe that it was a suggestion by Dr Leopold Kohr which was the kernel of what 'the three wise men' had to say; I was to be deeply indebted to them for their initiative. In his speech at Cambridge, Whitelaw had said that the Government would review in three years' time its plan for putting all Welsh-language programmes on two channels. Dr Kohr's suggestion in *The Times* was that they should be put on one channel and that that was the scheme which should be reviewed after three years. This was a way of allowing the Government to yield 'without losing face' and in the end it was accepted.

Another friend anxious to do what he could to help was Michael Foot, who invited me to have dinner with him at one of his favourite taverns, The Griffin Inn at Llyswen, on the banks of Wye near Builth. By this time it was becoming a bit of a joke that I was so often dining out before starting on my fast. Anyway, on a fine evening in the middle of August we had fresh salmon from the Wye with some delicious sauces to it. After discussing the situation, Michael Foot promised to see William Whitelaw and said he would insist on seeing him without there being a single civil servant present. After that we had a free-ranging discussion on various subjects in the course of which I managed to get him to talk about self-government for Wales. At Westminster he would refuse to deal with this subject whenever I tried to raise it in private conversation. He would say, 'There's no need for more divisions in the world,' and then the matter would be closed as far as he was concerned. But at The Griffin that evening, perhaps because his charming wife Jill Craigie was present, he was much readier to listen and discuss. Jill took a lively part in the discussion and Michael looked askance with an awkward smile when, at one point, she declared, 'If I were a Welshwoman I'd be in Plaid Cymru.'

Peter Hughes Griffiths and Dafydd Williams helped me in arranging, between 6th September and the night before the hunger-strike was due to start on 5th October, some twenty-two meetings in Wales and three others I had promised the S.N.P. in Scotland. Every one of these was successful, some of them remarkably so. Two thousand people turned up at the rally that launched the series on Saturday, 6th September, at Sophia Gardens in Cardiff. It wasn't difficult that day to believe that Wales might still live as a nation. On the following Monday night I was in Glasgow and a thousand people filled the McLellan Galleries, just as they had done after the Carmarthen by-election in July 1966, and the meeting there was a highly emotional occasion. Because I was late arriving, it was eleven o'clock before the meeting came to an end. Despite the lateness of the hour, at the request of Billy Wolfe, the S.N.P.'s Chairman, I had to stand at the exit and shake hands with each member of the audience as they made their way out, and every one of those thousand Scots offered me a word of approval or their good wishes. That meeting was followed by huge gatherings at Forfar and Edinburgh, with press-interviews and radio and television broadcasts filling the two hectic days I spent with my old Scottish friends. Back in Wales, there was a meeting at Aberdare, again with the hall full to overflowing and many people unable to find seats. The same day 'the three wise men' – the Archbishop and his two friends – went to see William Whitelaw. When Sir Goronwy Daniel rang me next day to give a report of the courteous reception they had received, it was clear that he feared the Government was not going to give in. That too was the day Michael Foot saw the Home Secretary. I received a letter from him immediately after the meeting. He was even more certain than Sir Goronwy that the Government would not change its mind. The meetings went on and on. At Welshpool and Denbigh and Swansea it was the same story – full halls and great enthusiasm everywhere. The signs were so numerous that it seemed as if there were reason to believe that Welsh Nationalism was stirring again and threatening to become a really overwhelming force. That's the only thing the Government fears in Wales, and it fears it greatly. Over the last twenty years or so the price has been paid time and again for holding it back, and this time the price it had to pay was the concession of a Welsh TV Channel.

On Wednesday, 17th September, exactly a week after Michael Foot and 'the three wise men' had seen Whitelaw, Nicholas Edwards announced that Wales was to get a Welsh television service broadcasting at peak hours on the Fourth Channel and that an independent board was to be set up which would run it with adequate finance at its disposal. My first reaction was one of disappointment that the Government had relented at least a month too early. If only we had been given five or six more weeks of excitement and national awakening, Plaid Cymru – on which the nation's future completely depends – would have been established in an unassailable position. Not everything had been conceded. Twenty-two hours a week were allowed at first (in fact it was 23¼ hours), and not the twenty-five demanded, and there was no guarantee that the Welsh Channel would be launched in advance of the Fourth Channel in England. We had given up hope of seeing it start months earlier than the English Channel as we watched the weeks and months slipping by, but we still hoped for a head-start of at least a month so that the Welsh Channel could get going properly before having to face competition from London. For these reasons I wasn't entirely sure whether I should abandon my plan. Emyr Daniel, then of HTV, happened to be at Talar Wen that Wednesday and he was firmly of the opinion that the scale of the victory was so huge as to justify dropping my intention of going on hunger strike. I saw the sense of what he had to say, but I didn't let on to the media people immediately. Although we hadn't won every smidgen of what we had hoped for, the Welsh service would start with an average of three and a quarter hours each evening, an uninterrupted flow of hours at peak times if that were to be preferred. It would, moreover, be an independent, self-governing service in receipt of adequate finance enabling it to make programmes of a high quality. The position of the Welsh language would be reinforced by a brand-new Welsh-speaking organization that would be an important asset the likes of which had never before been seen in Wales.

The meeting scheduled for that evening was to be held in Crymych. Although only a small village, some eight hundred people packed into the hall, seething with the news about the Government's climb-down. When I announced that I was calling off my intention of going on hunger-strike, the crowd exploded in a wave of emotional relief. Their feelings were reflected in the collection. In response to an appeal by Merfyn Phillips, Plaid Cymru's organizer in Pembrokeshire, the sum of £2,100 was collected; that collection at Crymych has long since passed into legend. There was a similar experience on the following night at Porthmadog, with the platform as crowded as the hall and a collection of nearly a thousand pounds. At Llangefni on the Friday evening I had to address the three or four hundred people who had failed to get into the large Town Hall from the balcony outside. The enthusiasm showed no sign of subsiding at large meetings and dinners in the Rhondda, at Criccieth, Mold, Cardiff, Newbridge in Gwent, Aberaeron, Merthyr Tydfil, Maesteg, Pontypridd, Llandeilo, and on the evening of Sunday, 5th October, the night before my fast had been due to start, in Carmarthen. Even if Wales wasn't on fire, there were quite a few flames leaping from the embers. Someone painted the score in letters three feet high on the wall of the Thames embankment facing the Parliament at Westminster – Gwynfor 1, Thatcher 0.

After battle, silence. Quietly the foundations of the new order were put into place. There was no more talk about the lack of talent among the half-million Welsh-speakers, though they aren't many more in number than the population of Bristol. If the Welsh had the guts to go with their abundant talent, they would be among the leading nations of the world. The Government's behaviour after it had been beaten was entirely honourable and there was no quibbling about the cost. The BBC in Wales took enthusiastically to preparing Welsh programmes for the new Channel. An exciting lot of independent producers who were capable of making Welsh television known abroad came into their own. Only HTV tended to drag its feet, but of course everything took second place to profit with that company. First-class appointments were made to the Board of S4C, as the Fourth Channel in Wales came to be known, and to its staff. Sir Goronwy Daniel was the ideal man to be the authority's Chairman, while Owen Edwards, its Chief Executive, and Euryn Ogwen, the Head of Programmes, were notable examples of having the right men in the right jobs. This was a company of people who were entirely committed to the work that now lay before them, and they worked with other splendid members of the Board and staff as an inspired team. Filled with the infectious enthusiasm of its programme-makers – there were at the outset 120 of them in the Society of Welsh Broadcasters under the chairmanship of Emyr Daniel – S4C is going to leave a lasting impression on the life of the nation, and as a result Wales is going to become much better known on the television screens of Europe and America. It's possible that Wales will soon have a television service as good as, if not better than, any other small country in the world. The talent is here, the commitment is here, and now the finance is also available.

There's good reason to believe that S4C will help to reinvigorate the position of the Welsh language and fill, at least in part, the vacuum which awaits the tens of thousands of pupils in our Welsh-medium education system when they leave school and have to live in English-speaking areas. Already the nation's morale has received an enormous boost. Perhaps we shall now see another manifestation of that marvellous ability it has for rejuvenation which Wales has shown so many times in the past. If its spirit continues to improve, it won't be completely unrealistic to expect to see the Welsh-speaking minority, despite all the pressures on it, binding together the English-speaking Welsh and the others who have made their home among us into one living whole.

Chapter 23

Facing the Holocaust

Since such a dangerous deterioration has taken place in the international situation over the last twenty-five years or so, with a terrifying increase in the number of nuclear bombs, and in their accuracy, pacifists have had to concentrate their attention more and more on the nuclear threat to Europe and humanity. Although most opponents of Welsh Nationalism in the British political parties support this cosmic terrorism, they persist in accusing Plaid Cymru of being in favour of violence, for ever claiming that it's encouraging the kind of violence that we see in the six counties of Northern Ireland. We were given an opportunity of putting the case for non-violent Nationalism when I accepted an invitation from the Fellowship of Reconciliation to give the Alex Wood Memorial Lecture on this subject, and to do so moreover in Welsh. With Pennar Davies in the chair, I delivered it at the Temple of Peace in Cardiff, taking as my theme the Party's attitude to violence. The lecture was later published by the Fellowship, in both Welsh and English, under the titles *Cenedlaetholdeb Di-drais* and *Non-violent Nationalism*.

I had been used to addressing meetings on pacificism, including those of the Union of Independents, the Baptist Union, and the Methodist Synod, on one occasion in the company of the writer E. Tegla Davies, and at Westminster I had made speeches in debates on defence. My lecture on George M.Ll. Davies, which the Union of Independents' Peace Society had asked me to deliver to mark the hundredth anniversary of his birth, was published in 1980. The Temple of Peace in Cardiff was full for a peace meeting which I addressed there under the chairmanship of Archbishop Glyn Simon. I note this last point because it gives me an opportunity of paying a small tribute to the bravest and most modest of Archbishops, one who has proclaimed his pacificism quite openly in the face of whatever the generals and colonels who belong to the Church in Wales may have had to say on that score. Of course, he was on wholly firm ground. During the greater part of the first three centuries of the early Church, the period nearest in time to Jesus Christ, no member was allowed to be a soldier. The pacificism of the great fathers of the Church in that period was unshakeable. A great change came over Christians' attitude to war after the Emperor Constantine gave his blessing to the Church. Christianity thereafter became fashionable and the sign of the Cross was carried at the head of the armed forces. After that, Christianity turned into the bloodiest religion the world had ever seen.

I recall the astonishment I felt when first I went to see Glyn Simon at his home in the Bishop's Palace in Llandaf. When I knocked at the door it was he who opened it. After we'd been chatting for half an hour or so, his wife came in with a tray of tea and cakes. There were no servants in the house, though they had a woman in to help with the cleaning on some mornings. The Archbishop came to the meeting at the Temple of Peace straight from London; I was given to understand that he had travelled from the station to Cathays Park in a bus. He didn't have a car and I had the privilege of driving him home in mine after the meeting. A more different person from the proud prelates of old could not be imagined.

It is easy, indeed quite natural, for a Welshman who has put aside all things British to be a pacifist. He knows that Britain never fought a war in the defence of Wales. On the contrary, its wars have done far more harm than good to our Welsh heritage. He also knows that any future war will destroy Wales. Such a Welshman is free of the paranoia of people belonging to the military regimes of the United States and the Soviet Union which blinds them to the destruction they are preparing for the world as a result of nuclear conflict. Today, peace is a condition of humanity's survival, whereas war will be its death-knell. Since this has become clear to me, I have given a good deal of my time in recent years to working for the peace movement.

In order to have some idea of the destruction that would be caused by a single bomb of one megaton, let's imagine it exploding over Llangyfelach, some five miles from Swansea. Every building would collapse in rubble in the area between Loughor and Pontarddulais, and between Pontarddulais and Neath, including the whole of Swansea. Within a radius of four miles from the centre of the explosion the heat would melt all metal and glass. Every building between Llanelli and Port Talbot would suffer enormous damage. The glass from the windows would have the force of bullets. Within this area of two hundred square miles most of those trying to escape from the other effects of the explosion would be burned to death.

The fires would spread as far as Llandeilo and Maesteg. At the same time the whole area would be shrouded in clouds of dust and smoke, and when the mushroom cloud went up the sun would be obscured and day would be turned into night. In the darkness a tornado of huge flames would sweep through the buildings, burning everything in its path to a cinder. If anyone remained in Swansea, where would they flee? The radioactive dust would have preceded them wherever they chose to go, poisoning the air, the earth, and the water. If the wind were from the west, the deadly dust would fall for a day over Cardiff and Newport and the valleys of Glamorgan and Gwent. This deadly stuff could fall as far away as London and Brighton.

This account of the effects of a one-megaton bomb is based on experiments that have already been carried out. If a hundred such bombs were to be dropped on the countries of Britain, some sixty per cent of their populations would be killed. Most of the others would die within months from the effects of the radioactive fall-out, or else from epidemics and famine. Obviously, the economy would be utterly destroyed. Three hundred one-megaton bombs would have similar effects on the United States. The Soviet Union has an arsenal of twenty-five thousand megatons. Well-informed sources in America expect an attack to the force of ten thousand megatons. The reason why such an enormous attack is possible is that the Soviet Union takes the view that the only hope it has of protecting some part of its territory would be to strike the first terrible blow. Since the United States take a similar view, a huge attack might always be possible at a time of mounting international tension. The recent war against Argentina demonstrates the fragility of the human situation. If there can be such hysteria at Westminster and in England over such a trifling issue, what will happen when the life of England itself is thought to be in the balance? The Argentinian attack on the Malvinas was an act that cannot be excused, though it followed a generation of futile discussions. But Britain should have insisted at once that the international community, through the United Nations and the International Court in The Hague, solved the dispute. This would have been a feather in the cap of the United Nations and it would have enhanced the status of the world community. But the political parties were in the grip of British Nationalism. They agreed, every one of them, at an emotional meeting of Parliament, that an armada should be sent eight thousand miles to drive the Argentinians from the islands by force. Michael Foot was praised for speaking up for England and Callaghan for declaring that his people would not suffer 'being kicked around by a tinpot dictatorship'. From the start, the Labour Party, like all the other British parties, insisted on the use of force, while at the same time making sure that they employed the rhetoric of pacifism. Since the use of force on this scale develops its own momentum, agreement became unlikely if not impossible, and it was hypocrisy on the part of Labour to call for moderation in the force employed. Up to that point Britain had been busy selling arms to Argentina and training its soldiers at Aberporth, at Llanbedr in Merioneth, and in Cardigan Bay. In the heat of the euphoria generated by British Nationalism, the use of conventional weapons wasn't enough for the head of the Falklands Office in London. He called for the exploding of a nuclear bomb over Buenos Aires.

I find it easier to understand how people can quietly accept that we are likely to be destroyed than to comprehend that they will not react with furious energy against the preparations made in their name for the slaughter of millions of innocent men, women, and children in another country. The general inertia of the Christians of Wales is a particularly worrying mystery to me. Despite the fact that the preparations are so satanically immoral, it seems as if they are tolerated in the belief that they are good for Britain and its people, and that their evil is somehow irrelevant in the face of the perceived needs of the British state. It was a similar attitude which made it possible for the Nazis to inflict the holocaust on the Jews. Although it was so unbelievably barbaric, the Nazis believed that it was for the good of Germany and, indeed, for Europe. This evil was personified in Hitler, who was undoubtedly a monster. He killed millions; whereas we, or the majority of us who don't lift a finger against nuclear villainy, are content to let the state make preparations for the killing of scores of millions. We acquiesce by our silence.

If humankind is to go on living for centuries more, its task is to rid itself of all the nuclear arms now in existence, together with the means of manufacturing them, including nuclear reactors which produce plutonium for the making of bombs. An international body must be set up to supervise disarmament effectively. Although this might seem impossible at the present time, unless the impossible is implemented the threat to humanity will remain. What we have here is a fundamental struggle against the forces of destruction and death. While the enormity of the task may dishearten us and make us feel powerless, it's not impossible that the huge scale of what is in the balance might inspire feats of energy and heroism of which we have never dared to dream we are capable.

We of all people ought not to allow ourselves to be overcome by a feeling of impotence in the face of the nuclear threat, for Wales as a nation has the ability to give an important lead to the rest of the world. The Welsh have so far responded with disappointing feebleness in comparison with the English at the scores of peace meetings I have addressed during the last year or so, including the fifteen nights in a row when I showed the film *The War Game* before speaking. If it hadn't been for the Nationalists, there would hardly have been any Welsh support at all. It is mostly English people who keep the peace groups going, distribute the leaflets, and attend the meetings and demonstrations, and it was mainly English women living in our midst who first marched from Cardiff to Greenham Common. It was mostly they too who walked from Cardiff to the RAF camp at Brawdy in Dyfed at the end of last May and who camped there over the summer. It was mainly English people who took responsibility for canvassing members of the County Councils prior to their deciding to declare their counties nuclear-free, although the splendid response of those Welsh councillors showed what was possible in our country. By its anti-nuclear declaration each of the eight counties made it clear that Wales wishes to be a nuclear-free country. The decision of all eight was embodied in the Clwyd Declaration. We may take pride in the fact that this initiative has raised the hearts of the peace movement from Iceland to Italy, from the United States to Japan. The historian and peace activist E.P. Thompson has said that audiences rose to their feet when he announced the news in Ireland and Iceland. In Glasgow the declaration caused a keen response to the idea of a chain of non-nuclear Celtic nations. The strong delegation of local councillors who came from Italy to Strasburg to welcome Dafydd Wigley and the Welsh contingent who took the Clwyd Declaration there were stimulated into deciding that they would try to get a similar declaration from all the local councils of their own country. The good news was published in a weekly Japanese paper which has a circulaion of millions. So, although its importance may only be symbolic, the declaration of the local councils of Wales was a good beginning and points to the important part Wales can play in the struggle for world peace and a future for humankind.

Wales, as a small country comparable in many ways with the Scandinavian countries, can make a unique contribution to adapting the world order to the needs of peace. The great powers were created in response to the demands of military might. What they produce is nuclear bombs and world wars. In such a situation the building of strong peace movements is not enough; we must also try to break up and decentralize the great powers and the large centralized systems. This will be more possible in the Soviet Union and the USA if there is less pressure on them from military demands. The large, centralist, anachronistic power that we in Wales can help to dismantle is

Britain. The means of accomplishing this are available to us and that is to gather in our hands sufficient political power to establish a Welsh state and to begin creating in our own country an oasis of peace. We have to strengthen the peace movement in every possible way, but the greatest contribution this small nation can make in the cause of world peace and the survival of humankind is to win full self-government for Wales.

With the growth in the Welsh national consciousness which enables its people to look objectively at the human situation, there's no need for despair. The war against Argentina over the Malvinas demonstrated both the danger and the possibilities. For the first time ever, Wales looked independently and critically on a British war. There is huge significance in the wide gap between, on the one hand, the British point of view that is fuelled by Britain's imperialistic and military tradition and, on the other, the attitude of Plaid Cymru, which springs naturally from the values of the Welsh heritage.

Chapter 24

Looking Ahead

Heavy though the damage has been to its national life, there is still hope in Wales because we have here a substantial and growing minority who are prepared to face the future with militant determination. They are the patriots who have decided that the nation is going to live and make its contribution to the world. It's true that the vast majority of the people of Wales continue to have a dull Britisher mentality, and that only some scores of thousands who can see that their country's future has to be fought for – they are the creative minority. Their energy and conviction, whether they be Welsh-speakers or English-speakers, will create a future for a nation that was born in the cradle of the Roman Empire some fifteen centuries before the advent of Great Britain on to history's stage.

Plaid Cymru is the political conduit of the nation's will to live. Within its ranks are gathered those Welsh people who are willing to fight on the nation's behalf. The Party is the hope of Wales. Other national movements and organizations have played an important role in Welsh life and they will go on making an indispensable contribution in future. But valuable though they be, it is only the strength and success of the National Party that can ensure a national future. If it should fail, the others won't be able to do much more than postpone the nation's demise. For this reason the Party's vigour is all-important to Wales.

Since my term of office had been such a long one, from 1st August 1945 to 31st October 1981, there was great interest in the election of a new President. My successor was chosen with dignity and in good spirit. Plaid Cymru and Wales were extremely fortunate that the two who stood as candidates were men of ability and uncommon back-bone – Dafydd Wigley and Dafydd Elis Thomas. For months the election focused attention on the Party and its status was raised in the eyes of the public by the quality of those taking part – two young Welsh politicians who are among the abst of their generation. The contest between them in the summer and autumn of 1981 underlined the fact that the leadership of Plaid Cymru is now wholly in the hands of my children's generation. The candidates' numerous meetings up and down the country were a medium for the membership's political education that was badly needed. The excitement continued right up to the Annual Conference, which turned out to be the best-attended and among the liveliest the Party had ever held. It took place for the first time in Carmarthen. When Dafydd Wigley was elected, Plaid Cymru recognized that it had a leader in whom it could put its complete confidence, and it came together around him.

The striking fact about Plaid Cymru is its unity, which is firmly behind its main policies. This is the only party which has been completely united in its opposition to nuclear arms and war – the greatest scourge of the age. Only it among all the parties in the countries of Britain opposed the war in the Malvinas. The others were drowned by a wave of British militarism and imperialism. I am terribly proud of its record, which seems to me utterly worthy of the party which has inherited the radical tradition of Wales. In the same way it is united on its economic and industrial, constitutional and educational, cultural and social policies. About the form of words used to describe its objectives in two of these fields there has been some disagreement, and so I shall go into a little detail about them both.

Everyone in Plaid Cymru agrees that it must aim at complete self-government, that is to say, full national status that will give its people, through the creation of a Welsh state, control over its own life, including defence, and its relations with other countries. The establishment of a Welsh state and the winning of a seat at the United Nations – and the League of Nations before that – have been among Plaid Cymru's aims for more than half a century. It's a disgrace that our country does not belong to the international organization of which some fifty countries with smaller populations are now members. The word used by Saunders Lewis in the 1930s to describe this objective was 'freedom'. More recently, pressure has been brought to bear in favour of 'independence'. I opposed the change, because to me 'independence' is an inflexible word and a rather dangerous one as well. There are no degrees of independence: a country is either independent or it is not. The word fails to suggest the interdependence of countries. The meaning it conveys is one of unfettered sovereignty, which is a curse underlying many an instance of international discord and which throughout the world is a barrier to international co-operation. The concept is so often a cause of international conflict. The word 'freedom' doesn't have these unhappy connotations. It suggests that nations are dependent on one another, while having the moral right to run their own lives. It also suggests that there are limits to sovereignty and that the nations are prepared to accept them. There are degrees to freedom. What Wales needs, and what it has a moral right to, is the degree of national freedom that will give it control over its domestic affairs and external relations. All are agreed that this would mean accepting the economic and constitutional limits which a peaceful international order would lay down. That is to say, the word 'freedom' suggests a willingness to co-operate with other nations without taking an intransigent stand over sovereignty; the concept is of a political nature. The words 'independence' and 'sovereignty' suggest standing apart, a country standing on its rights; they are by nature legalistic.

What has to be won for Wales is national freedom. The British system which locks Wales up as an indistinguishable part of England without allowing its people any real control over its national life has been a disastrous failure. This failure is to be seen in every sector of its life, in its economy as well as in its culture. Behind the British polity lie military and imperialist aims. Not often does *The New Statesman* publish the truth about this situation, but it did so in April of this year when it said: 'The thing we still have to call our government – the United Kingdom state – was never designed to rule nations such as the English, the Scots, the Welsh and the Irish are capable of being. It was brought into existence to run, by bluff and cheap contrivance, a shabby world-wide empire that was assembled by blunder, force and fraud in varying proportions.'

The second example was to bring the phrase 'decentralized socialism' into the wording of the Party's principal aim at its Annual Conference in Carmarthen last year. It is a well-known fact that over the years I have consistently objected to using the word 'socialism' (which I always write with a small first letter) to describe one part of our policies. It goes without saying that I don't object to the policies as such; on the contrary, I have been strongly in favour of them. They have been upheld by Plaid Cymru over the years ever since the early days of D.J. Davies, who helped to place workers' co-operative control firmly among them, and several times we have endeavoured to carry them out in a practical way. Such policies as these have a long tradition in Wales, including the Guild Socialism that was supported by many after the First World War and the Syndicalism of Noah Ablett and *The Miners' Next Step*. This last was a good deal closer to what Plaid Cymru stands for than any of the centralist policies formulated by the Webbs for the Labour Party. Plaid Cymru has stuck to the policies of D.J. Davies, and has of course refined them from time to time.

There's been a great deal of talk during the last fifteen years that Plaid Cymru is moving to the left. But what it has done is stick to its original policies. If it is way out on the left today, that is where it was fifteen years ago. In an article for *The Guardian*, Raymond Williams, the distinguished Welsh thinker and writer from Pandy in Gwent, said that Plaid Cymru was part of the New Left. The reason why I objected to the use of 'Socialism' was that this was the word used by Communists in the centralized, oppressive states of Eastern Europe. It was the Labour Party's word for describing the centralized nationalization of Clause 4 in its constitution. It was also used by the Nazis to describe the National Socialism of their centralized, totalitarian regime. Plaid Cymru's policies have always been completely decentralist, aiming not at bureaucratic state control but at placing power in the hands of the people to the greatest possible extent. It seems to me misleading to use the word 'Socialism' to describe policies which are self-contradictory. But there was great pressure from some quarters in favour of its use, and my own opposition to it, and that of others, gave the impression that we were somehow out of sympathy with the policies themselves. Furthermore, when Plaid Cymru's Research Commission recommended the adoption of the phrase 'decentralized community socialism' as a formula, I readily agreed to it. The Carmarthen Conference took this a step further. It decided to ensure that decentralized socialism would henceforth be among the Party's main aims. None of this changed anything in the Party's policies; only the wording was changed. This step was of great importance in the view of a strong section of Plaid Cymru, and it was hoped it would increase the Party's appeal among industrial workers and others whose allegiance to the national cause is essential for its success. With that in mind, and with some trepidation, I cast my vote at the Conference in favour. So I accept some of the responsibility for the alteration in the wording. Whatever we may think of all this, the unity of Plaid Cymru – given the wide range of its policies – remains as impressive as ever.

The political life of Wales today is more unstable than it has ever been before. Four British parties are competing for the support of its people, and one Welsh party. The other four are British Nationalist Parties in the sense that they support military and imperialist British Nationalism, as was so clearly seen in the Falklands war. They give their allegiance to Britain, on Britain's behalf they operate, and about Britian they are wholly concerned. There is a chasm between their values and aims and those of Plaid Cymru, which is inspired by the sense of belonging to a nation and empowered by remembering its past. Plaid Cymru – the Party of Wales – is the Welsh National Party, which embraces peaceful, non-violent, internationalist Welsh

Nationalism. Its allegiance is to Wales, it works for Wales, and it's concerned wholly with Wales. This is the only truly radical party in Wales today and the only one that is truly internationalist. Only Plaid Cymru endeavours to win a place for this nation in the international community. It alone has stood up for the wondrous heritage of Wales, rousing the country's national consciousness. It has achieved this with a unanimity which in my judgement is quite inspiring. With the slow unravelling of its old enemy, the Labour Party, the hour of its great opportunity is not far off.

Plaid Cymru is winning growing respect for Wales and for itself in many a country in Europe and other parts of the world. This was made clear at the Conference of the Fourth World at which I presided in August 1981, when some four hundred delegates from many nations and small communities in four continents gathered in London. It was also evident at this year's International Symposium in Salzburg where I was asked to speak about the freedom movement in Wales as a model for others in similar situations. Increasingly the smaller, stateless nations and regions of the world are looking to Wales for a lead. I receive letters all the time, and other evidence, which bear witness to the inspiration given by the work and success of the national movement in Wales to many Nationalists in countries overseas.

Today in Wales, despite the erosion of its life and the continuing damage done to it, I sense a new hope and confidence which could renew allegiance and commitment to the nation. Doubtless S4C, as the Welsh Television Channel is now known, has played its part in this process. With the zeal of young people, both Welsh and English-speaking, for the British parties that once used to offer them dazzling careers now falling away, I can foresee the tide rising under the Nationalist Party which offers them a life of struggle on behalf of Wales. Although the winning of the English-speaking industrial valleys of the South is essential to the national cause, the inspiration for deepening the sense of national commitment may yet again spring from the Welsh-speaking parts of our country and among Welsh-speakers wherever they may be, for it is the language that is the vehicle for traditional Welsh values. I have done my share of criticizing the shortcomings of the Welsh-speaking Welsh, but the fact remains that the half-million Welsh-speakers have abundant talent and creative energy. It may be that, with the help of our new television service, their Welshness will penetrate and inspire the English-speaking majority on an increasing scale from now on. We must aim at creating a Welsh synthesis that will have significance for the world. A combination of the Welsh people's talents and the values of their splendid heritage could make a contribution that is creatively explosive and brimming with hope. It is my belief that a commitment to those values will ensure that the small nation living in this corner of the earth will at last realize its great potential.

Gwynfor Evans: a Bibliography

Pamphlets

Y Radio yng Nghymru, 1944
The Radio in Wales, 1944
They Cry Wolf, 1946
Havoc in Wales – The War Office Demands, 1946
Eu Hiaith a Gadwant: A Oes Dyfodol i'r Iaith Gymraeg?, 1948
Wales as an Economic Entity, 1948
Yr Her i Siroedd Cymru, 1949
The Challenge to the Welsh Counties, 1949
Monmouthshire is in Wales, 1950
Coedwigaeth yng Nghymru, 1950
Cyfle Olaf y Gymraeg, 1952
70 Cwestiwn ac Ateb ar Blaid Cymru, 1953
Cristnogaeth a'r Gymdeithas Gymreig, 1954
The Labour Party and Welsh Home Rule, 1955
The Political Broadcasts Ban in Wales, 1955
Welsh Nationalist Aims, 1956
Wales against Conscription, 1956
The Wicked Ban, 1956
Save Cwm Tryweryn for Wales, 1956
Our Three Nations, (with others), 1956
Ymreolaeth i Gymru a'r Pleidiau Gwleidyddol, 1957
Gwersi Tryweryn, 1957
We Learn from Tryweryn, 1957
Tryweryn: New Proposals, 1957
TV in Wales, 1958
80 Cwestiwn ac Ateb ar Blaid Cymru, 1958
80 Questions and Answers on Plaid Cymru, 1958
Self-Government for Wales and a Common Market, 1959
Welsh Nationalist Aims, 1959
Cyfle Olaf y Gymraeg, 1962
Wales, the Next Step, 1964
Black Papers on Wales, 1967, 1968, 1969

Transport Bill Blow to Wales, 1968
Voice of Wales: Parliamentary Speeches, 1968
Non-violent Nationalism, 1973
Cenedlaetholdeb Di-drais, 1973
Great Britain, Parliament, House of Commons, 1974
Hanes Cymru: Gwynfor Evans yn Adrodd Stori ei Wlad, 1974
History of Wales: Gwynfor Evans tells the Story of his Country, 1974
George M. Ll. Davies, Pererin Heddwch, 1980
Byw neu Farw? Y Frwydr dros yr Iaith a'r Sianel Deledu Gymraeg, 1980
The End of Britishness, 1981
Emrys ap Iwan, 1982
Diwedd y Byd, 1982
Yr Arglwydd Rhys, 1982
Magnus Maximus and the Birth of the Welsh Nation, 1983
Macsen Wledig a Geni'r Genedl Gymreig, 1983
Wales: A Historic Community, 1988
Gwenllian, Arwres Gymraeg/Gwenllian, A Welsh Heroine, 1991
Yr Iaith yn y Nawdegau, 1992

Books

Argyfwng Amaethyddiaeth Cymru/The Crisis of Welsh Agriculture, n.d.
Plaid Cymru and Wales, 1950
Rhagom i Ryddid, 1964
Celtic Nationalism, with Ioan Rhys (Ioan Bowen Rees) and others, 1968
Wales Can Win, 1973
A National Future for Wales, 1975
Aros Mae, 1971
Land of my Fathers, trans. by Elin Garlick, 1974
Diwedd Prydeindod, 1981
Bywyd Cymro, 1982
Seiri Cenedl, 1986
Welsh Nation Builders, 1987
Pe Bai Cymru'n Rhydd, 1989
Fighting for Wales, 1991
Heddychiaeth Gristnogol yng Nghymru, 1992
For the Sake of Wales, trans. by Meic Stephens, 1996

I am grateful to Beti Jones of the National Library of Wales for help in compiling this bibliography.
M.S.

Index